# COLLINS
# COBUI[LD]

# VERBS:
# PATTERNS & PRACTICE

## CLASSROOM EDITION

THE UNIVERSITY
OF BIRMINGHAM

COLLINS
COBUILD

HarperCollins*Publishers*

HarperCollins Publishers
77-85 Fulham Palace Road
London W6 8JB

COBUILD is a trademark of William Collins Sons & Co Ltd

First published 1997

Reprinted 1998

2  4  6  8  10  9  7  5  3

ISBN 0 00 375090 6

Design and typesetting by
eMC Design, Bromham, Bedfordshire

## Corpus Acknowledgments

We would like to acknowledge the assistance of the many hundreds of
individuals and companies who have kindly given permission for
copyright material to be used in The Bank of English. The written
sources include many national and regional newspapers in Britain and
overseas; magazines and periodical publishers; and book publishers in
Britain, the United States, and Australia. Extensive spoken data has
been provided by radio and television broadcasting companies; research
workers at many universities and other institutions; and numerous
individual contributors. We are grateful to them all.

Printed and bound in Great Britain by
Caledonian International
Book Manufacturing Ltd,
Glasgow, G64

## Note

http://www.cobuild.collins.co.uk

## The COBUILD Series

| | |
|---|---|
| *Founding Editor-in-Chief* | John Sinclair |
| *Publishing Director* | Gwyneth Fox |

---

## Editorial Team

### Senior Editors

**Gill Francis**
**Elizabeth Manning**
Susan Hunston

| | |
|---|---|
| *Editorial Consultant* | Eugene Gatt Winter |
| *Computer Officer* | Tim Lane |
| *Illustrations* | Ela Bullon |

We would like to thank Elaine Watton and Deborah Orpin for their help with the Practice pages, and Philippe Humblé and John Todd for their detailed comments on the text.

# Contents

# Introduction

## Verb patterns

This book presents the major patterns of English verbs, and relates these patterns to meaning.

A verb pattern is, in most cases, a verb and the words that come after it. These words might be a noun group, an adjective group, a prepositional phrase, an adverb group, or a clause. In some cases, the Subject is restricted – for example it is always *it*, or always plural – and so can be considered part of the verb pattern.

We have devised a simple way of referring to patterns whereby the elements in each pattern are set out in the order in which they occur. For example:

| | |
|---|---|
| **V n** | means 'verb followed by a noun group' |
| **V n that** | means 'verb followed by a noun group and a that-clause' |
| **V *for* n** | means 'verb followed by *for* and a noun group' |
| **V n *for* n** | means 'verb followed by a noun group, *for* and another noun group' |

A list of the elements and their abbreviations is given at the end of this Introduction.

A pattern of a verb includes only those words that are significant for that particular verb, not those that are just part of general clause structure. For example, most verbs in English can be followed by adverb groups or prepositional phrases indicating manner, time, or place. When information about manner, time, or place is not essential, the adverb group or prepositional phrase is not considered to be part of the pattern.

## The Units

In this book, we present information on each verb pattern on the left-hand pages, with practice material on the right-hand pages. Sometimes a pattern is described in two or three successive Units. Sometimes a Unit deals with two or three major patterns, in which case each section is numbered.

## Left-hand pages: Patterns

Each Unit begins with a simple description of each pattern. For each major pattern, there is a table with a shaded area showing the pattern and simplified examples of verbs used with this pattern. There is also a table illustrating the passive pattern, if it occurs frequently.

### Meaning groups

The verbs with a particular pattern have been divided into groups according to their basic meaning. For example, in the Unit on **V n *into* -ing** (Unit 62), there is a group of verbs which indicate that someone makes someone do something by using force or pressure. This group includes the verbs *force*, *frighten*, *nag*, *pressure*, *push*, *scare*, and *terrify*. This division into meaning groups means that this book can be used as a grammatically-based thesaurus.

### Examples

Each meaning group has examples to show the verbs being used with the pattern in question. These examples are actual examples of current English, taken from the Bank of English. The verb pattern is highlighted in bold, and the verb group itself is underlined.

This example illustrates the pattern **V adj** with the verb *feel*:

> I <u>**was feeling**</u> a bit lonely.

Note that the verb group includes any auxiliaries (forms of *be*, *do*, and *have*), modals (for example *may* or *will*), and phrasal modals (for example *used to* or *have to*).

The negative word *not*, or its contracted form *n't*, is also included in the verb group:

> Chandler <u>**did not notice**</u> him enter.

A group of examples may contain active and passive examples, and examples of phrasal verbs. The passive examples are labelled.

### Lists

The lists contain the verbs which most frequently or typically have the pattern in question. Phrasal verbs are included, as well as ordinary verbs.

If a verb is usually or always used with a negative such as *not* or a modal such as *can* or *would*, that word is given in brackets before the verb. Verbs preceded by *can* in the lists can also be preceded by *could*.

If a verb is always passive when used with the pattern, its passive form (for example *be seen*) is given in the list. If a verb is usually used in continuous tenses, that form (for example *be dying*) is given.

Sometimes a verb may appear in more than one list in a Unit, because it has more than one meaning when used with the pattern concerned.

### Phrasal verbs

Where necessary, we give brief information on the position of the different parts of phrasal verbs in a pattern. We refer to the adverb or preposition in a phrasal verb as the **particle**. Where we say that the particle comes either after the noun group or after the verb, it should be noted that it does not come after the noun group if that noun group is a personal pronoun. For example, you should say *They pulled it down*, not *They pulled down it*. If we give no special information on phrasal verbs, the particle always comes immediately after the verb.

### Different forms of the pattern

One of the difficulties in recognising patterns comes about because patterns can take different forms, for example in questions or in relative clauses. At the end of the information on a pattern, we give some of the different forms a pattern can take.

For example, the verbs *do, buy, make, train* and *choose* are used with the pattern **V n *for* n** (see Units 51 and 52), as in these made-up examples:

(a) *I can do something for you.*

(b) *I will buy something for my mother.*

(c) *Her mother had made a dress for her.*

(d) *We've been trained for this job.* (passive)

(e) *I chose Roger, Lawrence and John for the interviews.*

But the order of elements in this pattern may be different. In a question or clause beginning with *what*, the *what* replaces the first noun group and comes at the beginning of the clause:

(a) *What can I do for you?*

(b) *I was trying to work out what to buy for my mother.*

If the verb comes in a relative clause, the relative pronoun may replace one of the noun groups and come at the beginning of the clause:

(c) *She was wearing a dress that her mother had made for her.*

(d) *This is a real opportunity to go and do the job that we've been trained for.*

The relative pronoun can be omitted: *She was wearing a dress her mother had made for her.*

If the first noun group is very long, it may be moved to the end of the clause:

(e) *I chose for these interviews Roger de Grey, Lawrence Gowing, and John Piper.*

### Productive uses

If a pattern is particularly productive – that is, many verbs with a particular basic meaning can be used with the pattern – we mention it in a special note.

## Right-hand pages: Practice

The right-hand pages contain practice material relating to the patterns on the left-hand pages. This material is based on real examples taken from the Bank of English. Where necessary, the first question has been done for you to provide a model. In the Self-Study edition, an Answer Key is given at the back of the book.

There are many different types of exercise in this book, so you should read the instructions carefully. Here are some comments on the most common types of exercise.

# Introduction

## 'Find the pattern' exercises

In these exercises, you are asked to put a dotted line under the verb used with the pattern being practised, and then to underline the other parts of the pattern. For instance, in Unit 42 you will see this example:

> Top executives around the country have rated Atlanta as the nation's best city for business.

and you are asked to pick out the pattern **V n** *as* **n**. The verb with this pattern is *rate*, and the parts of the pattern are:

**V**   have rated
**n**   Atlanta
*as*   as
**n**   the nation's best city for business

Using underlining to show the pattern, the example looks like this:

> Top executives around the country have rated Atlanta as the nation's best city for business.

Often, the example shows a different form of the pattern, and this is more difficult to identify (see 'Different forms of the pattern' above). In the following example, the verb which occurs in the pattern **V n** *as* **n** is *address*, but it is in a relative clause.

> When he reached the back porch, he met an officer, whom he addressed as captain.

The parts of the pattern are:

**V**   addressed
**n**   whom
*as*   as
**n**   captain

Using underlining to show the pattern, the example looks like this:

> When he reached the back porch, he met an officer, whom he addressed as captain.

Where we ask you to put a dotted line under the verb used with a pattern, we mean you to mark the whole verb group, including any auxiliaries or modals.

## 'Filling in gaps' exercises

Some of the exercises in this book ask you to fill in the gap in each of a number of sentences by choosing the correct word from a list. These exercises both practise the pattern and develop your knowledge of what words go together. Usually, some of the questions in these exercises are easier than others, so do the ones that you know first, then fill in the others. Unless you are told otherwise, each of the words in the list will be used in only one example. If you are filling in a verb, you should use an appropriate tense or form of the verb.

## 'Rewriting' exercises

In these exercises you are asked to rewrite an example so that it uses a given verb and the pattern you are practising. The examples also help you to understand what the verb and its pattern mean. For example, in Unit 47, you will see this example:

> He took hold of my hair and pushed me roughly up the trailer steps.

You are asked to rewrite this sentence using the verb *grab* in the pattern **V n** *by* **n**. So instead of *took hold of my hair* you write *grabbed me by the hair*. The complete answer is:

> He grabbed me by the hair and pushed me roughly up the trailer steps.

## 'Matching sentences' exercises

In the 'matching sentences' exercises you don't have to write anything. You simply draw a line to match the first part of the sentence with the second part. As with the 'filling in gaps' exercises, you are developing your knowledge of which verbs and nouns go together. Do the easy ones first, then puzzle out the others.

## Extra Practice

On pages 202-205 there is some extra practice material, in which each exercise tests your knowledge of more than one pattern.

## Verb Index

To find out which patterns a particular verb has, look it up in the **Verb Index** (p 206) and turn to the Unit(s) where it is listed, along with other verbs with the same pattern and meaning.

## Glossary

There is a Glossary of grammatical terms on page x.

More detailed information about verbs can be found in Collins Cobuild Grammar Patterns 1: Verbs. This book was the winner of the **Duke of Edinburgh English-Speaking Union Award 1996.**

## Words and abbreviations used in the patterns

| | |
|---|---|
| / | or |
| **adj** | an adjective group |
| **adv** | an adverb group |
| **amount** | a word or phrase indicating an amount |
| **as if** | a clause beginning with *as if* |
| **as though** | a clause beginning with *as though* |
| **inf** | the bare infinitive form of a verb |
| **-ed** | a clause beginning with the past participle of a verb |
| **-ing** | a clause beginning with the '-ing' form of a verb |
| *it* | 'introductory' or 'general' *it* |
| **like** | a clause beginning with *like* |
| **n** | a noun group |
| **pl-n** | a plural noun group |
| **prep** | a prepositional phrase |
| **pron-refl** | a reflexive pronoun |
| **quote** | a quoted clause in direct speech |
| **that** | a that-clause |
| **to-inf** | a clause beginning with the to-infinitive form of a verb |
| **V** | a verb group |
| *way* | *way* preceded by a possessive determiner |
| **wh** | a finite clause beginning with a wh-word |
| **when/if** | a finite clause beginning with *when* or *if* |
| **wh-to-inf** | a non-finite clause beginning with a wh-word and a to-infinitive form |
| **with** | more than one order of elements is possible |

# Glossary of grammatical terms

**active voice** If a verb is in the active voice, the Subject of the clause indicates the person or thing doing the action or responsible for it, e.g. *Anne **has given** me a tiny black kitten.* Compare **passive voice**.

**adjective group** An adjective group may consist of just one adjective, e.g. *I was **glad**.* Or the adjective may have words before it, such as an adverb, e.g. *I was **very happy**,* or words after it, such as a non-finite clause or a prepositional phrase, e.g. *I was **pleased to see her**... That was **kind of you**.* An adjective group is used to describe someone or something, or to give information about them.

**adverb group** An adverb group usually consists of just one adverb, e.g. *He swung **round** to see who was there... She is doing **well** at school,* but the adverb may also have another adverb before it, e.g. *Young skin burns **very easily**.* Adverb groups which are part of verb patterns are usually concerned with place or manner.

**amount** An amount is a word or phrase indicating an amount of something, for example *a lot, nothing, three percent, four hundred pounds, more, much,* e.g. *Her style of cooking owes **much** to her mother-in-law.*

**auxiliary** An auxiliary is one of the verbs *be, have,* and *do,* when they are used with a main verb to form tenses, passives, negatives, interrogatives, imperatives, etc.

**bare infinitive** A bare infinitive is the infinitive without *to,* e.g. *Thomas did not dare **approach** the great man... She heard the girl **laugh**.*

**bare infinitive** The base form is the most basic form of the verb, e.g. *go, run* and *walk.*

**co-ordinated** Two parts of a group or clause which are co-ordinated are joined together with a **co-ordinator** such as *and, or,* or *than,* e.g. *In his 68 years, **he and Diana** quarrelled only once.*

**'-ed' clause** An '-ed' clause is a non-finite clause beginning with the '-ed' form of a verb, e.g. *Rose had all her shops **decorated** in pink.*

**'-ed' form** The '-ed' form of a verb is its past participle form. This usually ends in '-ed' but it sometimes ends in '-en'. There are also several irregular verbs which have special forms, for example, the past participle of *put* is *put.* The '-ed' form is used, for example, in all passive patterns, e.g. *The cliffs were **formed** when the sea level was higher.*

**ergative verb** An ergative verb has two patterns, most commonly **V** and **V n**. The **V** pattern indicates that something happens to the Subject, or that the Subject does something, e.g. *The car **stopped**.* The **V n** pattern indicates that someone or something causes something to happen, e.g. *The driver **stopped** the car.* The Subject in the **V** pattern is the Object in the **V n** pattern. See Units 90-93.

**finite clause** In a finite clause, the verb group includes an indication of tense or modality, e.g. *A man **was swimming** fast to the canoe.* Compare **non-finite clause**.

**general it** General *it* is used in some patterns and phrases to refer vaguely to a general situation, e.g. *It's raining... Cut **it** out.* See Unit 99.

**imperative** When a clause is in the imperative, the base form of the verb is used and the clause usually has no Subject. The imperative is typically used to tell someone what to do, e.g. ***Stand** with your feet about a foot apart.*

**'-ing' clause** An '-ing' clause is a non-finite clause beginning with the '-ing' form of a verb, e.g. *His wife did not like him **drinking so much**... You should consider **supplementing your diet with vitamins and minerals**.*

**'-ing' form** The '-ing' form of a verb is the form that ends with '-ing'. It is used, for example, to form continuous tenses, e.g. *I've been **thinking** about it,* or to make an action nominal, e.g. ***Swimming** is good exercise.*

**introductory it** Introductory *it* functions as a 'dummy' Subject or Object in a sentence, without contributing to its meaning. It points forward to another clause in the sentence, e.g. ***It** is not clear who will get the money... He made **it** clear that he would not negotiate.* See Units 94-98.

**modal verb** There are eleven modal verbs in English: *can, could, dare, may, might, must, need, shall, should, will,* and *would.* They are used to add meaning to a main verb, for example to indicate how certain or possible something is, or whether a course of action is recommended or allowed. See also **phrasal modal**.

**non-finite clause** In a non-finite clause, the verb group does not include an indication of tense or modality, e.g. *I can just see him **swimming in clear blue water**.* Compare **finite clause**.

**noun group** A noun group may consist of just one noun, e.g. ***Children** roamed the streets.* Or the noun may have words before it, such as a determiner, adjective, or other modifier, e.g. *He and **the children** drove down to the beach... She was raising **two little children**;* or words after it, such as a prepositional phrase or a relative clause, e.g. ***Children under twelve** are half-price... **Children who eat with their parents** can choose from an adult menu.* A noun group may also consist of a pronoun, e.g. ***They** were enjoying **themselves**... **He** didn't say **anything**.* It may be an amount, e.g. *Jack owes his mother **a lot**.*

**Object** An Object is a part of an active clause that refers to the person or thing that is involved in an action but does not perform the action, e.g. *I was eating **my dinner**... They painted **the outside of the house**.* An Object is typically a noun group, but it may also be a non-finite clause, e.g. *I'd like **to see you**.* When an Object is a clause it indicates a situation or action. An Object typically comes after the verb, but in questions it may be a wh-word and occur at the beginning of the clause, e.g. ***What** do you want?*. See also **introductory it**.

**ordinal** An ordinal is a word such as *first, last,* or *tenth.* It is used to indicate where something comes in a sequence.

**particle** 'Particle' is the term used to refer to adverbs or prepositions such as *in, on, up,* or *down* when they combine with verbs to form phrasal verbs, e.g. *He was trying to break **up** the fight... They burned the school **down**... I'll look **after** it for you.*

**passive voice** If a verb is in the passive voice, the Subject of the clause is affected by the action and is not responsible for it, e.g. *He **was given** a bone marrow transplant.*

**personal pronoun** The personal pronouns are *I, me, you, he, him, she, her, it, we, us, they,* and *them.* They are used to refer to people or things whose identity is clear.

**phrasal modal** A phrasal modal is a phrase which forms a single verb group with another verb and which affects the meaning of that verb in the same way that a modal verb does, e.g. *I have to go... You're bound to like him.*

**phrasal verb** A phrasal verb consists of a verb and one or more particles. Its meaning is different from that of the verb and the particle(s) taken separately. Phrasal verbs have patterns that are similar to those of ordinary verbs, except for the presence of the particle(s). Some examples of phrasal verbs are *back down, die out, look after,* and *put up with.*

**plural noun group** With some verbs, the noun group which comes before the verb or after the verb has to be plural. A plural noun group may consist of one noun group which indicates two or more people or things, e.g. *Combine **all the ingredients** in a pan.* Or it may consist of two or more co-ordinated noun groups, linked by *and*, e.g. ***Molly and Simon** were always arguing.*

**prepositional phrase** A prepositional phrase typically consists of a preposition and a noun group, e.g. *He dived **into the river**,* but it may also consist of a preposition and an adjective group, e.g. *She is described **as critically ill**;* an '-ing' clause, e.g. *They will work **towards removing the underlying causes of famine**;* or a wh-clause, e.g. *They are preparing to vote **on whether to begin a full investigation**.* A prepositional phrase indicates the circumstances of an action or event, for example, its time or place, its frequency, its degree, or the manner in which it occurs. Prepositional phrases which are part of verb patterns are either concerned with place or manner, e.g. *Place the mixture **in a saucepan**,* or they indicate a person or thing that is directly involved in the action or state indicated by the verb, e.g. *A practical program of reform must be based **on firm principles**.*

**quote** A quote gives the words that someone has said, written, or thought. There are usually quotation marks round a quote, e.g. *'I don't want you to leave,' he said.*

**reciprocal pronoun** There are two reciprocal pronouns, *each other* and *one another.* They indicate that what one person or thing does to another, the other does to them, e.g. *They looked at **one another**... They hated **each other**.*

**reciprocal verb** A reciprocal verb indicates a process which two or more people, groups, or things are involved in mutually, for example, they do the same thing to each other or they take part jointly in the same action or event. Reciprocal verbs are used in patterns with a plural Subject, where the Subject indicates both people, groups, or things, e.g. *We **argued** about politics... The two leaders **met** in New York yesterday.* They are also used in patterns where the Subject indicates one person, group, or thing, in which case the other participant is mentioned in another part of the pattern, e.g. *I **argued** with Dick about the rules... I **met** him in Switzerland.*

**reflexive pronoun** The reflexive pronouns are *myself, yourself, himself, herself, itself, ourselves, yourselves,* and *themselves,* e.g. *The government will continue to dedicate **itself** to peace.*

**relative clause** A relative clause is a subordinate clause which gives more information about someone or something mentioned in the main clause. Relative clauses are often introduced with a relative pronoun, e.g. *who, that* or *which.*

**Subject** In an active clause, the Subject is the part of the clause that refers to the person or thing that does the action indicated by the verb, or that is in the state

indicated by the verb, e.g. ***The children** have eaten all the biscuits... **The brain** consists of billions of nerve cells.* In a passive clause, the Subject typically indicates the person or thing that is affected by an action, e.g. ***The house** has been restored.* It may be something that is in the state indicated by the verb, e.g. ***Her mother** was known to be a rich woman... **This factory** is comprised of just three rooms.* The Subject is typically a noun group, but it may also be a wh-word, e.g. ***What** is happening here?;* a clause beginning with *what* or *all*, e.g. ***What I need** is some accurate information;* a non-finite clause, e.g. ***Thinking about it** makes me feel unhappy;* or, infrequently, a that-clause. The Subject typically begins the clause, and comes before the verb, but in questions it may come after an auxiliary verb such as *do* or *have*, e.g. *Do **you** think he will make a good president?*

**subjunctive** The subjunctive form of a verb is in most cases the base form, used in certain clauses in place of the present or past tense, e.g. *I suggested that he **call** me Pinky.*

**that-clause** A that-clause is a finite clause that follows a verb group or a noun group and often, though not always, begins with *that*, e.g. *She thought **that he was heading west**... Gertrude told him **he would soon be a father**.*

**to-infinitive** A to-infinitive is the base form of a verb preceded by *to*, e.g. *The number of victims continues **to rise**.* A passive to-infinitive form consists of *to be*, and the '-ed' form of a verb, e.g. *He refused **to be silenced**.*

**to-infinitive clause** A to-infinitive clause is a clause beginning with the to-infinitive form of a verb, e.g. *She persuaded him **to leave the office**... The President agreed **to be interviewed** the next day.*

**verb group** A verb group may consist of just one verb, e.g. *I **went** to Wales last year;* or it may also contain one or more auxiliaries, e.g. *I **have been thinking** about your offer;* a modal, e.g. *Colleges **should provide** needed information;* a phrasal modal, e.g. *I **have to leave** immediately;* or the negative form *not*, e.g. *Grace **did not answer** the question directly.* A verb group tells you, for example, what someone or something does or what happens to them.

**wh-clause** A wh-clause is a finite clause that begins with a wh-word, e.g. *I wondered **why the children weren't home yet**... I asked her **whether I should inform the police**.* A wh-clause indicates that something is uncertain or unknown. Wh-clauses usually follow verb groups or noun groups, although they occasionally occur as the Subject of a clause. In this book, we sometimes use the term 'wh-clause' as a general term covering both the finite clause and the non-finite wh-to-inf clause. See **wh-to-inf clause**.

**when/if clause** The term 'when/if clause' is used in Units 96-98 to indicate a finite clause beginning with *when* or *if* which is not a wh-clause because it does not indicate that something is uncertain or unknown. It refers to a situation that occurs, or may occur, e.g. *I used to like it **when you came round for coffee and a game of cards**.*

**wh-to-inf clause** A wh-to-inf clause is a non-finite clause that begins with a wh-word and a to-infinitive, e.g. *I still have not decided **what to spend the money on**.* Wh-to-inf clauses refer to something that is uncertain or unknown.

**wh-word** The wh-words are *what, who, whom, when, where, why, which, whose, whether, how,* and *if.*

# Verbs used on their own

The simplest verb pattern of all is where the verb can be used on its own, without anything following it. For example, in *She laughed,* there is nothing following the verb *laugh.* This pattern is **V**.

|  | Verb group |
|---|---|
| The meeting | had ended. |
| The amount of desert in the world | is increasing. |

This is one of the most frequent patterns in English. In this book we can list only a small number of the verbs which have this pattern. Here are some of the meaning groups they belong to:

■ **verbs indicating that someone or something moves or stays where they are**

| | | | | |
|---|---|---|---|---|
| approach | fall | leave | set off | turn |
| arrive | fly | move | sit down | wait |
| climb | get up | open | stand up | walk |
| come | go | pass | stay | |
| dance | go out | remain | stop | |
| emerge | jump | return | swim | |
| enter | land | run | travel | |

*Menti shook hands with her and **left**.*

*She **turned** and stared at him.*

*At this moment the screen door **opened** and John McGinnis **emerged**.*

*The car **stopped**.*

■ **verbs indicating that something happens or exists**

| | | | |
|---|---|---|---|
| continue | go on | last | result |
| exist | happen | occur | |

*The accident **occurred** when a pilot crossed a runway during foggy conditions.*

*The relationship **didn't last**.*

*Hundreds of their villages no longer **exist**.*

■ **verbs concerned with beginning and ending**

| | | |
|---|---|---|
| begin | finish | start |
| end | open | stop |

*The talks **began** on Monday.*

*We'll never **finish** in time.*

*The rain **had stopped**.*

■ **verbs concerned with changing**

| | | | |
|---|---|---|---|
| change | expand | grow | increase |
| decline | fall | grow up | rise |
| develop | go up | improve | |

*Things **have changed** in the fashion world.*

*Inflation **is rising**.*

*Reading standards **have improved**.*

■ **verbs concerned with being successful, failing, or managing to do something in difficult circumstances**

| | | | | |
|---|---|---|---|---|
| cope | lose | pass | survive | work out |
| fail | manage | pay off | win | |
| lead | miss | succeed | work | |

*I've made a big effort to improve my discipline and, to a large extent, I think I**'ve succeeded**.*

*Many are finding it difficult to **cope** because of unpaid wages and lost savings.*

*Other swimmers got him ashore, but attempts to revive him **failed**.*

*Didn't I tell you things **would work out**?*

■ **verbs indicating that someone makes a sound or puts on an expression, or that someone's body does something involuntarily**

| | | | |
|---|---|---|---|
| cough | frown | shiver | sneeze |
| cry | laugh | sleep | wake up |
| faint | pass out | smile | |

*She **smiled** weakly.*

*We both **laughed**.*

*Then they both drank so much that they **passed out** in their hotel.*

■ **verbs concerned with talking or thinking**

| | | | | |
|---|---|---|---|---|
| agree | argue | explain | reply | talk |
| answer | care | lie | speak | think |

*'This is your last chance', her father said. Erin **didn't reply**.*

*He never **spoke** unless he was spoken to.*

*She pauses and **thinks** for a moment.*

■ **other common verbs**

| | | | | |
|---|---|---|---|---|
| break | draw | hurt | run out | teach |
| carry on | dress | (not) matter | settle down | wash |
| cook | drink | paint | show off | work |
| count | drive | pay | sing | write |
| die | eat | read | smoke | |

*From an early age he loved to **draw** and **paint**.*

*Suppose we meet somewhere for a drink? I'll **pay**.*

*She'd be late for work, but it **didn't matter**.*

*I went to Dent's to get some more books 'cos I**'ve run out**.*

*I **work** hard.*

# Practice

**A** Fill in the gaps in the sentences below using the verbs in this list. Use each verb once.

arrive   begin   continue   die   explain   go up   happen   jump   laugh   pay off   smoke

1 'What's ...................................?' she asked.
2 There was no way to escape from the building except to ...................................
3 The train ................................... on time this morning.
4 When she said that nothing seemed to be working right, I asked her to ...................................
5 Two boys were sitting close together, whispering and ...................................
6 I'm afraid, though, the price has ................................... a little bit.
7 I was happy that all of the hard work I had done in practice had finally ...................................
8 When he ................................... in 1985, few people noticed.
9 Most people are now aware of the risks to their health if they ...................................
10 The radio said the fighting ................................... on Sunday and was ................................... in the region around the capital.

**B** In the list of verbs beginning with *approach*, find:

1 five verbs which indicate that someone leaves a place
..............................................................................................................................................................
2 four verbs which indicate that someone or something does not move or no longer moves
..............................................................................................................................................................
3 three verbs which indicate that someone or something moves through the air
..............................................................................................................................................................
4 one verb which indicates that someone moves through water ............................................................

**C** From the list of verbs beginning with *cough*, select the right verb to put into the following dictionary definitions.

1 When you ..............................., tears come from your eyes, usually because you are unhappy or hurt.
2 When you ..............................., you suddenly and involuntarily take in your breath and then blow it down your nose noisily.
3 If you ............................... or ..............................., you lose consciousness for a short time, especially because of hunger, pain, heat, or shock.
4 When you ..............................., your body shakes slightly because you are cold or frightened.
5 When you ..............................., you force air out of your throat with a sudden, harsh noise.
6 When you ..............................., you become conscious again after being asleep.
7 When someone ..............................., their eyebrows become drawn together, because they are annoyed, worried, or puzzled, or because they are concentrating.
8 When you ..............................., the corners of your mouth curve upwards and you sometimes show your teeth. People ............................... when they are pleased or amused or when they are being friendly.

# UNIT 2 Verbs used with a noun group: 1

Some verbs are followed by a noun group. For example, in *She was eating a biscuit*, the verb *eat* is followed by the noun group *a biscuit*. This pattern is **V n**.

## Active pattern

|        | Verb group | noun group      |
|--------|------------|-----------------|
| He     | hit        | me.             |
| I      | made       | a shallow box.  |

## Passive pattern

|                           | Verb group        |
|---------------------------|-------------------|
| The system                | has been improved.|
| The posters on the fence  | were removed.     |

(With most of the phrasal verbs listed in these units, the particle comes either after the noun group or after the verb. With a few, the particle always comes after the verb. If there are two particles, as in *look forward to*, the particles come after the verb.)

This is the most frequent pattern in English. In this book we can list only a small number of the verbs which have this pattern. Here are some of the meaning groups they belong to:

■ **verbs concerned with harming, breaking, destroying, or attacking someone or something**

| attack  | burn      | fight     | injure    | shoot down  |
|---------|-----------|-----------|-----------|-------------|
| beat    | burn down | hang      | kill      | take apart  |
| beat up | cut       | harm      | pull down |             |
| blow up | cut down  | hit       | run over  |             |
| break   | destroy   | hurt      | shoot     |             |

*She broke her leg, and can't get to work.*

*One civilian and one soldier were killed.* (passive)

*A four-storey hotel in Hull has been destroyed by fire.* (passive)

■ **verbs concerned with mending things**

| do up | maintain | repair  |
|-------|----------|---------|
| fix   | mend     | restore |

*I hope Rudolph can fix your car.*

■ **verbs concerned with making or producing something**

| bring about | complete | design | found   | produce |
|-------------|----------|--------|---------|---------|
| build       | cook     | finish | make    |         |
| cause       | create   | form   | prepare |         |

*They're building a prison a few miles from town.*

*I have completed my greatest work of art.*

*It is doubtful if such a response would produce the required results.*

*The bridge was designed by Brunel.* (passive)

■ **verbs concerned with changing or affecting something**

| affect  | cut    | improve  | limit  | reduce |
|---------|--------|----------|--------|--------|
| change  | extend | increase | raise  |        |

*I am proud that we helped change the world.*

*We have to reduce our costs now.*

■ **verbs concerned with moving or holding something**

| add       | close      | hang up    | pick     | remove |
|-----------|------------|------------|----------|--------|
| arrange   | cut off    | hide       | pick up  | shake  |
| bear      | deliver    | hold       | press    | shut   |
| break off | draw       | lift       | pull     | take   |
| bring     | drop       | move       | push     | turn   |
| carry     | give back  | open       | put away |        |
| catch     | hand over  | pass round | raise    |        |

*Add the garlic, onion and carrots.*

*I'll bring some more plates and cutlery.*

*Opening her bag again, Nancy handed over another envelope.*

*Michelle remembers the first time she held the new baby.*

■ **verbs concerned with operating machinery or vehicles**

| blow  | operate   | ring    | start    | work |
|-------|-----------|---------|----------|------|
| drive | play      | set     | start up |      |
| fire  | play back | set off | stop     |      |
| fly   | ride      | sound   | use      |      |

*Charles came and operated the security lock.*

*The second time we played the record, it sounded twice as fast.*

*Well, you can't ride your bicycle today, and that's final.*

*Eileen smiled, and started up the engine without speaking.*

# Practice

**A** Put the different parts of these sentences in the right order.

1 he / with a knife / and / money and jewellery / stole / them / threatened

.............................................................................................................................

2 all their money / decided / they / they / away / should give

.............................................................................................................................

3 as a result of / people / might lose / market reform / four million / their jobs

.............................................................................................................................

4 chose / with / the best view / the bedroom / Simon ...............................................

5 and / crisps / the group / drank / ate / white wine .............................................

**B** In the piece of text below, put a dotted line under the verbs used with a noun group in the pattern **V n**. Then underline the noun groups. The verbs may not appear in the lists in this Unit.

The track passes a small lodge. On meeting a main road turn left up the approach to Abbey Lodge, which guards a fine avenue of trees. Cross the bridge and bear right to an iron gate. Walk along the weir and over the lock gates. To reach Henley turn right and follow the river for 2 miles.

**C** In the sentences below, there is a dotted line under a verb used with a noun group. Underline the noun group, which may occur before the verb.

1 What are you trying to say?
2 Who did this?
3 What I want is more money.
4 He was the best golfer I've ever seen.
5 That's a horrible thing to say.
6 I found the radar extremely easy to use.
7 I asked her what that meant.
8 This she agreed to do.
9 The fish here are not suitable for eating.
10 The present system does not give us the information that we require.

**D** Fill in the questions, starting with the words provided.

1 'I saw something.' 'What *did you see?'* ...........................................................
2 'I've forgotten something.' 'What ...........................................................
3 'Let's play a game.' 'What ...........................................................
4 'We need something else.' 'What ...........................................................
5 'Yes, I heard something about that.' 'What ...........................................................
6 'Let's go out and buy something.' 'What ...........................................................
7 'I was watching television.' 'What programme ...........................................................
8 'I would prefer someone else.' 'Who ...........................................................

# Verbs used with a noun group: 4

In the case of some verbs with the pattern **V n**, the noun group after the verb describes the Subject. Most of these verbs do not have passives.

|  | Verb group | noun group |
|---|---|---|
| My husband | is | a doctor. |
| It | seemed | an ordinary place. |

These verbs belong to the following meaning groups:

■ **verbs indicating that a person or thing is something, or is made up of something**

| be | constitute | make up | represent |
|---|---|---|---|
| compose | form | prove | stay |
| comprise | make | remain | |

*That story **is a good example** of Crane's greatness as a writer.*

*Do you think he'**d make a good president**?*

*Two and two **make four**.*

*How many players **comprise a team** in netball?*

*The agreement **represents an important victory** for the union.*

The verbs *compose*, *comprise*, and *make up* have a passive pattern in which the verb group is followed by a prepositional phrase beginning with *of*.

*This machine **is composed of three parts**.*

*The Chinese character for 'wise leader' **is made up of three symbols**.*

■ **verbs indicating that a person or thing becomes something**

| become | form | make | turn |
|---|---|---|---|

*She eventually gave up her job and **became a full-time singer**.*

*After about 10-15 minutes, the police quietly began **forming a line across the road**.*

In the case of *turn*, the noun group is always singular but without a determiner.

*Both **turned informer** and were the main prosecution witnesses in the trial of the other men.*

■ **verbs indicating that a person or thing seems to be something**

| appear | feel | look | seem | sound |
|---|---|---|---|---|

*He **seems a reasonable man**.*

*That **sounds a good idea**.*

*Feel* indicates how someone seems to themselves.

*For the first year after the divorce I **felt a real failure**.*

■ **verbs indicating that someone behaves like a kind of person they are not**

| act | play |
|---|---|

The noun group after the verb always begins with *the*.

*The more the parents **act the boss**, the less control they seem to have and the more miserable they are.*

■ **verbs used when indicating the size or weight of something or someone**

| average | cover | measure | weigh |
|---|---|---|---|
| be | extend | stand | |

*Twenty years ago, supermarkets **averaged 20,000 square feet**.*

*He **weighs 8st 7lb**.*

*Be* and *stand* are always followed by a noun group and an adjective group, adverb group, or prepositional phrase when used to indicate size, and *measure* and *extend* usually are.

*The fence **was two and a half metres high**.*

*The river **was only fifty yards across** and we were over in a minute.*

*The brooch **measures 2 inches in length**, and the clip-on earrings **are 1 inch in diameter**.*

## Different forms of the pattern

*Who **are** you?*

*What **is** your favourite book?*

*I did not know **what** the problem **was**.*

*What it **is** is a civil war.*

Some verbs are sometimes used in a pattern with *than*.

*I feel I am a better player than I **was** in 1985.*

**A** The sentences below indicate someone's opinion of a person or thing. Fill in the gaps using the nouns in this list. Use each noun once.

arrangement  boy  business  experience  girl  people  place  thing

1  He's a charming ....................................

2  She seems a bright, happy .................................... who will fit in well here.

3  That looks a nice ....................................

4  That sounds a sensible ....................................

5  That sounds a ridiculous .................................... to say, but it's exactly how it felt.

6  They were decent ....................................

7  Growing up is a painful ....................................

8  A holiday in the Himalayas is an unforgettable ....................................

**B** For each pair of sentences, say whether the noun group after the verb describes the Subject or not.

1  a) She weighed 175 pounds. ...*yes*......
    b) He weighed the gun in his hands. ...*no*........

2  a) They make some good music. ................
    b) They would have made very good teachers. ................

3  a) He felt a stranger in this country. ................
    b) He felt a strange mix of emotions. ................

4  a) He represents a group of five artists, none of them yet over 30. ................
    b) The $4.7 billion deal represents a major victory for McDonnell Douglas. ................

5  a) The individual cells that make up the brain are well understood. ................
    b) Parliament can make up the rules as it goes along. ................

6  a) Riot police formed a human barrier between the two sides. ................
    b) He had formed a poor opinion of his forthcoming rival, Jimmy Carter. ................

**C** Express these measurements in sentences. There may be more than one way of doing it.

1  a hole – width: 12 feet; depth: 2 feet.
   *The hole was 12 feet wide and 2 feet deep.*

2  a bridge – length: 130 metres; height: 30 metres.
   ....................................................................................................

3  an insect – length: 2 inches; diameter: 1 inch.
   ....................................................................................................

4  an oil slick – length: 10 miles; width: 2 miles.
   ....................................................................................................

5  a man – height: 5 feet 8 inches; weight: 11 stone.
   ....................................................................................................

# Verbs used with or without a noun group

Many verbs can be used on their own (the pattern **V**) or can be followed by a noun group (the pattern **V n**).

Some verbs that have these two patterns are **ergative verbs**, for example *break*, as in *A window broke*, *They broke the window*. These verbs are dealt with in Units 90-92.

The other verbs with these two patterns can be divided into two groups:

## Group 1

When the verb is used on its own, something else involved in the action must have been previously mentioned or indicated. For example, you do not say *I'll check* unless it is clear what you will check.

| | | | | |
|---|---|---|---|---|
| accept | cut down | hear | pay | sell |
| answer | defend | help | play | start |
| approach | do without | help out | promise | stop by |
| ask | drink | investigate | publish | strike |
| attack | enter | know | pull | survive |
| attend | explain | lead | push | take over |
| call | fight | leave | remember | visit |
| call back | find out | lose | repeat | watch |
| check | finish | (not) mind | resign | win |
| choose | fire | miss | ring | |
| claim | fit | notice | ring back | |
| clear up | follow | order | rule | |
| count | give up | pass | see | |

Here are some pairs of examples, one with the pattern **V** and one with the pattern **V n**.

*To our great relief, she **accepted**.*
*He offered to help me, and I **accepted** the offer.*

*But what if Jay **found out**?*
*__Have__ you **found out** something?*

*__Have__ you **finished**?*
*There were further cheers when the old man **had finished** his speech.*

*He took his pistol and **fired**.*
*Pagan **fired** his gun again.*

*He talked softly so that nobody **could hear**.*
*I thought I **heard a noise**.*

*Tony grabbed the wire and **pulled**.*
*Reggie put a gun to his head and **pulled the trigger**.*

*You helped him once before, **do** you **remember**?*
*I **remember the day he was born**.*

*She'**ll ring back** later.*
*I'**ll ring** you **back** in the morning.*

*The chauffeur **survived** and identified Garcia.*
*Several people **survived** the crash.*

## Group 2

The verb can be used freely on its own because the general type of thing involved is obvious from the meaning of the verb. For example, you can say *She was singing*, and it is obvious that she was singing a song of some kind. More detail about the thing involved can be given with the pattern **V n**, as in *She was singing a song about me*.

| | | | | |
|---|---|---|---|---|
| act | draw | marry | run | study |
| adopt | drive | move | save | suffer |
| answer back | eat | negotiate | score | teach |
| change | fly | paint | shoot | travel |
| charge | go without | perform | sing | wait |
| cook | kill | please | speak | write |
| deliver | learn | read | steal | |

Here are some pairs of examples.

*She taught me how to **cook**.*
*__Cook the carrots, onions, celery and diced bacon__ until golden.*

*Cocaine **can kill**.*
*A series of explosions **have killed three soldiers** and wounded at least three others.*

*He never **married**.*
*He **married a local woman**.*

*I was thrilled when we **scored**.*
*Carey **scored five runs**.*

*He **has taught** at Princeton, Harvard and Yale.*
*She **taught English Literature**.*

With many of these verbs, the noun group in the **V n** pattern sometimes does not add any meaning. For example, *Uruguay had just scored a goal* means the same as *Uruguay had just scored*. Here are some further examples:

*She went upstairs to **change**.*
*When he came out he'**d changed his clothes**.*

*Unable to have children of their own, Penny and Rodney decided to **adopt**.*
*Eventually we decided to **adopt a child** instead.*

# Practice

**A** Fill in the gaps in the pairs of sentences below using the verbs in this list. Say which sentence shows the pattern **V** and which shows the pattern **V n** or its passive.

attack   attend   enter   follow   help   notice   pay   push

1  a) Your hotel bill's been ........*paid.*................  ........*V n (passive)*.........
  b) You must let me .........*pay.*.............  .........*V*.......................

2  a) Sutcliffe knocked on the door and ...............................  ...............................
  b) Quickly Nancy ............................... the shop. ...............................

3  a) Then I ............................... her eyes. ...............................
  b) The cake was trampled under their feet, but they didn't ...........................  ...........................

4  a) The message merely reported that the French had ............................... at dawn. .........................
  b) The victim was ............................... at about midnight on Thursday last week. ..........................

5  a) I can ............................... you. ...............................
  b) I just wanted to ...............................  ...............................

6  a) The public was invited to ...............................  ...............................
  b) About eight-hundred delegates ............................... the conference. ...............................

7  a) Don't look now, but I think we're being ...............................  ...............................
  b) She went up the stairs, and Jake ...............................  ...............................

8  a) He ............................... harder, and then fell on his face as the door was opened suddenly.
  ...............................
  b) She ............................... the buttons, but they didn't light up. ...............................

**B** In each case, say whether sentence b) means the same as sentence a).

1  a) He has never bothered to learn to drive.
  b) He has never bothered to learn to drive a car. .....*yes*.....

2  a) I love learning.
  b) I love learning English. ................

3  a) The sport has given me the opportunity to travel.
  b) The sport has given me the opportunity to travel the world. ................

4  a) You can easily take it with you when you move.
  b) You can easily take it with you when you move house. ................

5  a) She was reading.
  b) She was reading a magazine. ................

6  a) They cheated. They stole. And they lied.
  b) They cheated. They stole cars. And they lied. ................

7  a) Trying too hard to please can be harmful.
  b) Trying too hard to please others can be harmful. ................

8  a) He scored twice in their comfortable 3-nil win over Norway.
  b) He scored two goals in their comfortable 3-nil win over Norway. ................

# Verbs used with a reflexive pronoun

Some verbs are followed by a reflexive pronoun. For example, in *She enjoyed herself*, the verb *enjoy* is followed by the reflexive pronoun *herself*. This pattern is **V pron-refl**.

|  | Verb group | reflexive pronoun |
|---|---|---|
| History | Behave<br>repeats | yourself!<br>itself. |

(With phrasal verbs, the particle comes after the reflexive pronoun.)

Verbs with this pattern belong to the following meaning groups:

■ **verbs concerned with injuring yourself accidentally, or killing yourself**

| burn | drown | hurt | kill |
|---|---|---|---|
| cut | hang | injure | starve |

If you **burn yourself** in the kitchen, put your hand into the freezer and put ice on the burn.

She wanted to die and tried to **drown herself** in the river.

Police say he **hanged himself**, but there are suspicions that he may have been killed.

■ **verbs concerned with doing something with a lot of effort or enthusiasm, or taking something seriously**

| apply | commit | stir |
|---|---|---|
| assert | exert | wear out |

Potential buyers had been reluctant to **commit themselves**.

He never seemed to hurry or **exert himself**.

■ **verbs concerned with controlling your feelings or behaviour**

| behave | compose | limit | pull together |
|---|---|---|---|
| collect | control | organize | |

She tried to **control herself**, but there were tears in her eyes.

**Pull yourself together.** Go wash your face. Freshen up.

■ **verbs concerned with talking, often about yourself**

| explain | express | introduce | repeat |
|---|---|---|---|

Godard sat down and prepared to **explain himself**.

Johnson pretended not to be able to hear anything Shaw said, so Shaw **had to repeat himself** in a louder voice.

■ **verbs indicating that someone moves their body or changes position**

| cross | raise | shake | support |
|---|---|---|---|
| draw up | seat | stretch out | |

The old woman glared at him, **drew herself up** and stormed into the building.

'Nothing is wrong now,' laughed Bess as she **stretched herself out** lazily.

She knelt, **crossed herself** and prayed.

■ **verbs concerned with enjoying yourself or treating yourself well**

| enjoy | help | spoil |
|---|---|---|
| fulfil | indulge | suit |

I **do enjoy myself**, I love sports, travelling and socializing.

This is the time to **indulge yourself**. Go on, treat yourself to a new dress.

He has already arranged his life to **suit himself**.

■ **verbs concerned with hiding or keeping away from other people**

| hide | isolate | lock away | shut away | shut off |
|---|---|---|---|---|

His first instinct was to **hide himself**.

I always **lock myself away** to write.

■ **verbs concerned with being or becoming successful**

| better | distinguish | excel | prove |
|---|---|---|---|

Sheppard **excelled herself**, breaking her own 50m time and setting a new British record.

He never felt pressured to **prove himself** in a fight.

■ **other common verbs**

| be | dress | present | reproach |
|---|---|---|---|
| disgrace | kid | repeat | work out |

'What do I have to do?' I asked. Tony laughed. 'Just **be yourself**. Nothing more.'

An opportunity soon **presented itself**, which he eagerly seized.

Just how this situation **will work itself out** remains to be seen.

**A** Fill in the gaps in these sentences with a reflexive pronoun.

1 Losing her balance, she had landed on her back and hurt ................................ badly.

2 All the children in the class have to behave ................................

3 How often do I have to repeat ................................ ?

4 It's your body and your life, so don't be frightened to assert ................................

5 Let me introduce ................................

6 If we isolate ................................, we die.

7 The problem is not going to work ................................ out.

8 You must pull ................................ together.

9 He cut ................................ shaving.

10 Don't work so hard. You'll wear ................................ out.

11 She was allowed to leave the court for a few minutes to compose ................................

12 He'd been terrified of making a wrong step and disgracing ................................

**B** Rewrite these sentences using the verb given in brackets with the pattern **V pron-refl**.

1 He committed suicide. (kill)
*He killed himself.* ................................................................................................

2 You must get your personal life in order. (organize)
................................................................................................

3 He refused to give any explanation. (explain)
................................................................................................

4 Have a good time! (enjoy)
................................................................................................

5 He was finding it difficult to describe how he felt. (express)
................................................................................................

6 It is only with friends that most people feel they can relax and behave naturally. (be)
................................................................................................

7 She took an unnecessarily long time to bath and put her clothes on. (dress)
................................................................................................

8 He worked really hard and got into Magdalene, his father's college. (apply)
................................................................................................

9 They appear to be rewriting the rules to fit in with what they want. (suit)
................................................................................................

10 He was poor at maths and English but did very well in French. (distinguish)
................................................................................................

# Verbs used with two noun groups: 1

Some verbs are followed by two noun groups. For example, in *I bought him lunch*, the verb *buy* is followed by the noun groups *him* and *lunch*. This pattern is **V n n**. The first noun group always indicates a person, and the second noun group indicates the thing that is involved in the action.

## Active pattern

|  | Verb group | noun group | noun group |
|---|---|---|---|
| Her boyfriend | gave | her | a diamond ring. |
| I | wrote | him | a letter. |

## Passive pattern

|  | Verb group | noun group |
|---|---|---|
| Natalia | was offered | a job in New York. |
| We | were brought | the lunch menu. |

(With phrasal verbs, the particle comes either after the first noun group or after the second noun group.)

Verbs with this pattern belong to the following meaning groups:

■ **verbs concerned with giving, selling, or offering someone something, or refusing to do so**

| | | | | |
|---|---|---|---|---|
| accord | deny | hand back | pay | serve |
| advance | feed | lease | pay back | slip |
| allow | give | leave | permit | throw |
| assign | give back | lend | promise | tip |
| award | grant | offer | refuse | toss |
| deal | hand | pass | sell | |

That year for Christmas my parents **gave** me a microscope kit.

She **gave** me **back** my ring.

The club's representative had arranged to **sell** him a ticket for the match.

Throughout history, females **have been denied** many roles in society. (passive)

■ **verbs concerned with doing something for someone, usually something which is beneficial to them**

| | | | | |
|---|---|---|---|---|
| assure | cook | fix | order | sing |
| bear | cut | get | play | |
| book | do | guarantee | pour | |
| bring | fetch | make | prescribe | |
| buy | find | mix | secure | |

She asked me to **bring** her some tea.

They offered to **cook** us a Swiss lunch the following day.

They **can book** you a room by phone and tell you how to get there.

■ **verbs concerned with communicating**

| | | | | |
|---|---|---|---|---|
| ask | give | post | shoot | write |
| bid | kiss | quote | teach | |
| cast | mail | read | tell | |
| fax | make | send | throw | |

She asked me to **read** her a story.

I **sent** you a postcard from Nevada.

He's a good man and I've **taught** him everything I know.

Let me **give** you some advice.

Paul and Penny came to **bid** us good-bye.

*Cast, shoot,* and *throw* indicate that someone looks or smiles at someone else.

She **shot** Brian a quick look.

■ **verbs concerned with causing someone to gain, lose, or suffer something**

| | | | | |
|---|---|---|---|---|
| cause | cost | earn | save | spare |
| charge | do | lose | set back | win |

He's **caused** us all sorts of problems this season.

The man's identity is not being revealed to **spare** him further embarrassment.

It was a fight that **cost** him his life.

A basic meal **will set** you **back** about eight to ten pounds.

■ **other common verbs**

| | | | | |
|---|---|---|---|---|
| envy | let off | put off | show | wish |
| forgive | owe | set | take | |

She **envied** them their freedom.

Putting too much on the plate **may put** your child **off** his food.

It didn't turn out to be a difficult job, though it **took** me two hours.

In the case of *owe*, the second noun group is often an amount.

Now more and more I see I **owe** her everything.

## Different forms of the pattern

**What did** she **give** you?

Robina did not know **what** Martha **told** the police.

He refused to accept **the six dollars** she **offered** him.

I can't think of **anything** to **tell** him.

'**Thirty-five pounds** it **cost** me,' she said.

# Practice

**A** In the sentences below, put a dotted line under the verb used with the pattern described in this Unit. Then underline each of the other parts of the pattern.

1 I'll show you a photograph.

2 On the way out of town, he stopped by the florist and bought her a bouquet of white flowers.

3 Children between 1 and 5 are charged a small flat daily rate.

4 Dr Brock was extremely helpful and promised me a written report in a week's time.

5 Dad handed me a big box wrapped in gold foil and tied with a red ribbon.

6 The message you send your adolescent about drug and alcohol use is important.

7 I would do a 12-hour shift, come home and spring-clean the flat and then cook my flatmates a wonderful meal.

8 That will set you back a few pounds.

9 Elizabeth Dekker was refused employment as a teacher at a training centre on the grounds that she was three months pregnant.

10 What were you offered, George?

**B** Match up the two halves of each sentence.

1 My homework took me ...          a ... every success.
2 I envy him ...                    b ... money.
3 He owes me ...                    c ... hours.
4 We wish them ...                  d ... a lovely birthday card.
5 He poured her ...                 e ... his cheerful good nature.
6 He sent me ...                    f ... a glass of soda.

**C** Rewrite these sentences using the verb given in brackets with the pattern **V n n**.

1 Ginny said goodbye to her with a kiss at Victoria station. (kiss)
   *Ginny kissed her goodbye at Victoria station.*

2 Tod looked at them angrily. (throw)

3 He smiled at me gratefully. (shoot)

4 There had been barely time for Rose to say good-bye to Philip. (bid)

5 From time to time a passer-by would glance suspiciously at him. (cast)

6 I thought you might be able to advise me. (give)

17

# Verbs used with two noun groups: 2

In addition to those described in Unit 8, there are other verbs which are followed by two noun groups. For example, in *I considered him a friend*, the verb *consider* is followed by the noun groups *him* and *a friend*. The second noun group – *a friend* – describes the first noun group – *him*.

Verbs of this kind are very frequently used in the passive.

## Active pattern

|  | Verb group | noun group | noun group |
|---|---|---|---|
| They<br>He | named<br>proclaimed | their daughter<br>it | Mary.<br>a masterpiece. |

## Passive pattern

|  | Verb group | noun group |
|---|---|---|
| He<br>The hotel | will be nominated<br>is rated | prime minister.<br>one of the best in town. |

These verbs belong to the following meaning groups:

■ **verbs concerned with naming or labelling someone or something in a particular way**

| acclaim | christen | dub | name | rename |
|---|---|---|---|---|
| brand | code-name | hail | nickname | tag |
| call | declare | label | pronounce | term |

*My children **called** him Uncle Frankie and were always delighted to see him.*

*If she makes a mess of this marriage she'**ll be labelled** a complete and utter failure for the rest of her life.* (passive)

*I **was branded** a liar and a show-off.* (passive)

■ **verbs concerned with nominating or choosing someone for a particular position**

| anoint | declare | name | proclaim | vote |
|---|---|---|---|---|
| appoint | elect | nominate | pronounce |  |
| crown | make | ordain | rule |  |

*In 1987, the BBC **appointed** him their Deputy Editor of News and Current Affairs.*

*If you **elect** me president, you will be better off four years from now than you are today.*

*He **was named** full professor in 1941 and chaired the university's economics department for 10 years.* (passive)

■ **verbs concerned with having a particular idea regarding someone or something**

| account | consider | deem | feel | prove |
|---|---|---|---|---|
| adjudge | count | fancy | find | rate |

*The government **considers** him a threat.*

*I've always **found** him a pleasant man.*

*We have 10 industries in the constituency that **are rated** a pollution risk.* (passive)

In the case of *fancy* and *feel*, the noun group following the verb is always a reflexive pronoun.

*His son **fancied** himself a poet and a man of letters.*

■ **other common verbs**

| be born | bring up | hold | make | prove |
|---|---|---|---|---|

*In Mexico, his writing **has made** him a well-known public figure.*

*Two furious motorists **held** a man prisoner in his own car when they found him drunk on a motorway.*

*I **was brought up** a strict Catholic.* (passive)

In the case of *prove*, the noun group following the verb is always a reflexive pronoun.

*He **proved** himself a remarkably effective prime minister.*

## Different forms of the pattern

*What **are** you **going to call** it?*

*In 1722 he accompanied a missionary from Canton back to France, **which** he **found** an altogether bewildering place.*

*The Lodge, they **call** it.*

*They are displeased with **what** they **consider** a lack of concern for patients' needs.*

Some verbs are sometimes used in a pattern with *as*.

*Bob III, as he **is called**, shares his father's pride in the business.*

# Practice

**A** In the sentences below, put a dotted line under the verb used with the pattern described in this Unit. Then underline each of the other parts of the pattern.

1  He felt himself a fraud.

2  In 594 he proclaimed Buddhism the official state religion.

3  September 9 has been declared a day of action for press freedom.

4  We haven't got what you might term a school policy on assessment.

5  He consistently underestimated the Englishman, whom he considered an idiot.

6  It's not surprising, then, that fans throughout the United States have now voted him Entertainer of the Decade.

7  It was among the oldest of the Academy's buildings and was nicknamed 'Perilous Hall', with good reason.

8  I had been driving at about 35mph, which I considered a safe speed for the narrow, wet and winding road.

**B** Rewrite these sentences using the verb given in brackets with the pattern **V n n** or its passive.

1  They gave her the name of 'The Angel'. (call)
*They called her 'The Angel'.*

2  He was referred to as 'The King of Wessex'. (dub)

3  He was made into a priest. (ordain)

4  US officials are saying that the mission was a military success. (hail)

5  Always sun-tanned, he believed he was an athlete. (fancy)

6  Some people discover that relaxation is a useful way of calming down. (find)

7  He claimed he had been given the reputation of a liar and a hypocrite. (brand)

8  General Powell could be chosen as the country's first black President. (elect)

**C** *Find* and *make* have the pattern **V n n** with more than one meaning. For each sentence, say whether or not the second noun group after the verb describes the first one.

1  You find him a stupid man, I think. ....*yes*......

2  We have to find him a job. ................

3  Joanna found her an inspiration to work with. ................

4  The next morning she made them a real farmhand's breakfast. ................

5  His business had made him a very wealthy man. ................

6  She had made us an offer too good to refuse. ................

# Verbs used with an adjective group: 1

Some verbs are followed by an adjective group. For example, in *I was hungry*, the verb *be* is followed by the adjective *hungry*. This pattern is **V adj**.

|  | Verb group | adjective group |
|---|---|---|
| He | was feeling | unwell. |
| She | looked | happy. |
| The door | slammed | shut. |

Verbs with this pattern belong to the following meaning groups:

■ **verbs indicating that someone or something has a particular quality or is in a particular state**

| be | go | lie | prove | stand |
|---|---|---|---|---|
| feel | keep | pass | remain | stay |

She **was not young**, but she **was beautiful**.

I **was feeling** a bit lonely.

The law **has proved** difficult to implement.

The verbs *go* and *pass* are followed by negative adjectives such as *unnoticed* and *undetected*.

Adler wasn't going to let such behaviour **go unnoticed**.

*Be* is sometimes followed by an '-ed' clause indicating the state someone or something is in.

An old, yellowing card **was fixed** to the gate.

■ **verbs indicating that someone or something starts to have a particular quality or be in a particular state**

| become | come over | finish up | grow | wind up |
|---|---|---|---|---|
| come | end up | get | turn |  |
| come out | fall | go | turn out |  |

If your boss is opposed to your idea, your task **becomes more difficult**.

**Does** your father ever **get cross**?

He **came over** all dizzy, he said, when he stood up.

Swanson's face **turned white** as he realized what was about to happen.

*Become* and *get* are sometimes followed by an '-ed' clause indicating the state someone or something ends up in.

The whales often **become trapped** in fishing nets.

A thorny branch **had** just **got tangled** in my hair.

■ **verbs indicating that someone or something seems to have a particular quality or be in a particular state**

| appear | look | smell | taste |
|---|---|---|---|
| feel | seem | sound |  |

The Government **seems unable** to take control of the situation.

Bottled fruit not only **tastes delicious** but it also **looks terrific** displayed in the kitchen.

*Appear, feel, look,* and *seem* are sometimes followed by an '-ed' clause indicating the state someone or something seems to be in. *Feel* indicates how someone seems to themselves.

The enemy **seemed stunned** by the suddenness of the attack.

He **felt betrayed**.

■ **verbs indicating that something such as a door moves, or makes a sound as it moves**

| bang | burst | slide | spring |
|---|---|---|---|
| blow | slam | snap | swing |

As Adam and Zelikov entered, the heavy steel doors **banged shut** behind them.

The door **slid open** to admit Blake.

■ **verbs indicating that a person manages to get free, or that an object comes away from or out of something**

| break | roll | spring | work |
|---|---|---|---|
| pull | shake | struggle |  |

The more I struggled to **break free**, the more I became entangled.

The cable **had worked loose**.

■ **verbs indicating that something gives out or reflects light**

| flash | gleam | glisten | shine |
|---|---|---|---|

The metal box **gleamed silver** in the sun.

Behind us the white cliffs of Dover **shone bright** in the morning sun.

## Different forms of the pattern

I see now **how stupid** I **was**.

**Terrible** he **was**.

He's smarter than I **am**.

Note that questions are often asked using *what...like* or *how*:

**What did** it **look like**?

**How do** you **feel**?

**A** Fill in the gaps in the sentences below using the verbs in this list. Use each verb once.

fall   feel   get   look   pass   seem

1 He keeps buying me things and trying to make me ................................. guilty.
2 I found it hard to ................................. fit this season.
3 It now ................................. certain that the country's next President will be a woman.
4 She was ................................. strikingly attractive, as usual.
5 A health alert has been issued after 29 people ................................. ill after eating cucumber.
6 Without that, my mistake would have ................................. unnoticed.

**B** Fill in the gaps in the sentences below using the adjectives in this list. Use each one once.

bright   free   loose   open   shut   silver

1 The stream glistened ................................. in the sunlight.
2 Gordon tried to grab him by the arm, but the boy pulled .................................
3 The heavy door swung ................................. and the lock snapped into place.
4 His eyes still shone ................................. in the wrinkled face.
5 Noting that the ropes around the bags on my sled had worked ................................., I retied them carefully.
6 In the same moment, the outer door burst ................................. and several police constables stormed in.

**C** Put the different parts of these questions in the right order.

1 your brother / what / does / look / like ................................................................................................
2 the party / how / was ................................................................................................
3 it / what / did / feel / like ................................................................................................
4 I / how / do / look ................................................................................................
5 the food / what / was / like ................................................................................................

**D** Complete the second sentence in each pair.

1 Life was dull.
   He complained about how ..*dull life was.*..................................................................................
2 Middle America is flat and empty.
   I had forgotten how ................................................................................................
3 She looked fresh and pretty.
   I thought how ................................................................................................
4 His family are important to him.
   He told them how ................................................................................................
5 She seemed modest.
   I was struck by how ................................................................................................
6 This must have sounded suspicious.
   I was uncomfortably aware how ................................................................................................

# Verbs used with an adjective group: 2

Here are some more groups of verbs which are followed by an adjective group:

■ **verbs concerned with actions or processes**

| arrive | die | emerge | grow up | return |

*My father **died young**.*

*I want him to **grow up** happy and healthy.*

*None of them **returned alive**.*

The verbs listed above are the ones most frequently used with this meaning. However, it is often the adjective, rather than the verb, which makes this pattern possible. There are a lot of adjectives which are used with a much wider variety of verbs referring to actions and processes. Most of these adjectives have a negative meaning, especially those formed with 'un'. Here is a list of adjectives which are often used after an action verb.

| barefoot | unafraid | unescorted | unnoticed |
| blindfold | unaided | unharmed | unprotected |
| breathless | unannounced | unheard | unpunished |
| drunk | unarmed | unhurt | unread |
| empty-handed | unasked | unimpaired | unrecognized |
| free | unassisted | uninjured | unseen |
| naked | unattended | uninterrupted | untouched |
| straight-faced | undetected | uninvited | |

*A teenager named John Rush **came uninvited** to one of Stef's parties.*

*The man's car was hit by rifle fire but he **escaped unhurt**.*

*They all **walked barefoot** across the damp sand to the water's edge.*

■ **verbs indicating the position or posture of someone or something, or indicating that something stays in the same state**

| hang | lie | sit | stand |

The following adjectives are frequently used with *hang*:

| loose | low | motionless | open |

*Straight ahead of me the thunderclouds **hung low** over the highway.*

*Her head was on her knees, long dark hair **hanging loose**.*

The following adjectives are frequently used with *lie*:

| awake | empty | idle | open | unconscious |
| dead | flat | motionless | quiet | undiscovered |
| deep | helpless | naked | silent | undisturbed |

*He went in and found Stevens **lying dead** on the floor in the library.*

*The cave's entrance **lies deep** beneath the sea.*

The following adjectives are frequently used with *sit*:

| empty | idle | naked | silent |
| erect | low | quiet | straight |
| high | motionless | rigid | |

*The man **sat silent and motionless**.*

*8,000 unsold flats **are sitting empty**.*

The following adjectives are frequently used with *stand*:

| empty | high | naked | ready | straight |
| erect | idle | open | rigid | tall |
| free | motionless | proud | silent | unused |

*The corn **stood higher** than the car.*

*Very little work has been done and the flats still **stand empty**.*

■ There are a lot of other verbs which are followed by an adjective, but in many cases only one or two adjectives are used. Examples are *marry young, plead guilty/innocent, wear thin, sit up straight* and *fall down dead*.

*Her grandmother **married young** and divorced soon afterwards.*

*She was advised to **plead guilty** and accept a fine.*

**Practice**

**A** Rewrite the sentences below using the adjectives in this list. Use each adjective once.

barefoot    blindfold    empty-handed    unaided    uninterrupted    unseen

1  He was unable to walk without help. ....*He was unable to walk unaided.*....

2  The troops were marching without shoes to maintain silence.

.....................................................................................................................

3  His opponent was playing with a blindfold on. ................................................

4  I was hoping to work without anyone interrupting me.

.....................................................................................................................

5  There was barely time for the two boys to escape without anyone seeing them.

.....................................................................................................................

6  Her home was broken into by robbers, who miraculously left without taking anything.

.....................................................................................................................

**B** Fill in the gaps in the sentences below using the adjectives in this list. Use each one once.

alive    unheard    uninjured    uninvited    unpunished

1  His house was demolished but he escaped ...................................

2  Celebrities are welcome to show up ...................................

3  Women who say they feel unsafe are going ...................................

4  I don't think the man who killed that little girl should go ...................................

5  We didn't know whether they would return ...................................

**C** In each of the sentences below, one of the verbs from this list is missing. Mark where it goes and say what it is.

hang    lie    sit    stand

1  His mouth ⁀ open, his eyes grew wide, the blood drained from his face. ....*hung*....

2  Grace lifted the child into a corner of a deep chair. 'You have to quiet while Mommy makes a little music.' ...................................

3  When the newly-weds emerged from the church, a gleaming horse-drawn carriage ready to transport them to their reception. ...................................

4  Fiona fell to the ground and motionless for a few seconds. ...................................

5  Her fair hair loose on her shoulders. ...................................

**D** Fill in the gaps in these sentences with the correct adjectives.

1  There was a terrible flash of lightning and he fell down ...................................

2  Crook's expression made it clear that his patience was wearing ...................................

3  The actor vehemently denies the charges and will plead ................................... when the case opens on February 15 next year.

4  Sit up ................................... when you are having your hair cut to ensure an even line.

5  Lunn had married ................................... and had a boy and a girl aged four and six.

Some verbs are followed by a noun group and an adjective group. For example, in *I like my tea sweet*, the verb *like* is followed by the noun group *my tea* and the adjective *sweet*. This pattern is **V n adj**.

## Active pattern

|  | Verb group | noun group | adjective group |
|---|---|---|---|
| They | considered | these meetings | important. |
| He | wished | both of them | dead. |

## Passive pattern

|  | Verb group | adjective group |
|---|---|---|
| The party | was declared | illegal. |
| He | was proved | wrong. |

Verbs with this pattern belong to the following meaning groups:

- **verbs concerned with declaring or proving someone or something to have a particular quality**

| brand | confess | find | pronounce | rule |
|---|---|---|---|---|
| call | declare | label | prove | |
| certify | diagnose | pass | report | |

*The journal 'Nature' **called** this book dangerous.*

*Keating sampled the wine and **pronounced** it drinkable.*

*I **was** placed in a mental institution and **diagnosed** schizophrenic.* (passive)

*At the last moment he **was passed** fit to compete.* (passive)

In the case of *confess*, the noun group following the verb is always a reflexive pronoun. *Prove* often has this pattern as well.

*I **confess** myself very hurt by this neglect.*

*He **proved** himself worthy of the task in front of him.*

- **verbs indicating that someone has a particular opinion about someone or something**

| account | count | hold | rate |
|---|---|---|---|
| believe | deem | judge | think |
| consider | find | presume | |

*I **cannot believe** him capable of feeling for another human person.*

*At 48 he **is considered** too young to be prime minister.* (passive)

*The pair **are thought** likely to divorce later this year.* (passive)

Some of these verbs are used only with a very restricted range of adjectives; for example *hold* is used only with *accountable*, *liable*, and *responsible*.

*They **were held** responsible for the harm they caused.* (passive)

- **verbs indicating that someone likes, wants, or needs someone or something to have a particular quality or to be in a particular state**

| like | need | prefer | want | wish |
|---|---|---|---|---|

*The Dutch spread jam on bread for breakfast, so they **like** it smooth.*

*I **want** everything perfect.*

Note that these verbs cannot be used in the passive with this pattern.

## Practice

**A** In the sentences below, put a dotted line under the verb used with an adjective group. Then underline each of the other parts of the pattern. (For different forms of the pattern, see Unit 13.)

1  Readers, it seems, prefer their authors female.
2  Surveys suggest that people like their councils small and local.
3  It was six months before Joanna was diagnosed pregnant.
4  Courts should be given the power to declare invalid contracts written in complex or obscure language.
5  Mr. Schorr showed that the news media consider financial gains more important than ethics.
6  According to his mother he was a sober character, but I found him capable of profound emotion.
7  All the crew members of the oil tanker are reported safe, but a huge oil slick is reported to be spreading around the two vessels.
8  He presented himself at the library at a little after ten-thirty – an hour he judged appropriate for cornering an American scholar.
9  The lighting crew avoided directing very bright lights at him, which he found uncomfortable.
10  Whatever your reasons for pursuing a language course, you will soon find yourself able to speak and write with much greater confidence and clarity.

**B** Rewrite these sentences using the verb given in brackets and the pattern **V n adj** or its passive.

1  You're lucky it's still necessary to me that you remain alive. (need)
   *You're lucky I still need you alive.*
2  She admits that she is unable to give a definite view of the situation. (confess)
   ................................................................................................................................
3  Her doctor said she was unfit to travel. (rule)
   ................................................................................................................................
4  We think that we are lucky to have such a skilled worker around. (count)
   ................................................................................................................................
5  According to Patterson's wife, he was intelligent and well educated. (think)
   ................................................................................................................................
6  The owner cannot be regarded as responsible for injury or damage. (hold)
   ................................................................................................................................
7  Everyone knows the railway line should be built, but no one is in favour of having it close to their own village. (want)
   ................................................................................................................................
8  The jury decided that he was guilty. (find)
   ................................................................................................................................
9  In this instance a fine was considered to be appropriate. (deem)
   ................................................................................................................................
10  Sammy was not a nice man. Many people hoped he would die. (wish)
   ................................................................................................................................

# Verbs used with an adjective group: 4

Here are some more groups of verbs which are followed by a noun group and an adjective group:

■ **verbs used to indicate that something is opened or shut**

| blow | force | pull | slide |
|------|-------|------|-------|
| close | kick | push | tear |
| ease | open | shut | |

They **had to force** *the door open* to get in.

He went inside his cell and **pulled** *the door shut* behind him.

**Close** *your eyes tight*.

He rose, **opened** *the window wide*, and let in a blast of freezing air.

■ **verbs used with adjectives indicating the physical state of a person or thing after an action has been completed**

| draw | set | squash | sweep |
|------|-----|--------|-------|
| leave | shake | squeeze | wipe |
| pull | shoot | stuff | |

She took off her cap and threw it in Leigh's direction, **shaking** *her hair loose*.

A head-on collision between a bus and another passenger vehicle **has left** *eighteen people dead and two more injured*.

Whole neighbourhoods **have been squashed** *flat* by shelling. (passive)

■ **verbs concerned with holding or keeping someone or something in a particular position or state**

| have | hold | keep | leave |
|------|------|------|-------|

I had problems **holding** *the camera steady*.

His snores **kept** *me awake* all night.

■ **verbs used with adjectives indicating someone's mental or psychological state after an action has been completed**

| beat | knock | send |
|------|-------|------|
| drive | scare | strike |

I won't take this new job, it **scares** *me silly*.

It turns out he was in a fight and **was knocked** *unconscious*. (passive)

■ **verbs concerned with changing the colour of something**

| colour | paint | spray | turn |
|--------|-------|-------|------|

We **painted** *the walls white*.

Cut a rectangle from the card and **colour** *it green*.

■ **verbs concerned with catching or finding someone or something in a particular state**

| capture | catch | find |
|---------|-------|------|

He is a different man if ever you **catch** *him relaxed*.

One inmate **had been found** *dead* after a fire in his cell. (passive)

■ **verbs indicating ways in which people or animals get killed**

| boil | burn | bury | skin | swallow |
|------|------|------|------|---------|

The adjective used with these verbs is *alive*.

For many centuries the Christian Church **burned** *heretics alive*.

We feel terror at the thought of **being buried** *alive*. (passive)

Some of these verbs are sometimes used metaphorically.

They are fiercely competitive. If they **can skin** *us alive* in business, they will.

■ **other common verbs**

| be born | imagine | render |
|---------|---------|--------|
| get | make | serve |

Bake them for 8 to 10 minutes and **serve** *them hot* from the oven.

The government considered **making** *such experiments illegal*.

All men, whites and blacks, **are born** *free and equal*. (passive)

## Different forms of the pattern

What **do** people **consider** *important*?

Army commanders have been given full powers to carry out *any operation* they **consider** *necessary* to restore law and order.

The Court of Appeal yesterday **declared** *illegal* prison rules allowing the authorities to censor prisoners' letters.

*Black leather jeans* are easy to **keep** *clean*.

**A** Put the different parts of these sentences into the right order.

1 removed / in order to / his glasses / them / dry / wipe / he

......................................................................................................................................................

2 after / John / kicked / the door / him / shut

......................................................................................................................................................

3 the unlocked door / he / a wall cupboard / of / eased / open

......................................................................................................................................................

4 well / with / a few pistachio nuts / chilled / the pudding / serve

......................................................................................................................................................

5 maybe / think / unlucky / I / I / was born

......................................................................................................................................................

**B** Fill in the gaps in the sentences below using the adjectives in this list. Use each one once.

alight  alive  brown  exhausted  loose  mad  shut  steady  unconscious  white

1 Large quantities of iron may turn the water .................................

2 Eye-witnesses said that cars were set ................................., shop windows were broken and people passing by were beaten up.

3 They knew that the darkness could drive a man .................................

4 The man picked up the tool and left. Gibson kicked the door ................................. after him.

5 German houses were usually painted ................................., with blue roofs.

6 Bill recalls, 'I had problems holding the camera ................................. while shaking from loss of energy in the heat.'

7 I'd rather be buried ................................. than stuck in a lift with you.

8 They beat him ................................. with their pistols.

9 It is tragic when a rock shaken ................................. by an earthquake causes the death of a child.

10 It seemed to take him forever to get out of the river, and the effort left him .................................

**C** Fill in the gaps in the sentences below using the verbs in this list. Use each verb once.

be born  capture  force  keep  make  send  squash  tear

1 The man escaped from the back of the house, while his captors slept, after ................................. a window open with a spoon.

2 No one ................................. happy. Everyone has to make his own happiness.

3 Shock can ................................. people sad or angry.

4 They ................................. animals alive to sell to animal dealers, who sold them to zoos.

5 They've installed an irrigation scheme to ................................. the trees alive.

6 I stood outside with my suitcases and ................................. open the letter.

7 She made clay models and ................................. them flat again.

8 I can't help but feel that an obsessive search for our inner selves – far from saving the world – could ................................. us all mad.

# UNIT 14 Verbs used with an '-ing' clause: 1

Some verbs are followed by an '-ing' clause. For example, in *She started walking away*, the verb *start* is followed by the '-ing' clause *walking away*. This pattern is **V -ing**.

| | Verb group | -ing clause |
|---|---|---|
| He<br>You<br>She | kept<br>risk<br>hated | saying he was sorry.<br>losing everything.<br>being called Dora. |

Verbs with this pattern belong to the following meaning groups:

■ **verbs concerned with starting, stopping, continuing, or doing an action**

| | | | | |
|---|---|---|---|---|
| begin | come | give up | keep | resume |
| burst out | continue | go | keep on | start |
| carry on | finish | go around | leave off | stop |
| cease | get | go on | quit | take to |

I hope you**'re not going to start** crying.

**Stop** treating me like a schoolgirl.

I **gave up** swimming in the sea years ago.

Rather than correct her, I **kept trying to change the subject**.

■ **verbs indicating that someone does not do something**

| | | | | |
|---|---|---|---|---|
| avoid | (not) bother | escape | omit | resist |

I thought, I **won't bother** washing my hair – I'll wash it tomorrow.

He left word that he had rung, but carefully **omitted leaving his own number**.

He moved silently in the darkness to **avoid awakening his wife and two sons**.

■ **verbs concerned with doing something which may not be successful or may be dangerous**

| | | |
|---|---|---|
| chance | risk | try |

I **tried ringing his home**, but they told me he wasn't there.

He did not want to **risk going back to his apartment**.

Since race cars aren't insured, you **risk losing everything** if you hit something solid.

Note that these two examples of *risk* are different. In the first the '-ing' clause refers to an action which might have unpleasant consequences, and in the second the '-ing' clause refers to something that might happen as a result of an action.

■ **verbs indicating that someone takes part in an activity, often shopping or a leisure activity**

| | |
|---|---|
| come | go |

The next afternoon Amy **went riding with Gerald**.

■ **verbs indicating that someone likes or dislikes something**

| | | | |
|---|---|---|---|
| adore | dislike | like | resent |
| appreciate | (cannot) endure | love | (cannot) stand |
| (cannot) bear | enjoy | mind | (not) tolerate |
| detest | hate | prefer | |

I **don't** really **like having people round**.

Many people **prefer living alone**, even if it means loneliness.

I **don't appreciate being treated like a suspect**.

I hate the sight of guns and **dislike touching them**.

Many other people today said they **could not tolerate doing nothing**.

■ **verbs concerned with attitudes towards the future, for example looking forward to something or being afraid of something**

| | | | | |
|---|---|---|---|---|
| dread | (cannot) face | fancy | fear | look forward to |

She **was looking forward to taking a two-week holiday at the beach**.

She was hungry, but she **couldn't face eating**.

■ **verbs concerned with plans or ideas about the future**

| | | | |
|---|---|---|---|
| anticipate | count on | imagine | plan on |
| consider | debate | intend | reckon on |
| contemplate | figure on | look into | see about |

I haven't been in any trouble and I **don't intend getting into any**.

In this case, you **should consider seeking professional help**.

He **debated taking his car**, but decided to go on foot.

**A** Rewrite these sentences using the verb given in brackets in combination with the underlined verb.

1 We <u>wrote</u> our witty letters again as if nothing was wrong. (begin)
*We began writing our witty letters again as if nothing was wrong.*

2 I <u>lived</u> with my mum right up until we moved into this house. (carry on)
...............................................................................................

3 The team <u>has not analysed</u> that data yet. (finish) .....................................

4 I <u>asked</u> people how they felt about America. (go around)
...............................................................................................

5 I couldn't sleep and <u>thought</u> of the wonderful dancing I'd seen. (keep)
...............................................................................................

6 Dunne looked up at the ceiling and then <u>stared</u> at the fire. (resume)
...............................................................................................

7 He <u>walked</u> long distances in an attempt to physically exhaust himself. (take to)
...............................................................................................

**B** Rewrite these sentences using the verb given in brackets.

1 People did not talk about the problem. (avoid) *People avoided talking about the problem.*

2 When I was young, people didn't lock their doors. (not bother)
...............................................................................................

3 The dustmen made so much noise that I did not try to sleep. (give up)
...............................................................................................

4 'Don't read those books,' he said. 'They put ideas into your head.' (quit)
...............................................................................................

5 Hughes didn't use a wheelchair for almost two years. (resist)
...............................................................................................

6 His old comrades don't write to him any more. (stop) .....................................

**C** Rewrite these sentences using the verb given in brackets with the pattern **V -ing**.

1 45 per cent of British people might possibly vote Green in a general election. (consider)
*45 per cent of British people would consider voting Green in a general election.*

2 They are hoping that they will get money from the government. (count on)
...............................................................................................

3 I had been self-employed for so long that I couldn't think what it would be like to work for someone else. (imagine)
...............................................................................................

4 He thought he'd continue work on his writing. (intend) .....................................

5 You should expect to pay around £25,000 for a one-bedroomed flat. (reckon on)
...............................................................................................

6 I shall go and consult my lawyer. Then I must make arrangements to sell the house. (see about)
...............................................................................................

29

# Verbs used with an '-ing' clause: 2

Here are some more groups of verbs which are followed by an '-ing' clause:

■ **verbs concerned with attitudes and ideas about the past, for example remembering or forgetting something, or regretting something**

| | | | | |
|---|---|---|---|---|
| forget | miss | recall | regret | remember |

She **can't remember committing the murder**, although all the evidence points to her guilt.

**I'll** never **forget going to Sunday school as a kid**.

Whatever the future holds, **I will** never **regret meeting him**.

■ **verbs concerned with speaking or writing**

| | | | | |
|---|---|---|---|---|
| acknowledge | advocate | describe | mention | report |
| admit | debate | forbid | propose | suggest |
| advise | deny | justify | recommend | urge |

He **denied causing death by reckless driving**.

The judges **recommended giving more modest prizes**.

I **suggest following a simple rule**: never ask anyone anything about his or her life that you are not prepared to reveal about your own.

■ **verbs concerned with a logical relation between two actions, events, or states**

| | | | |
|---|---|---|---|
| allow | justify | permit | save |
| involve | mean | prevent | |

His route to school **involves crossing three main roads**.

Nothing **could** ever **justify destroying such a life**.

My brother had suggested that I take the bus because it **would save having to find a place to park in Manhattan**.

■ **verbs indicating that someone postpones an action**

| | | |
|---|---|---|
| delay | postpone | put off |

Many young couples **have postponed having families** because of the recession.

■ **verbs concerned with needing or deserving action or treatment of some kind**

| | | | |
|---|---|---|---|
| deserve | need | require | want |

I asked if there were any more problems that **needed sorting out**.

Miles is in good health and doesn't cry unless he **wants feeding or changing**.

■ **verbs concerned with beginning, ending, or spending time in a particular way**

| | | |
|---|---|---|
| die | finish up | start off |
| end up | hang around | wind up |

The soldiers reasoned that they'd prefer to **die fighting rather than waiting**.

Their boat **finished up pointing the wrong way**.

■ **other common verbs**

| | | |
|---|---|---|
| discourage | get away with | (cannot) help |
| encourage | go towards | play at |
| endure | go without | practise |

Parents **should encourage learning** but not push children beyond their current abilities.

The profits **will go towards fighting pollution and the destruction of rainforests**.

They say that when you're playing chess you **can go without eating**.

I **couldn't help feeling ashamed**.

**Practise giving your speech** in front of a mirror.

**A** Rewrite each of the following pairs of sentences as one sentence.

1 I used to be homeless. I'll never forget that.
*I'll never forget being homeless.*

2 He made the telephone calls. He admitted it.

3 I feel resentful. I can't help it.

4 She didn't want to tell Ida. She put it off until the last minute.

5 He cheated. He believed he might be able to get away with it.

6 They charge £22.50 for a fishing licence. I don't know how they can justify this.

7 People cannot campaign in the final two days before voting. The law forbids it.


**B** For each of the sentences below, say whether the underlined phrase indicates a past action or a possible future action.

1 The boys were expelled after admitting smoking cannabis. .........*past*..............
2 For best results, Virginia advises using olive oil rather than vegetable oil. ...............................
3 Witnesses described hearing a loud bang. ...................................
4 The committee recommended increasing the tax on fuels. ...................................
5 I don't regret telling her my suspicions. ...................................
6 I can remember sitting on the floor and eating an egg sandwich. ...................................
7 Several passengers reported seeing smoke coming from the engine. ...................................
8 They suggest opening up unused land around the airport. ...................................

**C** Match up the two halves of each sentence.

1 Many women delay ...
2 These criminals deserve ...
3 To improve your skills, practise ...
4 He appears gentle but ends up ...
5 The official policy is not to encourage ...
6 This technique involves ...

a ... removing the surface layer of the bone.
b ... doing harm.
c ... cycling on major roads.
d ... throwing and catching balls.
e ... having children until later in life.
f ... locking up.

# UNIT 16 Verbs used with a to-infinitive: 1

Some verbs are followed by a to-infinitive clause. For example, in *He expects to fly to Paris soon*, the verb *expect* is followed by the to-infinitive clause *to fly to Paris soon*. This pattern is **V to-inf**.

|  | Verb group | to-infinitive clause |
|---|---|---|
| The arrangements | appeared | to be satisfactory. |
| The President | agreed | to be interviewed. |

Verbs with this pattern belong to the following meaning groups:

■ **verbs concerned with starting, stopping, or continuing an action, or doing something next**

| begin | come | get | grow | start |
|---|---|---|---|---|
| cease | continue | go on | proceed | |

Edgar **began to laugh** again.

He treated us okay but I never **got to like him**.

Linda **continued to lose weight**.

Phil **went on to enjoy more success at cricket** than he had at football.

■ **verbs concerned with what something is or appears to be**

| appear | pretend | prove | seem | turn out |
|---|---|---|---|---|

The diagnosis **turned out to be her worst nightmare**.

He**'d** only **pretended to be sleeping**. He'd really been watching her all the time.

■ **verbs indicating that someone tries to achieve something**

| attempt | fight | strive | try |
|---|---|---|---|
| battle | labour | struggle | |

That's what he's doing, though he **tries to ignore it**.

A lot of people **struggled to understand** why they were doing this.

■ **verbs emphasizing that something is successfully done, especially something that is difficult or is easily forgotten**

| get | manage | remember | serve |
|---|---|---|---|

With some difficulty he **managed to stretch out an arm and get hold of the chocolate**.

**Remember to tell us** if you change your address.

What he learned **served to improve the managerial skills** needed in his present employment.

■ **verbs indicating that someone does not, need not, or cannot do something**

| (cannot) begin | decline | forget | omit | (not) trouble |
|---|---|---|---|---|
| (not) bother | fail | neglect | refuse | |

The peace talks collapsed when the rebels **failed to turn up**.

Jane went back to bed and fell promptly asleep, **forgetting to turn off the light**.

I **cannot begin to describe the things I miss**.

■ **verbs concerned with the manner or attitude of the person doing an action**

| care | dare | hesitate | regret |
|---|---|---|---|

I **regret to tell you that** very many American lives have been lost.

Each time the phone rings I **hesitate to answer**.

The roads are safer now, and people **dare to emerge from their homes at night**.

■ **verbs concerned with talking or thinking about a future action, or preparing for something that will happen in the future**

| agree | determine | intend | pledge | set out |
|---|---|---|---|---|
| arrange | elect | mean | prepare | swear |
| choose | fix | offer | promise | threaten |
| contract | go out | opt | propose | undertake |
| decide | guarantee | plan | resolve | vote |

Chloe **had promised to take her shopping** as soon as she arrived.

At one stage in the political crisis, the prime minister himself **threatened to resign**.

I **had planned to stay longer**, but something came up.

You **can choose to repay your loan over 60 months**.

**A** These sentences are about actions that are done or not done. Rewrite them using the verb given in brackets with the pattern **V to-inf**.

1 I didn't tell Ellen about this development. (neglect)
   *I neglected to tell Ellen about this development.*

2 Keep the list in a safe place. (remember) .................................................................

3 He escaped during the night. (manage) ................................................................

4 I hadn't brought a towel. (forget) .........................................................................

5 The man was nervous and would not give his name. (refuse)
   ..............................................................................................................................

6 The number of people who vote in these elections is small. (bother)
   ..............................................................................................................................

7 And did you meet Warhol? (get) ............................................................................

8 Mr. King, the contractor, has not answered our numerous phone calls. (decline)
   ..............................................................................................................................

9 This is the first time in nine years that the Lakers have not reached the finals. (fail)
   ..............................................................................................................................

**B** These sentences show the pattern **V that** (see Units 24 and 25). Rewrite them using the pattern **V to-inf**.

1 Lorraine just pretended she didn't hear. *Lorraine just pretended not to hear.*

2 He decided he would ask Claire to marry him. ....................................................

3 I promised I would have a word with Nick when he returned.
   ..............................................................................................................................

4 We have agreed that we have to follow up this incident.
   ..............................................................................................................................

5 She swore she wouldn't tell anyone. .....................................................................

6 He had already resolved that he would agree to nothing at this first meeting.
   ..............................................................................................................................

7 He kept threatening that he'd push the button on this remote control bomb device.
   ..............................................................................................................................

**C** Fill in the gaps in the sentences below using the verbs in this list. Use each verb once.

begin   cease   intend   seem   struggle

1 This was the first death in Trish's life and she had to ................................... to control her tears.

2 I ................................... to find that the subject of opera was becoming interesting.

3 It's funny how I never ................................... to get a thing accomplished on my day off.

4 We ................................... to invest 238 billion roubles over the next fifteen years.

5 Well, you never ................................... to learn in this life is what I always say.

# Verbs used with a to-infinitive: 2

Here are some more groups of verbs which are followed by a to-infinitive clause:

■ **verbs concerned with asking to do something or asking for something to be done**

| apply | beg | campaign | plead |
|-------|-----|----------|-------|
| ask   | bid | demand   | pray  |

The police **asked to use Keith's video as evidence**.

He **demanded to be flown to Sweden**, but the pilot landed instead at Helsinki.

■ **verbs concerned with wanting or expecting to do something**

| aim | fear | long | reckon | want |
|-----|------|------|--------|------|
| be dying | hope | (would) love | seek | wish |
| expect | (would) like | queue up | (cannot) wait | |

He **wanted to forget**.

We **expect to see her back on the screen in the autumn**.

He'd had his eyes on the telephone all during breakfast and he **couldn't wait to get out of his chair and get at it**.

■ **verbs concerned with liking or disliking something**

| (cannot) bear | like | prefer |
|---------------|------|--------|
| hate | love | (cannot) stand |

She **likes to entertain, shop and go to the theatre**.

Douglas **preferred to do his own driving**.

■ **verbs concerned with going somewhere in order to do something**

| come | flock | go | hurry | rush |
|------|-------|-----|-------|------|

Franklin **hurried to catch the last train back to Washington**.

Audiences **flocked to see the Beatles in their screen appearances**.

■ **other common verbs**

| (can) afford | happen | need | remain | train |
|--------------|--------|------|--------|-------|
| claim | help | negotiate | stop | wait |
| compete | learn | pay | survive | |
| deserve | live | qualify | tend | |

I want my books to be as cheap as possible so that more people **can afford to buy them**.

He **claims to have had no inside knowledge**.

Women **deserve to be treated as professionals**.

She never **learned to read or write**.

If you take Joey's advice, I'm convinced you'**ll live to regret it**.

Britain's 27 million motorists **may have to pay to drive on motorways within five years**.

Low-heeled comfortable shoes are best, too, as feet **tend to swell if you sit still for too long**.

Women **can** also **train to become fast jet pilots**.

The entire household **waited to greet them**.

In the case of *remain*, the verb is always followed by a passive to-infinitive.

A lot of questions **remain to be answered**.

**Productive use:** A to-infinitive clause after a verb often has the meaning 'in order to do something'. An example is *He smiled to hide his fear*, which means that hiding his fear was the purpose of his smiling.

## Different forms of the pattern

Don't **take me**, if you **don't want to**.

Some verbs are sometimes used in a pattern with *as* or *than*.

He did as his sister **asked**.

Kelly stayed at the disco much later than she**'d planned**.

**A** Fill in the gaps in these sentences using the to-infinitive form or the '-ing' form of the verb given in brackets. (See also Units 14 to 16.)

1 He longed ................................. her voice. (hear)

2 The woman admitted ................................. the bombing. (carry out)

3 We couldn't afford ................................. another actor. (hire)

4 She asked ................................. home. (be taken)

5 Lisa suggested ................................. a bonfire. (make)

6 He couldn't practise ................................. much, except when he hunted. (shoot)

7 I tend ................................. a bit of a perfectionist. (be)

8 He decided ................................. the matter to the women. (leave)

9 I would recommend ................................. your doctor. (consult)

10 Always give a toddler who is learning ................................. something to hold on to. (walk)

11 At least six states have passed laws that discourage ................................. by car. (commute)

12 The number of people applying ................................. physics and chemistry at British universities fell last year. (study)

**B** Fill in or complete the replies, using the verb given in brackets.

1 'Do you intend to keep playing until then?' (hope) .............*Yes, I hope to.*.............

2 'Would you like to have coffee?' (would love) ........................................................

3 'Put a T-shirt on.' (don't want) 'No, ........................................................

4 'So you're learning Italian?' (try) ........................................................

5 'Are you leaving tomorrow?' (plan) ........................................................

6 'Are you finding plenty of work?' (would like)
'Well, not as much as ........................................................

7 'You could have phoned me.' (mean)
........................................ but I didn't get the chance.'

8 'Does he in fact have most of the power at the moment?' (appear)
'Well, this is always hard to say, but ........................................................

**C** Put the different parts of these sentences into the right order.

1 all / the most popular / they / in the school / to be / long / girl

.............................................................................................................

2 in the competition / would love / more women / they / to see

.............................................................................................................

3 for / expect / in hospital / I / about / to be / five days

.............................................................................................................

4 everything / dropped / to help / and / rushed / everyone

.............................................................................................................

5 to be / with young children / most mothers / at home / would prefer

.............................................................................................................

35

# 18 Verbs used with an '-ing' clause or a to-infinitive

Some verbs may be followed either by an '-ing' clause or by a to-infinitive clause.

**A** With some verbs, the meaning is almost the same.

■ verbs concerned with beginning, ending, or continuing an action
■ verbs concerned with someone's feelings or attitudes
■ verbs concerned with not doing something

| (cannot) bear | cease | intend | omit |
| begin | continue | like | prefer |
| (not) bother | hate | love | start |

*They **began going out together** and some ten months later decided to marry.*
*As time passed and he grew colder, he also **began to grow tired**.*

*I **can't bear** being shouted at.*
*I **cannot bear** to watch the film from beginning to end because of the bad memories it brings back.*

*Some people have said they **will not** even **bother going back to their destroyed homes**.*
*He ran out, **not bothering to close the door**.*

Note that you use a to-infinitive clause after *would like* or *would love* meaning 'want'. You cannot use an '-ing' clause.

*She **would like to be more financially independent**.*

**B** With some verbs, the two meanings are different.

**1** After *come* and *go*, you use an '-ing' clause to indicate that someone moves or does something in a particular way.

*Bob **came running from the room next door**.*
*They **go looking for trouble** just for something to do.*

You use a to-infinitive clause to indicate that someone goes somewhere in order to do something.

*I actually **came to apologize**.*
*I **went to see him** last week.*

After *go*, you can also use an '-ing' clause to indicate that someone goes shopping or takes part in a leisure activity.

*My kids **go swimming in the sea**.*

After *come*, you can also use a to-infinitive clause to indicate that someone gradually begins to do something, or does something eventually.

*Phil **came to understand that it is impossible to control another person**.*

**2** If you *go on* doing something, you continue to do it. If you *go on* to do something, you do it after you have finished doing something else.

*He disregards what others say, quietly planning to **go on doing things his own way**.*
*After the calf muscles, **go on to exercise the knees, then the upper leg**.*

**3** After *remember*, *forget*, and *regret*, you use an '-ing' clause if you are referring to an event which actually happened.

*I **remember** visiting them just before his sixtieth birthday.*
*I'll never **forget** living next to her.*
*I think they **regret** selling it to us now.*

After *remember* and *forget*, you use a to-infinitive clause when talking about something that you had planned or are planning to do, or that you should do.

***Remember** to lock the door.*
*Too often we **forget** to laugh, taking ourselves and life too seriously.*

After *regret*, in formal English, you use a to-infinitive clause with verbs like *say* and *inform* to indicate that you are sorry for what you are saying.

*I **regret** to inform you he died as a consequence of his injuries.*

**4** After *need* and *deserve*, you use a to-infinitive clause if the Subject of the verb is also the Subject of the to-infinitive clause.

*I **need to talk to you**.*
*The gunmen **deserve to be locked up**.*

You can use an '-ing' clause instead of a passive to-infinitive clause.

*The plants **need watering**.*
*Local residents agree that the wildlife **deserves protecting**.*

**5** If someone or something *helps* to do something, they assist in an action. If you *cannot help* doing something, you cannot prevent yourself from doing it.

*Careful exercise or gentle massage **can help** to relax the muscles.*
*I **couldn't help** overhearing the argument.*

**6** If you *try* to do something, you make an effort to do it. If you *try* doing something, you do it as an experiment, for example to see if you like it or if it solves a problem.

*Defence lawyers **tried** to have the case dismissed.*
***Try** drinking your tea or coffee without sugar.*

**A** These sentences show the pattern **V -ing**. Rewrite them using the pattern **V to-inf**.

1 James started talking about the quiz show.

........................................................................................................................

2 The sport continued growing through the Seventies.

........................................................................................................................

3 She said that she wouldn't bother coming to the meeting.

........................................................................................................................

4 I tried to remember what I like eating.

........................................................................................................................

5 I can't bear not seeing him.

........................................................................................................................

**B** These sentences show the pattern **V to-inf**. Rewrite them using the pattern **V -ing**.

1 The team will begin to build the observatory later this year.

........................................................................................................................

2 The firm ceased to operate three weeks ago.

........................................................................................................................

3 He'd omitted to tell the police about the missing cash.

........................................................................................................................

4 First of all, he loves to make movies, he loves the process.

........................................................................................................................

5 You prefer to be taught by somebody who has actually done the job rather than somebody who's studied the job.

........................................................................................................................

**C** Fill in the gaps in these sentences using the '-ing' form or the to-infinitive form of the verb given in brackets.

1 He came ............................................. me on Monday. (see)
2 I went ............................................. down the stairs and bruised my thigh. (tumble)
3 She enjoyed talking to her neighbour, and they often went ............................................. together. (shop)
4 Did you remember ............................................. your voting form? (post)
5 I'll never forget ............................................. Barcelona to win the Cup-Winner's Cup. (beat)
6 I regret ............................................. that I am unfamiliar with her work. (say)
7 The rule needs ............................................. at. It should be changed. (look)
8 They were a better team than us and deserved ............................................. (win)
9 Again and again I tried ............................................., but no sound came. (speak)
10 I couldn't help ............................................. sorry for him. (feel)

# Verbs used with an '-ing' clause: 3

Some verbs are followed by a noun group and an '-ing' clause. For example, in *They caught him stealing money*, the verb *catch* is followed by the noun group *him* and the '-ing' clause *stealing money*. This pattern is **V n -ing**.

|       | Verb group | noun group | -ing clause |
|-------|-----------|-----------|-------------|
| I     | don't like | them      | pointing at me. |
| She   | noticed   | a man     | sitting alone on the grass. |

Verbs with this pattern belong to the following meaning groups:

- **verbs indicating that someone thinks about an event, or has a particular feeling about an event or situation**

| | | | |
|---|---|---|---|
| anticipate | forget | (not) mind | (cannot) stand |
| appreciate | hate | put up with | tolerate |
| (cannot) bear | (will not) have | recall | (not) want |
| contemplate | imagine | remember | |
| fear | like | (can) see | |

Nobody **can** ever **recall** *him firing anybody*.

Her husband **doesn't like** *her talking to us*.

I hope you **don't mind** *me calling in like this*, without an appointment.

- **verbs concerned with a logical relation between two processes or things**

| | | | |
|---|---|---|---|
| entail | involve | justify | mean |

A move there **would involve** *him taking a cut in salary*.

We get another customer for our hospital, and this **justifies** *us spending money on new equipment*.

- **verbs concerned with stopping someone doing something, or preventing something happening**

| | | | | |
|---|---|---|---|---|
| avoid | prevent | resist | save | stop |

They hope to reach an agreement to **avoid** *the case ending up in court*.

I think she really would have liked to **stop** *us seeing each other*.

- **verbs concerned with perceiving, finding, or showing someone doing something**

| | | | | |
|---|---|---|---|---|
| catch | find | notice | see | watch |
| feel | hear | observe | show | |

As she left, she **could feel** *his eyes following her*.

Most of these verbs are sometimes used in the passive.

Men **had been observed** *entering and leaving the house with large bags*, the police were told. (passive)

The Subject usually indicates a human being, but *see* and *show* sometimes have inanimate Subjects.

*The picture* **showed** *Joey jumping into the air, his arms and legs spread wide*.

In the case of *catch, feel*, and *find*, the noun group is often a reflexive pronoun.

I **caught** *myself wondering why we ever imagine children will bring us happiness*.

She **felt** *herself beginning to cry*.

- **verbs concerned with causing someone or something to do something or remain in a particular state**

| | | |
|---|---|---|
| bring | keep | send |
| have | leave | set |

Edna Lawrence survived a gas blast which **brought** *her home crashing down on top of her*.

The film **had** *the audience cheering and crying*.

All these verbs except *have* are sometimes used in the passive.

Mathis **was sent** *flying onto his back*.

- **verbs concerned with passing time in a particular way, or starting or ending a period of time in a particular way**

| | | | |
|---|---|---|---|
| begin | finish | pass | take |
| busy | kill | spend | waste |
| end | occupy | start | |

Don't **waste** *time talking*.

Liberal Democrats **started** *this day making their objections to the Republican plan clear*.

In the case of *busy* and *occupy*, the noun group is always a reflexive pronoun.

He **busied** *himself rinsing the washcloth*, soaping it again.

- *Risk* also has this pattern.

Glover **could not risk** *four men standing up in court and telling the judge he had ordered them to kill someone*.

## Different forms of the pattern

He was the first man I**'d seen** *wearing blue jeans*.

**A** In the sentences below, put a dotted line under the verb used with an '-ing' clause. Then underline each of the other parts of the pattern.

1 She wouldn't tolerate any of us going into the armed services.
2 When I was in my twenties, she put up with me drifting in and out of her life.
3 Despite Robin's importance he was kept waiting a long time.
4 I was amazed that I could watch Nicholas being delivered without feeling funny.
5 She wrote in her diary of two small boys she had seen begging in the street.
6 All the unaccompanied children had been taken away, except for the boys whom she had heard being rejected.

**B** Rewrite these sentences using the verb given in brackets with a noun group and an '-ing' clause.

1 They saw that a police car was following them. (notice)
   *They noticed a police car following them.*

2 He pulled in three or four huge lungfuls of smoke that made him cough. (set)

3 At the start of his career he played in dance bands. (begin)

4 Every day I keep myself busy by doing chores about the house. (occupy)

5 When she came back with the vase, he was staring at the picture of himself. (find)

6 During the process of digestion, the animal uses energy. (involve)

**C** Rewrite each of the following pairs of sentences as one sentence.

1 He was about to go into hospital. I couldn't bear that.
   *I couldn't bear him going into hospital.*

2 He said, 'You don't have to say anything, just be here.' I'll never forget that.
   I'll never forget ....................................................................................

3 The room is hot. You have to put up with that.
   You have to put up with .....................................................................

4 Don't chase around the streets. That's a waste of time.
   Don't waste .........................................................................................

5 Her father might see them together. Erin didn't want to risk that.
   Erin didn't want to risk ......................................................................

6 He could not see whether he had done any damage. The rifle's smoke prevented him.
   The rifle's smoke prevented ...............................................................

# Verbs used with a to-infinitive: 3

Some verbs are followed by a noun group and a to-infinitive clause. For example, in *She persuaded him to leave*, the verb *persuade* is followed by the noun group *him* and the to-infinitive clause *to leave*. This pattern is **V n to-inf**.

## Active pattern

|  | Verb group | noun group | to-infinitive clause |
|---|---|---|---|
| They | would prefer | the truth | to remain untold. |
| She | nagged | me | to cut my hair. |

## Passive pattern

|  | Verb group | to-infinitive clause |
|---|---|---|
| He | was begged | to stay on. |
| We | will be forced | to make some difficult decisions. |

(With phrasal verbs, the particle comes either after the noun group or after the verb.)

Verbs with this pattern belong to the following meaning groups:

■ **verbs concerned with what someone wants to happen**

| (would) hate | (would) love | prefer | wish |
|---|---|---|---|
| (would) like | need | want | |

*Treating others as you **would like** them to treat you is easier said than done.*

*I'**d love** her to go into politics or on the stage.*

*I **need** you to do something for me.*

Note that these verbs cannot be used in the passive with this pattern.

■ **verbs concerned with making requests, or giving advice or orders**

| advise | counsel | forbid | pressure | tell |
|---|---|---|---|---|
| ask | dare | invite | push | urge |
| beg | defy | nag | recommend | warn |
| challenge | direct | order | remind | |
| command | encourage | press | request | |

*She looked at him, waiting for him to **ask** her to come with him.*

*He **advised** me to go home and rest.*

*I **told** him to get out and stay out.*

*Last night, he **urged** them to give up their fight.*

■ **verbs concerned with making or causing someone to do something**

| (cannot) bring | force | lead | pay | tempt |
|---|---|---|---|---|
| cause | get | be made | persuade | |
| condemn | induce | motivate | prompt | |
| convince | influence | move | sentence | |
| drive | inspire | oblige | spur | |

*The force of her push **caused** me to crack my head against someone else's.*

*It was September 1982 when his love for books **drove** him to open his own shop.*

*Kim's guilt **led** her to overeat.*

*Their fairytale marriage **prompted** Jane to write a book on romantic living.*

*Make* occurs in this pattern only in the passive: the corresponding active pattern is **V n inf** (see Unit 22).

*I did nothing wrong, yet I'**m being made** to suffer like this.*

In the case of *bring*, the noun group is always a reflexive pronoun.

*Even now she **couldn't bring** herself to tell John the whole truth.*

■ **verbs concerned with allowing, enabling, or helping someone to do something**

| allow | entitle | help | qualify |
|---|---|---|---|
| assist | equip | permit | teach |
| enable | free | prepare | train |

*My dad **helped** me to buy it.*

*He **taught** us all to swim when we were quite young.*

*We obediently awaited the signal **permitting** us to enter.*

*The basic course **does not qualify** you to practise as a therapist, but it does give you an adequate foundation.*

**A** Rewrite these sentences using the verb given in brackets with the pattern **V n to-inf**.

1 It would be awful if he lost his job. (would hate) ...*I would hate him to lose his job.*...

2 It would be nice if you could see the house. (would like)
.................................................................................................................................

3 They would rather that the talks were held in a neutral country. (would prefer)
.................................................................................................................................

4 His wife wishes he would give up his job. (would love)
.................................................................................................................................

5 Why can't they leave me alone? (want) ...............................................................................

**B** Put these quotes into reported speech using the verb given in brackets and the words provided.

1 'You should go to bed immediately.' (tell)
The doctor ............*told*............ me ...........*to go to bed immediately.*...........

2 'Please don't go!' (beg)
I ................................. her ......................................................................................

3 'Tell me everything you can about the product.' (ask)
I ................................. him ....................................................................................

4 'Don't leave the room.' (forbid)
He ................................. me ...................................................................................

5 'You ought to take responsibility for yourself.' (urge)
I ................................. Jennifer ..............................................................................

6 'I wouldn't talk to the press, if I were you.' (advise)
His lawyer ................................. him .......................................................................

7 'The public should be on the look-out for other bombs.' (warn)
Police ................................. the public ......................................................................

**C** Fill in the gaps in these sentences using the '-ing' form or the to-infinitive form of the verb given in brackets. (See also Unit 15.)

1 It was Pam who finally persuaded him ............................................ to Britain. (return)

2 They said they were allowed ............................................ everything they wanted to see. (see)

3 Environmentalists advise ............................................ a damp cloth over the mouth and nose for protection. (wear)

4 All bicyclists are encouraged ............................................ helmets. (wear)

5 Donna taught herself ............................................ the piano. (play)

6 Guns enable men ............................................ at a distance. (kill)

7 The rules forbid ............................................ in the building. (cook)

8 I recommend ............................................ water or mild soap and water, depending on how dirty the surface is. (use)

# Verbs used with a to-infinitive: 4

Here are some more groups of verbs which are followed by a noun group and a to-infinitive clause:

■ **verbs concerned with appointing or choosing someone to do something, or with allocating or assigning something to a particular use**

| appoint | choose | detail | nominate | use |
|---------|--------|--------|----------|-----|
| assign | commission | employ | recruit | |

*Belgium **chose** her to represent the country again the following year and she became a star there.*

*It is never too late to **use** new information to improve the situation.*

*He **was nominated** to be the director of a computer company.* (passive)

■ **verbs concerned with thinking, saying, or showing something**

| acknowledge | declare | know | be reputed | think |
|-------------|---------|------|------------|-------|
| allege | discover | make out | be rumoured | understand |
| assume | feel | prove | be said | |
| believe | find | reckon | be seen | |
| consider | judge | report | show | |

*They **have declared** the north to be an independent republic.*

*60 per cent of 900 firms surveyed **judge** their business to be bad.*

*About eighty people **are believed** to have died in the attack.* (passive)

*Islands **are seen** to offer solitude, relaxation and a safe retreat.* (passive)

*She left the course by ambulance and **was thought** to have suffered a neck injury.* (passive)

In the case of *prove*, the noun group is often a reflexive pronoun.

*He **has proved** himself to be a highly skilled politician.*

■ **verbs concerned with intentions, predictions, and expectations**

| back | intend | project | schedule | trust |
|------|--------|---------|----------|-------|
| expect | mean | require | tip | |

*We **expect** you to show good judgement.*

*He **trusted** her to tell the truth because he knew that she always told the truth.*

*He **had been scheduled** to return to Washington, but now he clearly hoped to stay on.* (passive)

In the case of *trust*, the noun group is often a reflexive pronoun.

*I **don't trust** myself to handle this.*

■ **verbs concerned with someone or something being heard or seen to do something**

| be heard | be observed | be seen |
|----------|-------------|---------|

These verbs occur in this pattern only in the passive: the corresponding active pattern is **V n inf** (see Unit 22).

*New mothers **have been observed** to touch the feet and hands first, then the body, and then the baby's face.*

■ **other common verbs**

| be born | do | take | (not) trouble |
|---------|-----|------|---------------|

*That woman **was born** to be a teacher.* (passive)

In the case of *trouble*, the noun group is always a reflexive pronoun.

*Nobody **troubled** himself to tell me that anything was happening.*

In the case of *do*, the noun group is always an **amount**.

*We**'ve done** a lot to improve results, and a lot more will be done.*

In the case of *take*, the noun group indicates a period of time.

*The treatment **takes** up to twelve months to produce worthwhile improvement.*

## Different forms of the pattern

*Who **do** you **trust** to lead this country?*

*Michelle and Mark cheer on **the horse** they **want to win**.*

*I'd **die for her** if she **asked** me to.*

Some verbs, especially *tell*, are sometimes used in a pattern with *as*.

*He did as he **was told**.*

# UNIT 21 Practice

**A** Make these statements less direct or definite by rewriting them using the verb given in brackets with the passive of the pattern **V n to-inf**.

1 The Queen is deeply sensitive about the whole issue. (know)
*The Queen is known to be deeply sensitive about the whole issue.*

2 The two officers were poisoned 25 days ago. (believe)
......................................................................................................................................

3 The accused is a member of an extreme right-wing gang. (allege)
......................................................................................................................................

4 The round shape represents the sun. (be said)
......................................................................................................................................

5 The President favours more negotiations on environmental protection. (know)
......................................................................................................................................

6 This is one of the most powerful radar systems of its kind in the world. (be said)
......................................................................................................................................

7 Madonna is planning tours of the Far East and South America later this year. (be rumoured)
......................................................................................................................................

8 The German foreign minister is very annoyed that he was not consulted about the visit in advance. (understand)
......................................................................................................................................

**B** Match up the two halves of each sentence.

1 The management will require each employee ...   a ... to win the European Championship.
2 You could always trust them ...   b ... to fill in a questionnaire.
3 Paul Gascoigne last night tipped England ...   c ... to do what was necessary.
4 He intended the book ...   d ... to continue.
5 We expect the recovery ...   e ... to reflect ordinary American life.

**C** Rewrite these sentences using the passive of the pattern **V n to-inf**.

1 Someone heard her say he was 'madly attractive'.
*She was heard to say he was 'madly attractive'.*

2 People saw her weep during the Hungarian anthem.
......................................................................................................................................

3 People have observed that cats show strong maternal instincts.
......................................................................................................................................

4 In one outburst, the spectators heard him yell: 'You're so bloody wrong!'
......................................................................................................................................

5 Bystanders saw two other men shoot at him.
......................................................................................................................................

6 When he attended the summit earlier this week, people observed he was suffering from a heavy cold.
......................................................................................................................................

# Verbs used with a bare infinitive

**1** A few verbs are followed by a clause beginning with a **bare infinitive**, that is, an infinitive without *to*. For example, in *He didn't dare disagree with me*, the verb *dare* is followed by the infinitive clause *disagree with me*. This pattern is **V inf**.

|  | Verb group | infinitive clause |
|---|---|---|
| I | didn't dare | leave him. |
| He | helped | make her a star. |

There are only three verbs with this pattern.

| dare | help | need |
|---|---|---|

*It was some hours before she **need start preparations for the children's supper**.*

*The United Nations Security Council has taken another step to **help bring about a peaceful settlement to the conflict**.*

Note that the negative of *dare* in this pattern is either *do not dare* or *dare not*, while the negative of *need* is always *need not*. Both verbs are also frequently followed by a to-infinitive clause (see Units 16 and 17) where their negatives are like any normal verb.

*My blood boiled at the sight, but I **dared not speak**.*

*You **needn't worry about whether he will cope**.*

**2** Some verbs are followed by a noun group and a clause beginning with a bare infinitive. For example, in *I saw him leave the room*, the verb *see* is followed by the noun group *him* and the infinitive clause *leave the room*. This pattern is **V n inf**.

|  | Verb group | noun group | infinitive clause |
|---|---|---|---|
| She | heard | the man | laugh. |
| She | made | him | stop. |

Verbs with this pattern belong to the following meaning groups:

■ **verbs concerned with seeing, hearing, or feeling someone or something perform an action**

| feel | notice | see |
|---|---|---|
| hear | observe | watch |

*Chandler **did not notice** him enter.*

*When I turned back to **watch** him close the door, he seemed so utterly alone.*

In the case of *feel*, the noun group is often a reflexive pronoun.

*I **felt myself grow cold** and my hands trembled as I read: We have your son. He is safe so far. If you obey orders he will soon be back with you.*

■ **verbs concerned with making or letting someone do something, or making or letting something happen**

| have | let | make |
|---|---|---|

*Let's see what people want, and **make it happen**.*

*Angel eagerly awaited him, anxious to **have him meet Lara**.*

*She **let her head rest on his shoulder**.*

*They threatened him and **made him open the safe**.*

In the case of *let*, the noun group is often a reflexive pronoun.

*I don't think he really **let himself get close to anyone**.*

In the case of many senses of *let*, the noun group is always *me* or *us*. The verb is always in the imperative form.

***Let us look at the evidence**.*

■ *Help* also has this pattern.

*The money was an interest-free loan to **help him buy a Paris flat**.*

**A** In the sentences below, put a dotted line under the verb used with a pattern described in this Unit. Then underline each of the other parts of the pattern.

1 We can't just sit by and watch you throw your life away.
2 Let me say a few more words about economic affairs.
3 We had assembled a team of people to help advise us how to deal with the French government.
4 The first requirement for the undergraduate college is to help students achieve proficiency in written and oral language.
5 They whisper to me that James Hopper likes me, but I don't dare believe them.
6 But you do so much already and, really, you needn't do anything at all.

**B** Fill in the gaps in the sentences below using the phrases in this list.

didn't dare    did not help    needn't

1 I ............................................... tell my mother where I was going for fear of her having a heart attack.
2 You ............................................... worry, Mrs Dayton. We'll bring you back safely.
3 Sanctions ............................................... stop the war.
4 We ............................................... eat straightaway. You can read your paper.
5 He feared that the tradition would disappear if he ............................................... keep it alive.
6 For a terrible second I froze. I ............................................... turn around.

**C** Rewrite each of the following pairs of sentences as one sentence.

1 He went out of the tent. She heard him. *She heard him go out of the tent.* ...........................
2 A woman picked something up and handed it to another woman. Only one man noticed her.
...............................................................................................................
3 The students taught and conducted conferences. The university supervisor observed them.
...............................................................................................................
4 He dived into the deep end. I saw him. ...............................................................
5 The police car left the village. From her bedroom window, Jessica watched it.
...............................................................................................................

**D** Rewrite these sentences using the verb given in brackets with the pattern **V n inf**.

1 She took her daughter home and persuaded her to lie down on the couch. (have)
*She took her daughter home and had her lie down on the couch.* ..................................
2 She forced me to promise that I would not tell the others anything about it. (make)
...............................................................................................................
3 Don't accept a situation where you are overcharged. (let)
...............................................................................................................
4 Most women say that after using face masks their skin feels very smooth. (make)
...............................................................................................................

# Verbs used with an '-ed' clause

Some verbs are followed by a noun group and an '-ed' clause, which usually consists of just an '-ed' form. For example, in *I had my car repaired*, the verb *have* is followed by the noun group *my car* and the '-ed' clause *repaired*. This pattern is **V n -ed**.

|   | Verb group | noun group | -ed clause |
|---|---|---|---|
| I | must get | the car | serviced. |
| I | want | him | found. |

The verbs which most frequently have this pattern are *have* and *get*.

One use of these verbs is to indicate that you arrange for someone to do something or perform a service for you. In the case of medical procedures, the action is usually done because it is necessary rather than because you want it to happen, and the verb used is *have*.

Here are some of the more frequent combinations of *have* or *get*, a noun group, and an '-ed' clause:

| | |
|---|---|
| have a limb amputated | get/have your hair permed |
| get/have your hair cut | get/have your ears pierced |
| get/have your house decorated | get/have something repaired |
| get/have your house done up | get/have your house rewired |
| have a tooth extracted | get/have your car serviced |
| get/have something fixed | have someone tailed |
| have someone followed | have a tooth taken out |
| get/have someone immunized | get/have someone vaccinated |
| get/have something made | get/have something valued |
| get/have something mended | |

We **ought to get** the roof repaired before the house gets any damper.

You really **ought to get** your hair cut. It's starting to look ridiculous.

Before a purchaser can make a formal offer to buy, he **must have** the property valued.

At least 1 in 20 parents choose not to **have** their children immunised.

*Have* is also used to indicate that something happens to you which is caused by someone else.

Did I tell you Hazel**'s had** her car stolen again?

Press photographers on the scene **had** their exposed film confiscated by police.

*Get* is also used to indicate that someone or something causes something to happen.

Walsh made a determined effort to **get** me fired from my job at the Department of Justice.

'Anything at all that **can get** you noticed is good news in this business,' said Ms Swan.

*Get* is also used to indicate that someone achieves something.

How **will** I ever **get** all that cooking done?

Here are some more groups of verbs which have this pattern:

■ verbs concerned with **wanting or needing something to be done**

| (would) like | need | want |
|---|---|---|

The teachers' union says it **would like** the school shut down.

I **want this murder investigated**.

She came into the shop with a package saying: 'I **don't need** it changed, only re-wrapped.'

■ verbs concerned with **seeing, hearing, or feeling something happen**

| feel | hear | see | watch |
|---|---|---|---|

In the morning, everyone came out to **see** Nick carried into the ambulance.

It was the first time he **had heard** the name spoken in five years.

In the case of *feel*, the noun group is often a reflexive pronoun.

Watching her, Ellis **felt** himself overcome by love.

■ other common verbs

| find | keep | make | order | report |
|---|---|---|---|---|

Please **keep** me informed of your progress.

There's no way he **could have ordered** anyone killed, he says.

*Find*, *keep*, and *report* are sometimes used in the passive.

A man **was** last night **found** shot dead in the back of his car.

At least three people **were reported** killed when police opened fire in three areas of the capital.

In the case of *make*, the noun group is often a reflexive pronoun.

He had taught me a few words of his language and I **was able to make** myself understood now and then.

## Different forms of the pattern

It is a resource **which** the Majorcan authorities wish to **see used by a larger proportion of the island's visitors.**

**A** In the sentences below, put a dotted line under the verb used with an '-ed' form. Then underline each of the other parts of the pattern.

1 Readers who want a question answered should write to us.

2 Does the boss like to hear three possible courses of action discussed before a recommendation gets offered?

3 A search is going on after a yacht was found abandoned about eighty miles off Shetland.

4 The group would like EC laws changed to allow motorists to 'shop around' for cheaper deals abroad.

5 The door is kept locked at night, and they didn't come into the building.

6 To get you started, we've provided some favorite recipes.

**B** Fill in the gaps in these sentences using a form of *have* or *get* with the words given in brackets. Sometimes both *have* and *get* are possible.

1 I need to ...*get my amplifier fixed.*............................... (my amplifier / fix)

2 Alison says she wants to ................................................. (her ears / pierce)

3 He made a mental note to ................................................. (the car / service)

4 I asked him if he would ................................................. for insurance purposes. (my jewellery / value)

5 Henry eventually married Anne Boleyn and later ................................................. (her / behead)

6 Kevin was unfairly dismissed for refusing to ................................................. (his hair / cut)

7 Six months after the baby was born in 1964, Pauline ................................................. (her / adopt)

8 ................ you ................................................. against whooping cough? (your child / vaccinate)

**C** Rewrite the following sentences using *have*.

1 My friend's bike was stolen last week. ...*My friend had his bike stolen last week.*...........

2 Their salaries should be increased. .................................................

3 For the third time in three weeks my car's been vandalized.
................................................................................................................

4 My first novel was accepted for publication that year.
................................................................................................................

5 The driver's sentence has been reduced by the court of appeal.
................................................................................................................

6 Then I rang Doc and my suspicions were confirmed.
................................................................................................................

7 This is the second time Ms McInnes' work has been screened at Cannes.
................................................................................................................

8 His teaching certificate ought to be taken away from him.
................................................................................................................

9 Under the scheme, teachers' work will be reviewed by a senior colleague every two years
................................................................................................................

# Verbs used with a that-clause: 1

Some verbs are followed by a that-clause. For example, in *I said that I would do it*, the verb *say* is followed by the that-clause *that I would do it*. This pattern is **V that**.

After the more frequent verbs such as *say*, *think*, and *notice*, the word *that* is often left out, especially in speech.

|  | Verb group | that-clause |
|---|---|---|
| He | said | he knew nothing about it. |
| I | agree | that some progress has been made. |

Verbs with this pattern belong to the following meaning groups:

■ **verbs concerned with speaking, writing, and other forms of communication**

| | | | | |
|---|---|---|---|---|
| accept | comment | grant | point out | say |
| acknowledge | complain | guarantee | pray | signal |
| admit | concede | hint | predict | specify |
| advise | conclude | imply | proclaim | speculate |
| advocate | confess | indicate | promise | state |
| agree | declare | insist | propose | stress |
| allege | demand | (not) let on | protest | submit |
| announce | deny | maintain | recall | suggest |
| argue | dictate | make out | recommend | swear |
| ask | direct | mention | regret | testify |
| assert | disclose | note | remark | threaten |
| beg | emphasize | observe | report | urge |
| boast | estimate | order | request | warn |
| claim | explain | plead | reveal | write |
| command | forecast | pledge | rule | |

Taylor **said** he was delighted to be at the festival.

She **claims** she paid no money for it.

We **agreed** that she was not to be told.

Ordinary people **complain** that price rises have caused their standard of living to decline.

Western aid workers **point out** that the UN offer has come too late.

He **predicted** that the terms would be rejected and the war would continue.

George Orwell **wrote** that the great enemy of clear language is insincerity.

Verbs indicating that someone makes a request or suggestion can have *should* or a subjunctive in the that-clause.

The government **has ordered** that people should not gather in groups of more than two on the streets.

We all felt hungry, so I **suggested** that we stop for an early lunch.

■ **verbs indicating that someone says something after something else has been said**

| | | | |
|---|---|---|---|
| add | confirm | dispute | reply |
| agree | counter | object | respond |
| answer | disagree | repeat | |

She said he was in good health, and **added** that he had given up smoking.

I said: 'What a lovely morning,' and he **replied** that it would be very hot later.

■ **verbs indicating how loudly something is said**

| | | | |
|---|---|---|---|
| cry | murmur | scream | whisper |
| cry out | mutter | shout | yell |

Francis **murmured** that he would do anything he could and left the room.

She **screamed** that they'd killed her sons.

■ **verbs concerned with thinking, feeling, knowing, and understanding**

| | | | |
|---|---|---|---|
| accept | disagree | hold | resolve |
| acknowledge | doubt | hope | see |
| agree | dream | imagine | speculate |
| anticipate | estimate | intend | suppose |
| appreciate | expect | know | suspect |
| assume | fancy | (not) mind | think |
| believe | fear | pray | trust |
| bet | feel | realize | understand |
| calculate | figure | reckon | wish |
| consider | forget | reflect | worry |
| decide | gather | regret | |
| determine | guess | remember | |

I **thought** you were dead.

He was fantastically short of money, so everyone just **assumed** he sold the pictures.

I **decided** that nothing would be done in a hurry.

Officials **fear** that crop failure early next year will lead to serious food shortages.

'I **didn't know** you owned a camera,' said Michael.

# Practice

**A** Fill in the gaps in the sentences below using the verbs in this list. Use each verb once.

advise   boast   complain   dream   forecast   forget   pray   repeat

1 The report ................................. that up to 250,000 jobs could be lost in the industry.
2 He had never ................................. that his enemy would dare show his face in the town again.
3 She had ................................. that he was to leave so soon.
4 Hongkongers like to ................................. that there are more Rolls-Royces in their city than rickshaws.
5 The computer game market leaders ................................. that players should take regular breaks.
6 He ................................. again that the statement on independence was not negotiable.
7 I just ................................. that everything will come out all right in the end.
8 He ................................. that she never paid attention to him any more.

**B** Rewrite these sentences using the pattern **V that**.

1 'I'm from a small town in Vermont,' she explained.
   *She explained that she was from a small town in Vermont.*
2 'I'm going to call the police!' I shouted. ...................................................................................................
3 'I'd like an ice-cream,' she replied. ...................................................................................................
4 'I had no knowledge of the espionage operation,' insisted the officer.
   .........................................................................................................................................................
5 The President announced: 'The government will be lifting controls on the prices of luxury goods.'
   .........................................................................................................................................................
6 'I'm sorry I cannot reveal the decision yet,' he added.
   .........................................................................................................................................................

**C** Use a variety of verbs from this list to express your feelings on each of the issues mentioned below.

agree   believe   disagree   doubt   hope   wish   worry

1 Poverty should be eradicated from a civilized, affluent society.
   *I believe that poverty should be eradicated from a civilized, affluent society.*
2 People could easily be replaced by computers in the workplace.
   .........................................................................................................................................................
3 I won't be one of those parents who try to live their lives through their children.
   .........................................................................................................................................................
4 Racism is on the increase. ...................................................................................................
5 Brazil are the best football team in the world. ...................................................................................................
6 People form their own lives, and experience is the best teacher.
   .........................................................................................................................................................
7 More young people could be brought into the government.
   .........................................................................................................................................................

# Verbs used with a that-clause: 2

**1** Here are some more groups of verbs which are followed by a that-clause:

■ **verbs concerned with finding out and remembering**

| | | | | |
|---|---|---|---|---|
| calculate | establish | hear | read | see |
| conclude | figure out | learn | realize | sense |
| decide | find | note | recall | (can) tell |
| deduce | find out | notice | recognize | work out |
| determine | gather | observe | register | |
| discover | guess | perceive | remember | |

I **noticed** that a pane of glass was missing.

My boyfriend left me as soon as he **found out** I was pregnant.

Rigid with fear, Jessica **remembered** that the window was open.

Oh, I **see** you've already started.

■ **verbs concerned with indicating a fact or situation**

| | | | | |
|---|---|---|---|---|
| confirm | illustrate | indicate | prove | show |
| demonstrate | imply | mean | reveal | signal |

Research **shows** that more young women are taking up smoking.

An argument with a friend or relative **doesn't mean** that you don't get on with anyone.

■ **verbs concerned with making arrangements for the future, or influencing a situation**

| | | | |
|---|---|---|---|
| arrange | ensure | guarantee | mind |
| dictate | fix | mean | see |

He **had arranged** that all calls from there would be charged to the police.

I worked hard to **ensure** that everything would go smoothly.

The Argonne was one of the better small hotels, but not the best. This **meant** that at off-peak seasons they often had it nearly to themselves.

Mind is used only in the imperative, usually without the word that.

**Mind you don't slip.**

■ **other common verbs**

| | | | |
|---|---|---|---|
| check | gamble | pretend | require |

Anastasia **pretended** she hadn't heard his question.

She went upstairs and **checked** that her mother's bedside light was out.

The law **requires** that one-fifth of the apartments in large cities go to low-income families.

## Different forms of the pattern

Things didn't, he **admitted**, look good in Russia.

Some verbs are sometimes used in a pattern with as or than.

As Eamonn McCabe **says**, now it's up to the industry to prove him wrong.

The meeting lasted longer than he **had anticipated**.

**2** A small number of verbs with the pattern **V that** can also be followed by so, when referring back to a statement or thought. These verbs are assume, believe, fear, hope, imagine, presume, say, suspect, and think.

Janet considered the general incompetence appalling and **said so**.

With believe, imagine, say, and think, the negative can be expressed as in I **don't think** so, or as in I **think** not. With assume, fear, hope, presume, and suspect, the negative is always expressed by not after the verb.

'So for you it's not going to be a problem.' 'I **don't think so**. I **hope not**.'

**3** Some verbs cannot be followed by that alone, but are followed by the fact that.

But then the moment comes when they **have to face the fact that** they will never, ever see their child again.

I decided to give up smoking because I **can** no longer **ignore the fact that** it is bad for my health.

Some verbs with the pattern **V that** can also be followed by the fact that, for extra emphasis.

You **must accept the fact that** you are older than you used to be.

**A** In the sentences below, put a dotted line under the verb used with a pattern described in this Unit.

1  She noticed that the car was almost out of gasoline.

2  Mind you don't let the cat out.

3  I'd be surprised to find out that Spitt ever stole a penny from anybody.

4  As this example illustrates, people enjoy the sense of exercising control in difficult situations.

5  She also regrets the fact that modern children lack freedom.

6  He didn't think much of Goldstone's argument and said so.

7  As I walked back to the car, I decided I would say nothing to Bertie Owen and Charlie Hughes.

8  The papers confirm the fact that the murdered man was also a serving police officer.

9  The regulations will require that labels show the nutritional contents of every food product sold.

10  The audience, I noted, found it hilarious.

**B** Rewrite these sentences so that the underlined verb is followed by a that-clause.

1  My supervisor was, I <u>realized</u>, a second cousin.
  *I realized that my supervisor was a second cousin.*

2  She was, as you <u>may have guessed</u>, suffering from back pain.

3  This would allow more effective planning in the Royal Household, she <u>said</u>.

4  Children who take part in competitive sports are more likely to become winners in life, the survey <u>discovered</u>.

5  Yul Brynner was an excellent horseman, as he <u>demonstrated</u> in numerous films.

6  The intermission for each story would occur at different times, as I <u>had arranged</u>.

7  As we <u>revealed</u> in February, the famous Kent complex was sold by Ready Mixed Concrete.

8  No rail service, they <u>acknowledged</u>, would mean no future for the village.

**C** Respond to these questions using the verb given in brackets.

1  'Was he meeting someone?' (imagine) ...*'I imagine so.'*

2  'Do you suppose she could have had an accident?' (hope) ...........................

3  'So Susan will definitely be at the party?' (believe) ...........................

4  'So you don't think her husband is the murderer?' (suspect) ...........................

5  'Do all English people speak a foreign language?' (think) ...........................

6  'That's why Aubrey sent you, isn't it?' (presume) ...........................

# Verbs used with a that-clause: 3

**1** Some verbs are followed by a prepositional phrase beginning with *to*, and a that-clause. (The prepositional phrase indicates the hearer or reader.) This pattern is **V to n that**.

| | | | | |
|---|---|---|---|---|
| admit | demonstrate | point out | reveal | swear |
| announce | disclose | pray | say | whisper |
| boast | explain | prove | show | write |
| comment | hint | recommend | signal | |
| complain | indicate | remark | stress | |
| confess | (not) let on | repeat | submit | |
| declare | mention | report | suggest | |

He **admitted** *to me that he knew rather little about US law and politics*.

I **explained** *to him that my mother and father did not speak English*.

You **will have to demonstrate** *to the court that the repairs are necessary to preserve your property*.

**2** Some verbs are followed by a noun group and a that-clause. For example, in *I told her that there had been an accident*, the verb *tell* is followed by the noun group *her* and the that-clause *that there had been an accident*. This pattern is **V n that**.

After most of these verbs, the word *that* is often left out, especially in speech.

## Active pattern

| | Verb group | noun group | that-clause |
|---|---|---|---|
| He | told | me | he loved me. |
| They | had warned | me | that it would hurt. |

## Passive pattern

| | Verb group | that-clause |
|---|---|---|
| He | was informed | that he had been disqualified. |
| He | was told | that it could never happen. |

Verbs with this pattern are concerned with causing someone to know or think something.

| | | | | |
|---|---|---|---|---|
| assure | guarantee | promise | satisfy | tell |
| bet | inform | reassure | show | warn |
| convince | persuade | remind | teach | |

We are pleased to **inform** *you that we have been able to accept your application*.

I **reminded** *her that on several occasions she had remarked on the boy's improvement*.

*When she called at his studio, she* **was told** *that he had gone to Biarritz*. (passive)

*We've* **been promised** *that the telephone will be working in an hour*. (passive)

*Convince, remind, show, teach,* and *tell* sometimes have an inanimate Subject.

*By the time he was eighteen years old, something happened which* **convinced** *him that he was destined for great things*.

*Something* **told** *me she wasn't quite dead*.

In the case of the following verbs, the noun group is often a reflexive pronoun: *assure, convince, persuade, promise, reassure, remind, satisfy,* and *tell*. When used with a reflexive pronoun, these verbs indicate that someone has a particular idea or thought, often a comforting or confident one.

I **told** *myself I'd do better next time*.

**Remind** *yourself that the feelings will not last forever, and will become easier to cope with*.

## Different forms of the pattern

*Bobbie needed help, she* **told** *him*.

Some verbs are sometimes used in a pattern with *as*.

*The world, as Mr Hurd* **reminded us**, *is indeed entering a crucial period*.

**A** In the sentences below, put a dotted line under the verb used with a pattern described in this Unit. Then underline each of the other parts of the pattern.

1 They will prove to the world that they are serious about peace.
2 She promised herself that she would pay Granny back someday.
3 He persuaded the court that his basement was used exclusively as an office.
4 She'd been taught that when you said a word often enough, you understood its true meaning.
5 I could still convince myself that I was the victim of a subversive organisation.
6 I had to point out to him that gasoline was cascading down the side of the car.
7 A couple of editors mentioned to Kate that a research job was coming up.
8 Later that evening, I was informed that my father wished me to come to his study.
9 Sometimes I think he just needs to reassure himself that the place hasn't burnt down while he looked the other way.
10 She started hinting to him that he should take a course in business management.

**B** Rewrite these sentences using the pattern **V to n that** or **V n that**. The tense may have to change.

1 'The entire incident depresses me horribly,' I confessed to Stanley.
......................................................................................................................................
2 'We have a wedding to go to on Saturday,' I reminded him.
......................................................................................................................................
3 'My doctors have warned me to take care,' he said to me at lunch.
......................................................................................................................................
4 The President promises the people: 'The worst is over!'
......................................................................................................................................
5 'It's really not my business,' she told herself.
......................................................................................................................................
6 'He's Amanda's editor,' Mary Sweeny whispered to me.
......................................................................................................................................

**C** Rewrite these sentences in the passive.

1 They warned the directors that funds for new equipment were limited.
......................................................................................................................................
2 The beautician told me that my skin lacked moisture.
......................................................................................................................................
3 Our bosses promised us that there would be enough work for everyone.
......................................................................................................................................
4 However, when he arrived at the airport, a colleague informed him that the meeting was off.
......................................................................................................................................
5 The US navy has assured the Japanese government that there is no risk of further accidents.
......................................................................................................................................

53

# 27 Verbs used with a wh-clause: 1

Some verbs are followed by a finite wh-clause. For example, in *Can you suggest what I should say to her?*, the verb *suggest* is followed by the wh-clause *what I should say to her*. This pattern is **V wh**.

Many of these verbs can also be followed by a wh-clause consisting of a wh-word and a to-infinitive clause. For example, in *I knew what to do*, the verb *know* is followed by the clause *what to do*. This pattern is **V wh-to-inf**.

|  | Verb group | wh-clause |
|---|---|---|
| I | can understand | why your kids are worrying. |
| People | don't notice | whether it's winter or summer. |
| We | have to discuss | how to divide the land. |

Verbs with this pattern belong to the following meaning groups:

■ **verbs concerned with speaking or writing, for example asking questions, discussing things, and giving information**

| | | | | |
|---|---|---|---|---|
| acknowledge | describe | guarantee | point out | set out |
| advise | detail | hint | proclaim | specify |
| agree | dictate | illustrate | put down | state |
| announce | disclose | indicate | recall | stress |
| ask | discuss | inquire | recommend | suggest |
| confess | dispute | let on | remark | warn |
| confirm | emphasize | mention | report | |
| debate | explain | note | reveal | |
| declare | forecast | note down | say | |

*Don't ask who my informant was*, because I'm not going to tell you.

*Handing over the bag, she* **explained what had happened**.

*Did he* **say where he was taking the children**?

*A passer-by* **inquired why the television cameras were there**.

These verbs can be followed by a wh-word and a to-infinitive clause: *advise, ask, describe, discuss, explain, illustrate, indicate, reveal, say, specify,* and *suggest*.

*The book* **describes how to set up a self-help group**.

*Are your cosmetics past their sell-by date? We* **reveal how to make them last longer**.

■ **verbs concerned with thinking or having an opinion about something**

| | | | |
|---|---|---|---|
| accept | consider | imagine | resolve |
| acknowledge | debate | know | see |
| agree | decide | (not) mind | suspect |
| anticipate | determine | plan | think |
| appreciate | doubt | predict | understand |
| (cannot) believe | figure | recall | wonder |
| care | forget | reflect | worry |
| (cannot) conceive | guess | remember | |

*I* **doubt whether my parents said one unnecessary word to each other all their lives**.

*They don't stop to* **think who's going to do the actual basic work**.

*Brand* **wondered what thoughts were going through her mind**.

These verbs can be followed by a wh-word and a to-infinitive clause: *consider, debate, decide, determine, figure, forget, imagine, know, plan, recall, remember, see, think,* and *understand*.

*She began to* **plan how to get out of town without being caught**.

*Kemp* **didn't know whether to believe her or not**.

*I just* **couldn't remember how to spell the most simple of words**.

■ **verbs concerned with finding something out, realizing something, or working something out**

| | | | | |
|---|---|---|---|---|
| analyse | establish | investigate | piece together | (can) tell |
| assess | estimate | judge | prove | think |
| calculate | feel | learn | puzzle out | weigh up |
| check | figure out | make out | read | work out |
| decide | find | note | realize | |
| detect | find out | notice | recognize | |
| determine | guess | observe | see | |
| discover | hear | perceive | sense | |

*Investigators were last night trying to* **discover why the two planes had been flying so close**.

*I wanted to have a look at the book on my own to* **find out what was going on**.

These verbs can be followed by a wh-word and a to-infinitive clause: *assess, calculate, check, determine, discover, establish, figure out, find out, guess, investigate, judge, learn, puzzle out, realize, see, think, weigh up,* and *work out*.

*People* **discovered how to cultivate cereals** *thousands of years ago*.

*I* **couldn't see how to make money**.

# Practice

**A** In the sentences below, put a dotted line under the verb used with a wh-clause. Then underline the other part of the pattern.

1 I worried how I would cope mentally as well as financially.
2 You can easily guess what to expect from him.
3 Conservative MPs have until next Tuesday to decide who to vote for.
4 Bank customers found out why there were no staff when they heard cries coming from an office.
5 Most voters do not mind whether their representative is a man or a woman.
6 I won't ask why you've suddenly decided to write a book about him.

**B** Fill in the gaps in the sentences below using the wh-words in this list.

how    what    when    whether    who    why

1 Dr Fitzpatrick suggests ................................. to get the best from your family doctor.
2 How do you judge ................................. the significance of all this might be?
3 Simon wasn't in, and his flatmate didn't know exactly ................................. he'd be back.
4 Welles has said that he couldn't remember ................................. first thought of the idea.
5 Check that all students understand ................................. to use the answer books.
6 She didn't actually ever say ................................. she didn't want to do that.
7 I was trying to work out ................................. to run away from school or not.
8 David could not imagine ................................. anyone would wish to make such an ugly thing.
9 The newspaper has not yet decided ................................. to devote a full page every day to referendum coverage.

**C** Complete the sentences below using wh-clauses based on the questions. The tense may have to change.

1 How does it feel to live through that shock and pain?
He appreciates *how it feels to live through that shock and pain.*
2 Why are some men aggressive?
Scientists have discovered ................................................................
3 How would the room have looked to Jill?
He could see ................................................................
4 Where did Mr Young find the ornament?
Mr Young has refused to reveal ................................................................
5 Who were the fans shouting for?
They wondered ................................................................
6 Why do you sometimes come to see us here?
I've guessed ................................................................
7 How should children be tested?
The committee recommended ................................................................
8 What will the proposed changes mean?
We investigated ................................................................

# Verbs used with a wh-clause: 2

**1** Here are some more groups of verbs which are followed by a wh-clause:

■ **verbs concerned with showing something**

| | | | |
|---|---|---|---|
| confirm | illustrate | prove | show |
| demonstrate | indicate | reveal | signal |

*You'll be given the chance to **show** what you can do.*

*The records **do not indicate** whether they followed up their enquiries.*

*Demonstrate* and *show* can be followed by a wh-clause consisting of a wh-word and a to-infinitive clause.

*He **will show** how to make some of the restaurant's most popular dishes.*

■ **verbs indicating that something influences a situation**

| | | | | |
|---|---|---|---|---|
| decide | define | determine | dictate | influence |

*The final exam **determines** whether you can sit for university entrance or not.*

*These factors affect costs and **influence** what can be built.*

## Different forms of the pattern

*Why anybody should be interested, I **do not know**.*

**2** Some verbs are followed by a prepositional phrase beginning with *to*, and a wh-clause. The prepositional phrase indicates the hearer or reader. This pattern is **V to n wh**.

| | | | | |
|---|---|---|---|---|
| admit | dictate | indicate | prove | suggest |
| confess | disclose | let on | reveal | |
| demonstrate | explain | mention | show | |

*I don't like people **dictating** to me what I should do and what I shouldn't do.*

*Let me **explain** to you how this works.*

**3** Some verbs are followed by a noun group and a finite wh-clause. For example, in *He showed me where I should go*, the verb *show* is followed by the noun group *me* and the wh-clause *where I should go*. This pattern is **V n wh**.

The same verbs can also be followed by a to-infinitive clause introduced by a wh-word. For example, in *I'll show you how to do it*, the verb *show* is followed by the noun group *you* and the clause *how to do it*. This pattern is **V n wh-to-inf**.

### Active pattern

| | Verb group | noun group | wh-clause |
|---|---|---|---|
| He | asked | Paul | what he wanted. |
| I | 'll show | you | what to watch out for. |

### Passive pattern

| | Verb group | wh-clause |
|---|---|---|
| We | were shown | how beer is made. |
| They | were told | what to do. |

Verbs with this pattern are concerned with asking, telling, teaching, or showing someone something. The Subject may be human or inanimate, with the exception of *advise* and *ask*, which always have human Subjects.

| | | | |
|---|---|---|---|
| advise | inform | show | tell |
| ask | remind | teach | warn |

*About seven years ago she felt she **had to ask herself** whether she really wanted to spend her life teaching.*

*The authors wrote to them last week to **warn** them what was about to come out in the press.*

*It's time to **remind** people why they should feel good about the president.*

*She thinks it's her job to **tell** me how to run my life.*

*You'll also **be shown** how to check your baby's breathing pattern. (passive)*

**A** In the sentences below, put a dotted line under the verb used with a pattern described in this Unit. Then underline each of the other parts of the pattern.

1 They have proved to me how the system can work.
2 The video will show you what to eat on a food-combining diet.
3 Riddick Bowe has already warned Bruno what to expect.
4 Jurors are told who the key participants are.
5 Nancy was tempted to reveal to Mrs Struthers what she had learned.
6 They did not want to be advised what to do.
7 There are many other factors which influence what we choose to eat.
8 The producer mentioned to her who he was having dinner with.
9 Please indicate whether you require CD or vinyl.
10 Several times a day she would remind herself how lucky she was.


**B** Rewrite each of the following pairs of sentences as one sentence, using the wh-word given in brackets.

1 Personal computers let everyone explore their own ideas. He had explained that to me. (how)
*He had explained to me how personal computers let everyone explore their own ideas.*

2 I never abandon my patients. This incident reminded me why. (why)
..................................................................................................................................

3 My attitude has changed over the years. I told her how. (how)
..................................................................................................................................

4 Something has happened. It's difficult for him to admit it to anyone. (what)
..................................................................................................................................

5 Who planted the bomb? The police hope the security system video recording will show them. (who)
..................................................................................................................................

6 John had taken his shoes off. Shelley asked him why. (why)
..................................................................................................................................

7 On a boat, meals are served in different places. The weather determines the place. (where)
..................................................................................................................................

8 What steps should you take next? Our staff will advise you! (what)
..................................................................................................................................


**C** Fill in the gaps in the sentences below using the verbs in this list. Use each verb once.

demonstrate   dictate   disclose   inform   suggest

1 The climate ................................... which grapes will grow best in certain areas.
2 He did not ................................... anyone there what he was looking for.
3 The banks will have to ................................... to each other how much they lent the company.
4 Rick ................................... how to put long hair up into a casual style.
5 We're far too keen to ................................... to people how they might improve their lives.

# Verbs used with a quote: 1

Some verbs are used with a quote. For example, in *'I'm leaving,' he said*, the verb *say* is used with the quote *'I'm leaving'*. This pattern is **V with quote**.

The Subject, verb, and quote can be ordered in five different ways. Note, however, that if the Subject is a pronoun, it comes before the verb, not after it.

| quote | Verb group | |
|---|---|---|
| 'Don't be silly, Dawn!' | said | Quaver. |
| 'But the blood on the back seat?' | objected | Parslow. |

| quote | | Verb group |
|---|---|---|
| 'Someone in your family?' | Browne | suggested. |
| 'No, no, no,' | she | cried. |

| quote... | Verb group | | ...quote |
|---|---|---|---|
| 'This,' | said | Dan, | 'is Mr Freelove.' |
| 'Yes,' | replied | the man, | 'I am.' |

| quote... | | Verb group | ...quote |
|---|---|---|---|
| 'Yes,' | she | admitted, | 'it will.' |
| 'So why,' | he | asked, | 'don't they just leave?' |

| | Verb group | quote |
|---|---|---|
| A police spokesman | said: | 'It is a mystery.' |
| He | replied: | 'It's nothing.' |

The only verb that is frequently used with this pattern in conversation is *say*.

Verbs with this pattern belong to the following meaning groups:

■ **verbs concerned with speaking, writing, and other forms of communication**

| | | | | |
|---|---|---|---|---|
| admit | command | guess | proclaim | state |
| advise | comment | insist | promise | stress |
| allege | complain | maintain | protest | suggest |
| announce | concede | note | put | urge |
| argue | conclude | observe | read | warn |
| ask | confess | offer | recall | wonder |
| assert | declare | order | remark | write |
| beg | demand | plead | report | |
| boast | estimate | pray | request | |
| claim | explain | predict | say | |

*'Perhaps I should get the others,' he __said__, and made for the door.*

*'What's the matter?' she __asked__, backing away a step.*

*'Mr McClintock,' she __announced__, 'has decided to go and visit the bank in London.'*

*'We have been told nothing,' __claims__ Mr Matveyev.*

*'How he lost, I shall never know,' __remarked__ Lord Howard somewhat wistfully.*

*'Where the hell did these guys come from?' Kravis __wondered__ aloud.*

*'How depressed I am,' he __wrote__ in his diary.*

When *say* is used in conversation, the Subject and verb nearly always come before the quote.

*I called Lynda, and I __said__ 'Lynda, how can you do this to me?'*

■ **verbs indicating the relationship of something that is said to something else that is said**

| | | | | |
|---|---|---|---|---|
| add | continue | finish | prompt | resume |
| agree | correct | go on | put in | |
| answer | counter | interrupt | repeat | |
| begin | echo | intervene | reply | |
| conclude | end | object | respond | |

*He __added__: 'The important thing is to go out and win.'*

*'The fire seems to be behind that door,' Judy __began__.*

*'You knew her?' he asked. 'Of course,' she __replied__.*

■ **verbs indicating how something is said, for example how loudly or quickly, or at what pitch**

| | | | | |
|---|---|---|---|---|
| breathe | cry | exclaim | mutter | shout out |
| call | cry out | mumble | scream | sing |
| call out | drawl | murmur | shout | whisper |

*She __called out__, 'Nina, come in here and look at this.'*

*'I guess you guys don't mind if I smoke?' he __drawled__.*

*When he came back I asked him whether it was still raining. 'Don't know,' he __muttered__. 'I didn't notice.'*

*'Traitor!' she __screamed__.*

*'He's coming,' Egan __whispered__.*

**A** Fill in the gaps in the sentences below using the verbs in this list. Use each verb once. Use the past simple tense.

admit   ask   boast   echo   exclaim   insist   interrupt   order   pray   predict   reply   suggest

1 'I've done lots of big projects,' he ................................., 'hospitals, office blocks, all sorts of things.'

2 'Start turning the car around,' he ................................., 'and drive it out of here.'

3 'Oh, God,' she ................................., 'don't let there be a war.'

4 'What do you suppose the board would think of the plan?' I ................................. 'Not much,' he .................................

5 'Things aren't going too well at the moment,' Robyn .................................

6 'Let's go to a midnight movie,' she .................................

7 'I must see him. I must!' I .................................

8 Frank felt confused. 'I still don't see -' 'Take a look at this,' Joe .................................

9 'The fans will take the place over,' he ................................. 'They'll hold lots of parties and come dressed up for the occasion.'

10 Mr. Anders strode over and knelt down. Dipping a finger in the liquid, he sniffed it. 'Paint!' he ................................., astonished. 'Paint?' Sharon .................................

**B** These sentences show the pattern **V that**. Rewrite them using the pattern **V with quote**. In each answer, choose one of the ways of ordering the Subject, verb, and quote.

1 She confessed that she was terrified of heights.
*'I'm terrified of heights,' she confessed.* ............................................................................................

2 John announced that he had come to a decision.
............................................................................................

3 He predicted that they would start making a profit next year.
............................................................................................

4 She promised she would wait for me.
............................................................................................

5 Steve said he'd never seen anything like it before.
............................................................................................

6 The cab-driver complained that he had been out all night.
............................................................................................

7 Agnes murmured that Kathryn was acting strangely.
............................................................................................

8 Alice remarked that it was good to breathe fresh air again.
............................................................................................

**C** In the list of verbs which indicate how something is said, find:

1 five verbs which indicate that something is said softly
............................................................................................

2 seven verbs which indicate that something is said loudly
............................................................................................

# Verbs used with a quote: 2

**1** Here are some more groups of verbs which are used with a quote:

■ **verbs indicating speech accompanied by an expression, gesture, or non-verbal sound**

| | | |
|---|---|---|
| gasp | nod | smile |
| laugh | sigh | sob |

*'Do you know what this means?'* I **gasped**, *laying a hand on Sauter's shoulder.*

*'Go ahead,'* she **smiled**.

■ **verbs indicating the feeling expressed or felt by the person speaking, for example anger, scorn, or unhappiness**

| | | | |
|---|---|---|---|
| explode | groan | rage | sneer |
| fume | jeer | snap | sniff |

*'Can you believe that?'* Terry **fumed**.

*'Have you lost it, General?'* she **sneered**.

■ **verbs concerned with thinking**

| | | |
|---|---|---|
| muse | think | wonder |

Often quotation marks are not used around the quote.

*Someday, I* **thought***, I'll be grown up and have my own car.*

*About her hung a strong scent of Chanel No. 5.* **Where did she get it,** *wondered Stella.*

■ **verbs which are used when quoting a piece of writing or something such as a song or poem**

| | | | |
|---|---|---|---|
| go | read | run | say |

*'You can't kill the spirit, she is like a mountain,'* **went** *the women's chant.*

*The sign* **read***: SPEED ZONE AHEAD 35 MPH.*

**2** When they are used with a quote, some verbs are sometimes followed by a prepositional phrase beginning with *at*. This pattern is **V *at* n with quote**. The Subject usually comes before the verb.

These verbs indicate that someone is speaking loudly, angrily, or forcefully. The prepositional phrase indicates who is being addressed.

| | | | |
|---|---|---|---|
| scream | shout | snap | yell |

*'Hey, do something!'* Bobby **shouted** at them.

*'Don't panic,'* I **yelled** at him.

**3** When they are used with a quote, some verbs are sometimes followed by a prepositional phrase beginning with *to*. This pattern is **V *to* n with quote**. The Subject usually comes before the verb.

Verbs with this pattern belong to the following meaning groups:

■ **verbs indicating that someone says something to someone else**

| | | | | |
|---|---|---|---|---|
| admit | comment | explain | observe | scream |
| announce | complain | insist | proclaim | shout |
| boast | confess | mumble | protest | suggest |
| call | cry | murmur | remark | whisper |
| call out | declare | mutter | say | write |

*I* **said** *to Al, 'Wait a minute. What time did Steve call you?'*

*'This is all very well,'* he **muttered** *to himself, 'but what about my dinner?'*

*'Your cat isn't very friendly,'* a woman **complained** *to Reggie.*

■ **verbs indicating that someone thinks something**

| | | | | |
|---|---|---|---|---|
| muse | reason | say | think | wonder |

The noun group following the preposition is always a reflexive pronoun. Sometimes quotation marks are not used around the quote.

*Just what I was afraid of, Tatiana* **thought** *to herself.*

*'No,'* he **said** *to himself. 'It's not going to be like that.'*

**A** In the sentences below, put a dotted line under the verb used with a pattern described in this Unit. Then underline each of the other parts of the pattern.

1  'I don't know for sure,' Claire sighed, 'but I do keep wondering about it.'
2  'I'm a very selfish person on some levels,' he confesses to me.
3  'He's got a knife!' Jacky screamed at me, terror contorting her face.
4  'My dog eats anything that doesn't eat him first,' she remarked to John, who smiled.
5  'I feel sick!' Chet groaned, supporting himself against the cupboard.
6  'Relax, will you,' he snapped at her.
7  'We are eating vegetarian,' Mrs McCartney announced to the waiter in an officious manner.
8  'I wonder where the gang found that wreck?' Joe mused.
9  'I think I'd better go now,' she whispered to her table companions.
10  I said to myself, 'Settle down. Try to enjoy this.'

**B** Fill in the gaps in the sentences below using the verbs in this list. Use each verb once.

admit   explain   fume   go   mutter   nod   read   sob   think   wonder   write   yell

1  If you don't like the message kill the messenger, the old saying ...................................
2  'Help!' I ................................... at them at the top of my voice.
3  'What he did was scandalous – I'm furious with him,' she ...................................
4  He ................................... to The Sun newspaper: 'Yes, I am broke.'
5  They were wasting time, he ................................... to himself.
6  A notice ...................................: Please do not lean out of the windows.
7  I did ................................... to myself, why not just go into an embassy and get political asylum and leave the country?
8  'No such luck,' Lettie ................................... to me under her breath.
9  'Dearest, I shall be back soon,' she ................................... to Solita in early January 1969.
10  'Do you understand me?' 'Oh, yes,' she ................................... , 'I understand you very well.'
11  'Ali and I were once very good friends,' he ................................... to Izzy.
12  'Oh Dennis,' she ................................... 'I'm sorry, I really am.'

**C** In the lists in this Unit, find:

1  two verbs which indicate that someone is unhappy or dissatisfied ...................................................
2  three verbs which indicate that someone feels contempt ...................................................
3  four verbs which indicate that someone is angry ...................................................

61

# Verbs used with a quote: 3

**1** Some verbs are followed by a noun group and are used with a quote. For example, in *'I'm used to it,'* I told *him*, the verb *tell* is followed by the noun group *him*, and is used with the quote *'I'm used to it.'* This pattern is **V n with quote**.

## Active patterns

The Subject, verb, and noun group can come after, within, or before the quote.

| quote | | Verb group | noun group |
|-------|------|------------|------------|
| 'Absolutely,' | Cross | assured | her. |
| 'We'll do it,' | she | promised | him. |

| quote... | | Verb group | noun group | ...quote |
|----------|-----|------------|------------|----------|
| 'Why,' | I | asked | him, | 'are you here?' |
| 'Doreen,' | she | told | me, | 'something's wrong!' |

| | Verb group | noun group | quote |
|------|------------|------------|-------|
| He | asked | me, | 'Who are these people?' |
| She | had warned | me: | 'This guy means business.' |

## Passive patterns

The Subject and Verb can come after, within, or before the quote. They most frequently come after it, as shown below.

| quote | | Verb group |
|-------|-----|------------|
| 'Only include relevant achievements,' | I | was advised. |
| 'This is considered unacceptable,' | he | was told. |

Verbs with this pattern are all concerned with telling and asking. The person being addressed is indicated by the noun group.

| advise | beg | inform | promise | urge |
|--------|---------|-----------|---------|------|
| ask | command | interrupt | remind | warn |
| assure | correct | order | tell | |

*'A suite is always kept ready for me,'* Loveday **informed** *him* with a little laugh.

*'It changed me,'* she **told** me.

*'Don't move,'* I **warned** him and took out my clasp knife.

*After a while she* **asked** *me, 'Do you want to hear one of my songs?'*

*'Nothing to worry about,'* he **was assured**. (passive)

*Tell* is sometimes used with a reflexive pronoun following the verb to indicate that someone thinks something, usually something encouraging.

*'I am going to make it,'* I **told** myself.

Most of the verbs with this pattern also have the pattern **V with quote**. The exceptions are *assure*, *inform*, *remind*, and *tell*.

**2** With some verbs, the quote always comes after the noun group, or, when the verb is passive, after the verb. This pattern is **V n quote**.

Verbs with this pattern belong to the following meaning groups:

■ **verbs used when indicating the way a word is pronounced or spelled**

| pronounce | spell |
|-----------|-------|

*'This is your own Tuesday phone-in,'* the DJ intoned, **pronouncing** *it Chewsday*.

*Jimmy Savile, you see,* **spells** *his name S A V I L E.*

■ **verbs concerned with labelling or inscribing**

| be captioned | be headed | be inscribed | mark |
|--------------|--------------|--------------|--------------|
| be entitled | be headlined | label | be subtitled |

*Too often he merely read a report,* **marked** *it 'seen'* and took no action.

*The photograph* **is captioned** *'Farnborough, Friday, 5th September 1952'.* (passive)

The quote often occurs after an '-ed' form used to qualify a noun.

*It was a silver cigarette case* **inscribed** *'To Laura, with all my love, Leonard'.*

**A** In the sentences below, put a dotted line under the verb used with a quote (see this Unit and Units 29 and 30). Then underline each of the other parts of the pattern.

1 'Do you think I should call the police?' 'I'd wait a day or two,' Dad advised her.
2 'You'll need proof,' Frank reminded her. 'Then I'll get proof!' Miss Hardy declared.
3 One energetic 90-year-old was told by her doctor, 'You have the heart of a 20-year-old.'
4 'Come, eat!' the old woman urged.
5 'Bob and I were sitting around at Headquarters discussing the case and...' 'Headquarters?' the director interrupted him sharply.
6 I used to pronounce your name 'Bo-shomp' instead of 'Beechum'.
7 Even foods that are labelled 'additive-free' may have hidden preservatives.
8 'Get a doctor!' Eva begged. 'Somebody do something, quick!'
9 'But I know...' She corrected herself: '*We* know that you've seen Lily.'
10 'Look in that room,' the major ordered Hubert.

**B** Fill in the gaps in the sentences below using the verbs in this list. Use each verb once. Use the past simple tense.

ask   assure   beg   correct   be entitled   tell

1 'Everything will be all right,' he ................................ her.
2 'Just lay there,' said Joy. '*Lie* there,' Mr Abbott ................................ her and then passed out.
3 Her column ................................ 'Can this marriage be saved?'
4 'Was it crowded on the beach?' Kay ................................ her brother.
5 'Please forgive me,' he ................................ her.
6 'You're doing very well for a beginner,' I ................................ myself.

**C** Rewrite these sentences using the pattern **V n with quote**, putting the different parts in an appropriate order. The tense may have to change.

1 He reminded her that he had given up that kind of work.
*'I've given up that kind of work,' he reminded her.*

2 He told himself that everything would look different tomorrow.
................................................................................

3 She warned him that they would be late if he didn't hurry up.
................................................................................

4 Joe advised her to go and get some sleep.
................................................................................

5 Her secretary informed her that Mr Watson was on the line.
................................................................................

6 Jay promised her that he would take care of everything.
................................................................................

7 He urged her to smile for the camera.
................................................................................

# UNIT 32 Verbs used with prepositions and adverbs: 1

**1** Some verbs are always or typically followed by a prepositional phrase or adverb group. For example, in *She walked across the room*, the verb *walk* is followed by the prepositional phrase *across the room*; in *She walked away*, it is followed by the adverb *away*. This pattern is **V prep/adv**.

| | Verb group | prep. phrase/adverb group |
|---|---|---|
| I | hurried | home. |
| He | ran | down the path. |

Verbs with this pattern belong to the following meaning groups:

■ **verbs indicating that someone or something moves, goes somewhere, or arrives somewhere**

| | | | | |
|---|---|---|---|---|
| arrive | fall | head | push | slide |
| climb | fit | hurry | return | speed |
| come | flee | jump | roll | spread |
| continue | float | land | rush | swim |
| dive | flow | leap | set off | travel |
| drift | fly | move | set out | turn |
| drop | get | pass | sit | wander |
| end up | go | pour | sit down | |

She didn't want to **go home**.

Haig **arrived in Bombay** on 22 October 1909.

**Turn right** at the lights.

The sound of a printer **drifted through the open door**.

Ron became so ill with worry that he **ended up in hospital**.

■ **verbs indicating that someone walks or runs somewhere**

| | | | | |
|---|---|---|---|---|
| bound | leap | shuffle | storm | walk |
| burst | limp | slip | stroll | |
| charge | march | sneak | stumble | |
| crawl | race | stagger | sweep | |
| dance | run | step | tear | |

She **walked to the window** and looked out.

We **had to sneak out** because it was after nine at night.

He **stormed out of the apartment**, slamming the door furiously behind him.

■ **verbs indicating that a form of transport, or someone using a form of transport, goes or arrives somewhere**

| | | | |
|---|---|---|---|
| cycle | fly | park | pull in | sail |
| drive | land | pedal | ride | |

They **drove to Heathrow airport**, with Cathy sitting between them.

After the plane **landed in Miami**, the man surrendered peacefully.

■ **verbs used to indicate where someone or something is**

| | | | | |
|---|---|---|---|---|
| be | lie | remain | sit | stop |
| hang | live | rest | stand | |
| keep | occur | settle | stay | |

The restaurant **was in Cork Street, Mayfair**.

He **lives in the same village** as me.

She **was sitting at the kitchen table** when I came in.

*Live* is sometimes used in the passive, with *in*.

The cottage **has not been lived in** for several years.

■ **verbs indicating the shape of something, or where it is in relation to something else**

| | | | |
|---|---|---|---|
| extend | lead | pass | stick |
| face | look | point | stretch |
| go | look out | run | wind |

My garden **faces south**.

The pool and terrace **look out over the sea**.

The road **wound through the mountains**.

## Different forms of the pattern

*Where* **did** they **go**?

*Which way* **do** you **go**?

*Where* **is** it?

They asked me **where** my money **was**.

But one day, she had to say goodbye to **the house** she **had lived in** all her life.

I had to find **somewhere** to **stay**.

We were having a chat when **in walked** Stanley.

**2** Most verbs with the pattern **V prep/adv** can also be followed by an adverb and a prepositional phrase, or by two prepositional phrases.

They **drove off into the desert**.

He **walked over to his desk**.

He **ran down the stairs to the living room**.

64

**A** In the sentences below, put a dotted line under the verb used with a prepositional phrase or an adverb. Then underline the other part of the pattern.

1 She ran down the stairs.
2 Where are you going?
3 She tried to read his face, but he turned away and busied himself with the dishes.
4 Inside were half a dozen pill bottles she'd never seen before.
5 He put down the phone and sat there thinking for a bit.
6 She left the house and followed the moonlit path that led to the clearing beside the river.

**B** Now do the same with these longer pieces of text. The verb may be followed by an adverb and then a prepositional phrase.

1 'Well, I should probably go inside,' Erin said. 'Uh, sure. Well, see you at school tomorrow.' Zack turned and started to walk down the path. Erin went back into the house. She was shocked to find her whole family waiting for her. Her father was standing near the couch with his arms crossed. Her mother was sitting on the couch.

2 The sheriff turned right at the only traffic light, led him through the business district, turned left and headed up a low hill. On the left was an area of trees that might have been a park. A white church stood at the top of the hill.

3 I was walking down the hill near Crinan Bottom when a man with a parachute on his back suddenly dropped out of the skies and landed at our feet, having jumped off the summit a few moments earlier. 'Far more exciting than walking down,' he told us.

**C** Below are instructions on how to get from the post office to the police station shown on the map. Fill in the gaps using the words in these lists.

arrive   come   continue   get   passing   turn        along   at   left   out of   under

1 When you ................. ................. the post office, turn ................. up Bread Street. When you
   ................. to the traffic lights, ................. right and go ................. the High Street. .................
   down the High Street, ................. ................. the railway bridge, until you ................. .................
   the police station.

2 Now write similar instructions on how to get from the police station to the post office.

# 33 Verbs used with prepositions and adverbs: 2

**1** Here are some more groups of verbs which are followed by a prepositional phrase or an adverb group:

■ **verbs used to describe people's behaviour**

| | | | |
|---|---|---|---|
| act | dress | live | think |
| behave | eat | react | |

They **were behaving** like animals.

It's important to **eat sensibly** during pregnancy.

■ **verbs used when talking about how successful something or someone is**

| | | | |
|---|---|---|---|
| be coming along | fit | progress | sell |
| come off | go off | read | work |
| be coming on | handle | run | work out |

Her English **is coming along** well.

For once, the show **went off** without technical problems.

This book **will** probably **sell** well in Japan.

■ **verbs concerned with beginning or ending**

| | | | |
|---|---|---|---|
| begin | conclude | finish | start |
| close | end | open | |

Clinton's campaign **began** well.

The first full day of discussions **ended** on a note of **optimism**.

■ **verbs used when indicating how long something lasts**

| | | | |
|---|---|---|---|
| keep | last | live | run |

The mixture **will keep** for 2-3 days in the fridge.

The strike **did not last** long.

## Different forms of the pattern

How **are** things **working out** there?

How long **does** this effect **last**?

**2** Some verbs are always or typically followed by an adverb. This pattern is **V adv**.

| | Verb group | adverb group |
|---|---|---|
| She | is doing | well. |
| Wood | marks | easily. |

Verbs with this pattern belong to the following meaning groups:

■ **verbs concerned with success or failure**

| | | | |
|---|---|---|---|
| do | fare | go | perform |

The operation **went well**.

The Republicans **did badly** in the election.

■ **verbs used to indicate that something has a desirable quality, such as being easily cleaned, prepared, or used**

| | | | |
|---|---|---|---|
| clean | cut | fold | wash | wear |

His favorite wood is pine because it's perfect for carving and **cuts easily**.

■ **verbs used to indicate that something is damaged**

| | | | |
|---|---|---|---|
| break | burn | mark | tear |
| bruise | crack | scratch | |

Be sure to store bananas carefully, as they **bruise easily**.

Sarah has typically British fair skin that **burns easily**.

■ **verbs indicating that two or more people live together or spend time with each other**

| | | | |
|---|---|---|---|
| get | knock around | move in | run off |
| hang around | live | run away | sleep |

The adverb is always *together*.

They usually **hung around** together most of the time.

They decided to **live together** the following year.

■ **verbs indicating that people form a group, do something together, or support each other**

| | | | |
|---|---|---|---|
| band | club | pull | stick |

The adverb is always *together*.

Christian charities **have banded together** to call for action to stop the conflict in Southern Sudan.

**A** In the sentences below, put a dotted line under the verb used with a prepositional phrase or an adverb group. Then underline the other part of the pattern.

1 The concert went very well.
2 Why are you acting like this?
3 Cosmetics will last longer if stored in a cool, dark place.
4 Despite Mr Neil's nerves, the actual launch went off perfectly.
5 The cover is easy to remove and washes well.
6 An oak tree may live for hundreds of years.
7 Des and Raquel have moved in together.
8 She always dresses in black and I've started to copy her because it makes life so easy.
9 Flat owners now club together to hire security guards to police their blocks.
10 The other republics, increasingly pre-occupied with their own economic and political problems, have so far reacted cautiously.

**B** Fill in the gaps in the sentences below using the prepositions in this list. Two of the prepositions will be used twice.

by   in   on   with

1 She began ...................... telling me what the exhibition was about.
2 The meal ended ...................... toffee bananas and Chinese tea.
3 The conference began ...................... a debate on broadcasting.
4 Over the last few years, almost everything I've done has ended ...................... failure.
5 Today's opening round of peace talks ended ...................... a high note.
6 He ended ...................... saying, 'Long live the Brazilian people.'

**C** Match up the two halves of these dictionary definitions.

1 If someone performs well ...          a ... it stays fresh and suitable to eat for a long time.
2 If something wears well ...           b ... he or she works well or achieves a good result.
3 If something fits well ...            c ... it is operating well.
4 If a vehicle handles well ...         d ... it appears quite new or useful after a long time.
5 If a situation works out well ...     e ... it is the right size and shape.
6 If food keeps well ...                f ... what happens is satisfactory.
7 If a system is running smoothly ...   g ... it is easy to drive.

**D** Put the different parts of these sentences in the right order.

1 for / an hour / the interview / lasted / about ...................................................................................
2 nicely / were coming / the arrangements / along ...............................................................................
3 women / behave / why / do / in this way ..........................................................................................
4 with / the company / predictable outrage / has reacted .....................................................................
5 well / never / sold / his books ........................................................................................................
6 and / badly / got / started / the tour / worse ...................................................................................

# Verbs used with prepositions and adverbs: 3

Some verbs are always or typically followed by a noun group and a prepositional phrase or adverb group, or by an adverb group and a noun group. For example, in *I buried the box in the garden*, the verb *bury* is followed by the noun group *the box* and the prepositional phrase *in the garden*. These patterns are **V n prep/adv** and **V adv n**. With phrasal verbs, the particle comes either after the noun group or after the verb.

## Active patterns

|  | Verb group | noun group | prep. phrase/adverb |
|---|---|---|---|
| He | threw | a blanket | over my head. |
| The smoke | drove | the mosquitoes | away. |

|  | Verb group | adverb | noun group |
|---|---|---|---|
| He | Screw | down | any loose floorboards. |
|  | knocked | over | a glass of milk. |

## Passive pattern

|  | Verb group | prep. phrase/adverb |
|---|---|---|
| The sacks | were loaded | onto sixteen army lorries. |
| The protesters | were dragged | away. |

Verbs with this pattern belong to the following meaning groups:

■ **verbs concerned with putting something somewhere**

| | | | | |
|---|---|---|---|---|
| arrange | hang | plunge | put | spread |
| bury | lay | pop | replace | stand |
| drop | lean | position | rest | stuff |
| dump | load | pour | set | thrust |
| fit | place | press | slip | |

He *put* his cup down.

*Place the mixture in a saucepan* and boil for 1 minute.

She *slipped* the photograph into her bag.

■ **verbs concerned with attaching one thing to another**

| | | | | |
|---|---|---|---|---|
| bind | join | nail | screw | tie |
| fix | link | pin | stick | |

Apply glue to the back of this piece and *nail it to the wall*.

He *had pinned* up a map of Finland.

■ **verbs concerned with moving or sending something somewhere**

| | | | | |
|---|---|---|---|---|
| blow | knock | push | slide | transfer |
| brush | lift | raise | spill | turn |
| divert | lower | roll | sweep | |
| draw | move | scatter | throw | |
| drive | pass | send | tip | |
| kick | pull | shift | toss | |

He *kicked the ball into the crowd*.

The boy *pulled* out a pistol and shot another boy in the leg.

He accidentally *knocked his glass off the table*.

■ **verbs concerned with carrying something or someone somewhere or accompanying someone**

| | | | | |
|---|---|---|---|---|
| accompany | drag | lead | see | transfer |
| bear | drive | lift | ship | walk |
| bring | fly | run | show | |
| carry | guide | rush | take | |

The plane *was carrying relief supplies to Sarajevo*.

Carl *drove* him home at 12.15 and I *saw* him in.

The suspects *have* now *been brought* to London. (passive)

■ **verbs concerned with causing someone to go somewhere**

| | | | | |
|---|---|---|---|---|
| allow | drive | kick | post | tempt |
| ask | force | let | put | transfer |
| assign | get | march | settle | urge |
| call | help | move | sit | warn |
| direct | hurry | order | sit down | wave |
| drag | invite | persuade | steer | |

His men *have driven government troops from a number of towns*.

This was the man who *put me in hospital* for four days.

They *were invited there* by the government. (passive)

■ **verbs indicating that someone takes a vehicle somewhere**

| | | | | |
|---|---|---|---|---|
| drive | fly | ride | sail | steer |

He *drove the truck into the barn* and parked it.

He *flew the helicopter back* last night.

## Different forms of the pattern

*Where did you take her?*

She showed me *where to put my jacket*.

John *placed* on the table a jam jar full of worms.

You need a case to *put your clothes in*.

*In the centre of her garden* she *placed* a marble statue of a boy.

**A** In the sentences below, put a dotted line under the verb used with a prepositional phrase or adverb group. Then underline each of the other parts of the pattern.

1 Natasha fixed the star to the top of the tree.
2 The authorities might kick her out of Barbados.
3 Davenport removed his coat and brushed off the snow.
4 Let me show you to your rooms.
5 We know many more people have died but the army has taken the bodies away.
6 The cage was knocked over and the bird escaped.
7 On Mondays, Rachel often brought to school things she had made at the weekend.
8 Then you have to remember where you buried it.
9 There is no jail to put him in.
10 Within hours of the accident, Mr Graff had been flown to Brisbane for specialist treatment.

**B** Fill in the gaps in the sentences below using the prepositional phrases in this list. Use each phrase once.

| | | | |
|---|---|---|---|
| across the Atlantic | at the dining table | behind the shop | from the town |
| in a semi-circle | over the meat | to the wall | under Carl's nose |

1 The computers were arranged ......................................................................
2 Pour the sauce ...................................................... and garnish with the onions and herbs.
3 Bookcases and cabinets should be screwed ....................................................................
4 The rebels have been driven ......................................................................
5 He sailed the catamaran single-handed ...................................................... in 1934.
6 He sat himself down ......................................................................
7 He lifted the man and dragged the body ......................................................................
8 Microphones were pushed ...................................................... and flashbulbs popped.

**C** Put the different parts of these sentences in the right order.

1 into / he / the banknotes / stuffed / his wallet ..........................................................
2 a slice of wholemeal bread / spread / peanut butter / on / she
..........................................................................................................................
3 was shipped / the furniture / three huge containers / over / in
..........................................................................................................................
4 into / Wren / dropped / her purse / her lipstick ..........................................................
5 they / away / the UN trucks / sent ..........................................................
6 sheets of wood / the windows / I / over / nailed ..........................................................
7 put / on / the tray / the table / she ..........................................................
8 her / Christopher / offered / home / to drive ..........................................................

# Verbs used with prepositions and adverbs: 4

**1** Here are some more groups of verbs which are followed by a noun group and a prepositional phrase or adverb group, or by an adverb group and a noun group:

■ **verbs indicating that someone moves a part of their body**

| | | | | |
|---|---|---|---|---|
| fling | pull | stamp | toss | wave |
| hide | rub | stretch out | turn | |
| hold | run | throw | twist | |

*Turning to Henry, she **flung her arms round his neck** and **hid her face on his shoulder**.*

With *pull*, *stretch out*, and *throw*, the noun group following the verb is often a reflexive pronoun. This indicates that someone moves their whole body.

*Moira **stretched herself out** on the lower bench, lying on her side.*

■ **verbs concerned with keeping or holding someone or something in a particular place**

| | | |
|---|---|---|
| have | keep | shut |
| hold | leave | store |

*She sat rigidly upright, **holding her handbag to her chest**.*

*He **left his bike there**.*

■ **verbs concerned with seeing, finding, or meeting someone or something in a particular place**

| | | | | |
|---|---|---|---|---|
| catch | feel | find | meet | see |

*I **found the tape in a garage in Kingston**.*

*Martin **met us at the station**.*

■ **verbs concerned with causing something or someone to be or stay in a particular state**

| | | | | |
|---|---|---|---|---|
| bring | keep | place | put | throw |
| get | leave | push | set | |

*Cover the soup and **bring it to the boil** slowly.*

*They **kept us out of trouble**.*

*He **was placed under arrest**. (passive)*

■ **verbs indicating that one person hits or injures another**

| | | |
|---|---|---|
| bash | hit | slap |
| batter | knife | strike |

*He **knifed his attacker through the heart**.*

*He **was slapping a woman around** and I objected.*

■ **verbs concerned with starting, passing, or finishing a period of time in a particular way**

| | | | |
|---|---|---|---|
| begin | finish | pass | start |
| end | live out | spend | |

*Philip **begins each day with half an hour's meditation**.*

■ **other common verbs**

| | | | |
|---|---|---|---|
| approach | be found | regard | treat |
| bring up | handle | take | |

*When I'm tired – that's when I **handle everything least well**.*

*Michael broke the news to Brian. He **took it well**.*

*I **was brought up in Shanghai**. (passive)*

*Protein **is found in a wide variety of both animal and plant foods**. (passive)*

**2** Some verbs have the patterns **V n adv** and **V adv n** but not the pattern **V n prep** – that is, they are used with an adverb but not with a preposition.

## Active patterns

| | Verb group | noun group | adverb |
|---|---|---|---|
| He | switched | the television | on. |

| | Verb group | adverb | noun group |
|---|---|---|---|
| Howard | took | off | his jacket. |

## Passive pattern

| | Verb group | adverb |
|---|---|---|
| Street lighting | has been switched | off. |

Verbs with this pattern belong to the following meaning groups:

■ **verbs indicating that someone puts clothing on or takes it off**

| | | | | |
|---|---|---|---|---|
| put | rip | slip | take | tear |

*She **put her slippers on** and shuffled into the kitchen.*

*He **tore off his shirt** and threw it to the ground.*

■ **verbs indicating that someone turns machinery or equipment on or off**

| | | | | |
|---|---|---|---|---|
| click | flick | put | switch | turn |

*He **clicked on the lamp**.*

***Are** you **going to turn the machine off** now?*

**A** Fill in the gaps in the sentences below using the noun groups and the prepositional phrases and adverbs in these lists. Use each phrase once.

| his arms | her face | her feet | her hair | his hands | himself |
| around his wife | away from him | back | on the pavement | to his feet | together |

1 She stamped ..................................... ........................................ to keep out the cold.
2 He threw ..................................... ........................................ and told her not to worry.
3 She tossed ..................................... ........................................ with a jerk of her head.
4 Larry rubbed ..................................... ........................................ with satisfaction.
5 She turned ..................................... ........................................
6 Very slowly he pulled ........................... ........................................., using the table as an aid.

**B** Fill in the gaps in the sentences below using the verbs in this list. Use each verb once.

bring   get   keep   place   push   throw

1 He's the one that .................................. me out of trouble.
2 After releasing her, the doctors had .................................. her on anti-depressants.
3 Any emotional crisis could have .................................. either of them over the edge.
4 This was a campaign deliberately designed to .................................. me into disrepute.
5 Britain's Heathrow Airport was .................................. into chaos again last night after the third bomb attack in less than a week.
6 These relatives are .................................. in the awkward position of speaking on behalf of the person in a coma.

**C** The sentences below all contain the verb *run*. Identify the verb pattern (**V prep/adv** or **V n prep/adv**) and write it in the gap at the end of each sentence. Then select from the list the verb that means the same as *run* in that sentence.

flow   go   last   pass   race   take

1 The show was an instant success and ran for 300 days. ............... *V prep, last* ...............
2 I was relieved to get home and find everything running smoothly. .............................................
3 I'll run you back after the show. .............................................
4 Leo ran his fingers through his thick, graying hair. .............................................
5 The river runs past the town of Guben. .............................................
6 Chivers got out of the car and ran home but was later arrested. .............................................

**D** Fill in the gaps in the sentences below using the nouns in this list. Use each noun once.

coat   cooker   dressing-gown   light   switch   tee-shirts

1 They ripped off their ........................................... and started waving them above their heads.
2 Then he flicked down the ........................................... on the office intercom.
4 Just bring the peas to the boil, then turn the ........................................... off.
5 Robina put on her ..........................................., took a shopping basket and went out.
6 He saw that a ........................................... had been clicked on in the office next to him.

# 36 Verbs used with *way*

The verb is followed by a noun group which consists of a possessive determiner, such as *my, his, her,* or *their,* and the noun *way.* This is followed by a prepositional phrase or adverb group. For example, in *He pushed his way through the crowd,* the verb *push* is followed by the possessive determiner *his,* the noun *way,* and the prepositional phrase *through the crowd.* This pattern is **V way prep/adv.**

|   | Verb group | *way* | prep. phrase/adverb group |
|---|---|---|---|
| I | groped | my way | out. |
| She | ate | her way | through a pound of chocolate. |

This pattern is very productive: any verb indicating an action can be used with this pattern. Here we give the most typical.

Verbs with this pattern belong to the following meaning groups:

- **verbs which are used with *way* to indicate that someone or something manages to get somewhere**

| find | make | wend |
|---|---|---|

*Shirley and Boris **made their way home** in thoughtful silence.*

- **verbs indicating that someone moves or gets somewhere with difficulty or using force**

| barge | claw | fight | push | steamroller |
|---|---|---|---|---|
| battle | cut | force | shoot | tear |
| blast | dig | hack | shoulder | thrust |
| bore | drill | jostle | shove | |
| burrow | elbow | power | smash | |

*They're trying to **fight their way towards** the besieged army camp.*

*Four gunmen **forced their way into the house** and opened fire.*

- **verbs indicating that someone moves carefully or avoids obstacles**

| ease | grope | navigate | thread |
|---|---|---|---|
| edge | inch | pick | weave |
| feel | manoeuvre | squeeze | worm |

*We **edged our way past the soldiers** and turned up the staircase.*

*She turned her back on him and began to **thread her way through the dancers**.*

- **verbs indicating that someone or something moves or travels in a particular way**

| bump | hitchhike | pedal | splash |
|---|---|---|---|
| crawl | limp | shuffle | wing |
| flap | meander | sneak | zigzag |

*Ordinary Japanese people **had to pedal their way about** on bicycles.*

*They **splashed their way along the stream**.*

*She **zigzagged her way to the far corner of the cemetery** and stood at last at the foot of her father's grave.*

- **verbs concerned with talking persuasively or lying in order to get into or out of a situation or place**

| bluff | con | negotiate | sweet talk |
|---|---|---|---|
| charm | lie | reason | talk |

*I just **bluffed my way in**.*

*He **lied his way into power**.*

*He'd **talked his way out of awkward corners** before, but none like this.*

- **verbs which are used with *way* to indicate that someone achieves something by means of a legitimate activity**

| borrow | export | spend | work |
|---|---|---|---|
| buy | play | trade | |

*I do not believe governments **can spend their way out of** recession.*

- **verbs which are used with *way* to indicate that someone achieves something by doing something illegal or immoral**

| bribe | cheat | murder | wangle |
|---|---|---|---|
| bully | insinuate | trick | worm |

*He **has cheated his way to the title**.*

*He **tricked his way into a senior management job** at Guy's Hospital.*

- **verbs used with *way* to indicate that someone eats or drinks the whole of something**

| chew | drink | eat | munch | work |
|---|---|---|---|---|

*Mrs Lorimer **chewed her way through a large helping of apple tart**.*

*Work* is also used more generally to indicate that someone deals with all of a set of things.

*She **was working her way through a pile of correspondence**.*

- **verbs indicating that someone says, sings, or plays the whole of something**

| croon | mumble | shout | stammer | whistle |
|---|---|---|---|---|
| grunt | mutter | slur | strum | yell |

*Our chairman **mumbled his way through a couple of prayers**.*

**A** Match up the two halves of each sentence.

1 She elbowed ...          a ... her way through a tomato salad.
2 The police smashed ...   b ... their way home.
3 He inched ...            c ... his way out of jail.
4 We charmed ...           d ... our way through the litter-strewn streets.
5 Anne is munching ...     e ... her way through the crowd.
6 They couldn't find ...   f ... their way through the front door.
7 We picked ...            g ... our way out of trouble.
8 He bribed ...            h ... his way to the window.

**B** These sentences show the pattern **V prep/adv**. Rewrite them using the pattern **V *way* prep/adv**.

1 He limped along the corridor. ....*He limped his way along the corridor.*....................

2 She pushed to the front of the queue. ...................................................................

3 They zigzagged across the snow. ...........................................................................

4 We edged past the soldiers. ..................................................................................

5 Jack was working through a mountain of paperwork.

...............................................................................................................................

6 When the larvae hatch, they bore into the beans.

...............................................................................................................................

**Now rewrite these sentences using the verb given in brackets.**

7 William went to the door. (make) ..........................................................................

8 Somehow the news got into the Italian newspapers. (find)

...............................................................................................................................

**C** The ends of ten sentences are given below. Provide beginnings for them using verbs from this list with the pattern **V *way* prep/adv**. Use each verb once.

  bluff   borrow   eat   hack   hitchhike   inch   murder   shoulder   stammer   whistle

1 ............................................................... through the crowd.
2 ............................................................... along the narrow ledge.
3 ............................................................... through the National Anthem.
4 ............................................................... round Europe.
5 ............................................................... into the job.
6 ............................................................... through a bag of crisps.
7 ............................................................... out of the recession.
8 ............................................................... through the poem.
9 ............................................................... to the throne.
10 ............................................................... through the undergrowth.

# Verbs used with *about*: 1

**1** Some verbs are followed by a prepositional phrase which consists of *about* and a noun group. For example, in *I lied about my age*, the verb *lie* is followed by the preposition *about* and the noun group *my age*. This pattern is **V *about* n**. With most verbs, the preposition is sometimes followed by an '-ing' clause or a wh-clause.

|  | Verb group | *about* | noun group/-ing/wh |
|---|---|---|---|
| Other players | are grumbling | about | unpaid wages. |
| We | don't care | about | what you think. |
| I | dream | about | winning the 100 meters. |

Verbs with this pattern belong to the following meaning groups:

■ **verbs indicating that someone speaks or writes about something**

| argue | complain | inquire | quarrel | speak |
|---|---|---|---|---|
| ask | drone on | joke | rabbit on | talk |
| bang on | enthuse | keep on | rant | waffle on |
| boast | generalize | lie | rant on | whinge |
| brag | go on | moan | rave | witter on |
| burble on | grumble | mutter | sing | write |
| chat | harp on | protest | sound off | |

*He **talked** about all kinds of things.*

*Some of them could be heard **muttering** about the high prices of the clothes.*

*He **had boasted** about stabbing a woman.*

Note that the phrasal verbs in this list are fairly informal.

*'For God's sake, stop **going on** about Fate!' Alex shouted.*

In the case of the following verbs, the preposition *about* is sometimes followed by a wh-clause: *argue, ask, chat, inquire, joke, lie, quarrel,* and *talk*.

*He and Patra **argued** about what to wear.*

The more frequent verbs are sometimes used in the passive.

*This is an idea that **has been talked** about before.*

■ **verbs indicating that someone phones or writes to someone**

| call | phone up | ring up |
|---|---|---|
| phone | ring | write in |

*Hello? I**'m calling** about the ad for the car.*

*I hope many more people **write in** about this.*

■ **verbs concerned with thought or feeling**

| agree | care | dream | speculate | worry |
|---|---|---|---|---|
| bother | differ | forget | think | |
| brood | disagree | know | wonder | |

*For the most part, people **think** about themselves rather than others.*

*He told me he **had** always **dreamed** about being a star when he was a kid.*

*Different psychiatrists **might disagree** about what causes the condition.*

*Forget, know,* and *think* are sometimes used in the passive.

*It's a problem that **has been known** about for years.*

■ **verbs concerned with acquiring knowledge**

| find out | hear | learn | read |
|---|---|---|---|

*We **found out** about these changes by pure accident.*

*I **heard** about the trouble on the television early this morning, so I hurried on over.*

*The players **learned** about competing against quality opposition and improved each game.*

In the case of *learn*, the preposition *about* is sometimes followed by a wh-clause.

*Even in school, Hewitt **was learning** about how to use time.*

## Different forms of the pattern

*So **what** exactly **is** he **complaining** about?*

*I asked Pollard **what** he **was thinking** about.*

*That's **the man** you **were talking** about, isn't it?*

*Racism is quite difficult to **talk** about.*

*It's **a good subject** to **write** about.*

***All** you **care** about is money.*

**2** A number of verbs with the pattern **V *about* n** are sometimes followed by *about*, a noun group, and an '-ing' clause. These verbs include *complain, joke, go on, know, think, worry, hear,* and *read*.

*Terrified residents **complained** about aircraft flying low over their homes.*

*I think he still **worries** about me being the youngest.*

*And that's how you **heard** about Ron Hythe fighting with Doyle?*

**A** Put the different parts of these sentences in the right order.

1 about / the girls / were chatting / fashion ...........................................................................
2 my father / about / her / worries / being so tired ...........................................................
3 the woman / her daughter / I / about / and / asked ........................................................
4 do / how / you / know / the kidnapping / about ...............................................................
5 always / how ugly she was / about / going on / she / was ..............................................
6 write / know / about / about / something / you ................................................................


**B** Fill in the gaps in the sentences below using the verbs in this list. Use each verb once.

   disagree   forget   hear   phone   read   worry   write in

1 Hello Doctor, it's Mrs Jones again. I'm ................................. about my daughter.
2 They ................................. about her death in the newspapers.
3 We agreed about much more than we ................................. about.
4 I didn't tell her about my problem because I didn't want her to ................................. about it.
5 Our mail this week included a letter from George Farmer of Westchester, Ohio, who
   ................................. about a number of things.
6 I went into the attic and there I found something I had ................................. about.
7 The day after I wrote about a character falling down a lift shaft I ................................. about a
   similar tragedy on the radio.


**C** In the sentences below, put a dotted line under the verb used with *about*. Then underline each
of the other parts of the pattern.

1 In other words he does not care about you.
2 He seemed not to understand what I was talking about.
3 What have we got to worry about?
4 He shouldn't be a doctor if all he thinks about is money.
5 They are useful earplugs, and reasonably comfortable and easy to forget about.
6 Antonio's favourite dishes include mushrooms, about which he has written extensively.


**D** In each of the sentences below, one of the verbs from this list is missing. Mark where it goes
and say what it is. Use each verb once.

   complain   dream   find out   joke   know   lie   read

1 He'd / about his parents being friends of the owner. .........*lied*..............
2 Despite her enormous wealth, she was always about one thing or another. .........................
3 My sister is the only one who about my eating problem. .........................
4 How did the press about it? .........................
5 I know several players got really upset when they about him criticising the team. .........................
6 My mother and I about the fact that whatever she loves I'll hate, and vice versa. .........................
7 He was living the life that others only dared to about. .........................

# Verbs used with *about*: 2

Some verbs are followed by a noun group and a prepositional phrase which consists of *about* and a noun group. For example, in *She told him about her plan*, the verb *tell* is followed by the noun group *him*, the preposition *about*, and the noun group *her plan*. This pattern is **V n *about* n**. With some verbs, the preposition is sometimes followed by an '-ing' clause or a wh-clause.

## Active pattern

|  | Verb group | noun group | *about* | noun group/-ing/wh |
|---|---|---|---|---|
| She | warned | me | about | people like you. |
| They | tease | me | about | being overweight. |
| He | was telling | her | about | what had happened. |

## Passive pattern

|  | Verb group | *about* | noun group/-ing/wh |
|---|---|---|---|
| He | was grilled | about | his personal life. |
| They | were lectured | about | how to beat crime. |
| Nothing | can be done | about | changing it. |

Verbs with this pattern belong to the following meaning groups:

■ **verbs indicating that someone talks to someone else**

| | | | | |
|---|---|---|---|---|
| advise | inform | nag | remind | warn |
| ask | interrogate | press | teach | |
| consult | interview | question | tease | |
| grill | lecture | reassure | tell | |

*Tell me about your skiing holiday.*

*MPs were indignant that the government **had not consulted** them about starting price reforms.*

*They ruthlessly **questioned** him about why he hadn't bothered to see Christopher or even find out our address.*

*About 25 army officers **are** currently **being interrogated** about their part in the coup.* (passive)

With *teach* and *tell*, the prepositional phrase sometimes has an **amount** before it.

*She **taught** me a lot about plants.*

■ **verbs concerned with approaching or challenging someone about something**

| | | | | |
|---|---|---|---|---|
| approach | challenge | confront | contact | tackle |

*I **could** never **confront** people about the things that annoyed me.*

*One of the networks **approached** him about hosting a science show.*

*I **tackled** him about how one could live amidst so much poverty.*

■ **verbs concerned with thoughts or feelings**

| | | | | | |
|---|---|---|---|---|---|
| dislike | feel | hate | like | love | think |

These verbs usually occur in clauses and questions beginning with *what*.

*What **do** you **think** about this threatened strike by professional footballers*, then?

*What I **loved** about Gloria was her talent and her independence.*

■ **verbs indicating that someone knows or finds out about something**

| | | | |
|---|---|---|---|
| find out | hear | know | learn |

The noun group following the verb is always an **amount**.

*She frequented the library to **find out** all she could about the disease.*

*He may be a brilliant 'personality', but he **knows** nothing about producing a play.*

*We**'ve learned** a lot about how to travel with kids and how not to.*

*Very little **is known** about him.* (passive)

The preposition *about* is sometimes followed by a noun group and an '-ing' clause.

*I heard Wally **didn't know** anything about me going to Canberra and that he was upset about it.*

■ *Do* and *say* also have this pattern.

*My doctor kept telling me to **do something about my weight**, but I never bothered.*

*Did he **say** anything about being shot at?*

The preposition *about* is sometimes followed by a noun group and an '-ing' clause.

*Did he **say** anything about anyone stealing anything from him?*

## Different forms of the pattern

*What **do** you **know** about his family?*

*Joe asked his aunt what she **had found out** about Dr Montrose.*

*Remember the guys I **told** you about?*

**A** In the sentences below, put a dotted line under the verb used with *about*. Then underline each of the other parts of the pattern.

1  I never asked her about ghosts again.
2  Dr. Miller has been advising the government about milk production.
3  What do people think about your policy?
4  I didn't know what to do about it.
5  A senior lawyer said that several people had been contacted about taking part in the trial.
6  But what did he say about us?
7  Harry was questioned about where his father got the money.
8  As usual, they told me nothing about the case.
9  I reminded him about changing the name on the box.
10 Artie was probably one of the rogues Molly had warned her about.

**B** Match up the two halves of each sentence.

1 Parents should warn their children ...         a ... about my home life.
2 Her father teased her ...                       b ... about what he eats.
3 He kept asking me ...                           c ... about how much she is loved.
4 The president reminded reporters ...            d ... about the dangers of talking to strangers.
5 I still nag him ...                             e ... about her weight.
6 I try to reassure her ...                       f ... about his statement two days ago.

**C** Rewrite these sentences using the noun group in brackets in a clause beginning with *what*.

1  I like the fact that there are heaps of trees. (this school)
   *What I like about this school is that there are heaps of trees.*

2  I like the day-to-day contact with clients. (my job)

3  I like his evident determination to think things out for himself. (him)

4  I hate the uncomfortable seats. (my car)

5  I love the fact that you never know what you'll find. (these shops)

6  I love the fact that the people really love sport. (Australia)

7  I dislike the fact that it takes itself so seriously. (the fashion world)

# Verbs used with *against*: 1

Some verbs are followed by a prepositional phrase which consists of *against* and a noun group. For example, in *He voted against the proposal*, the verb *vote* is followed by the preposition *against* and the noun group *the proposal*. This pattern is **V *against* n.**

| | Verb group | *against* | noun group |
|---|---|---|---|
| You | 're competing | against | younger workers. |
| The bottle | smashed | against | a wall. |

Verbs with this pattern belong to the following meaning groups:

■ **verbs concerned with opposing someone, competing with someone, or doing something to harm someone**

| | | | | |
|---|---|---|---|---|
| battle | fight back | plot | rise up | win |
| compete | gang up | prevail | run | |
| draw | lose | race | stand | |
| fight | play | rise | testify | |

*The competition gave junior players the chance to* **compete** *against members of other clubs.*

*When I started at college, all the girls in my class seemed to* **gang up** *against me and talk and laugh about me.*

*He began to believe that colleagues and his wife* **were plotting** *against him.*

■ **verbs concerned with trying to stop something that is happening or is planned**

| | | | |
|---|---|---|---|
| campaign | fight | protest | vote |
| demonstrate | lobby | strike | |

*He* **has campaigned** *against apartheid all his life.*

*They* **were protesting** *against government plans to cut public spending.*

*Only twelve members* **voted** *against the plan.*

■ **verbs concerned with saying that something is bad in some way**

| | | | | |
|---|---|---|---|---|
| advise | argue | hit out | protest | speak out |
| appeal | come out | lash out | rule | warn |

*Church leaders* **have** *also* **spoken out** *against the killings.*

*The prime minister* **warned** *against an excess of nationalism.*

The preposition *against* is sometimes followed by an '-ing' clause.

*Doctors* **advise** *against putting a thermometer into your child's mouth because it may cause him to choke.*

■ **verbs indicating that something hits or touches something else**

| | | | | |
|---|---|---|---|---|
| beat | bump | rest | slam | strike |
| brush | knock | rub | smash | |

*They reversed until they* **bumped** *against a wall.*

*Something* **brushed** *against her leg.*

■ **other common verbs**

| | | | | |
|---|---|---|---|---|
| battle | decide | react | rebel | struggle |

*She is portrayed as a near saint who* **struggled** *against impossible odds.*

*Not surprisingly, she* **reacted** *against this treatment.*

In the case of *decide* and *react*, the preposition *against* is sometimes followed by an '-ing' clause.

*We* **decided** *against having a midday meal so as to save time.*

## Different forms of the pattern

*He tied the boat to the sturdy post* **against which** *it* **was resting**.

*I want* **my team** *to be difficult to* **play** *against.*

*I didn't have* **any structure** *to* **rebel** *against.*

*That is* **what** *we* **are fighting** *against.*

**A** In the sentences below, put a dotted line under the verb used with *against*. Then underline each of the other parts of the pattern.

1 An iron bed rested against the far wall.
2 He was the strongest man I have ever played against.
3 The victim refused to testify against him.
4 He was offered a place at the Royal College, but he'd already decided against becoming a classical musician.
5 There are a lot of young, fit guys out there to compete against.

**B** Match up the two halves of each sentence.

1 Reeves had been battling ...          a ... against his own brother?
2 What kind of man would testify ...    b ... against a corner of the table.
3 These magazines have campaigned ...   c ... against a referendum.
4 His head smashed ...                   d ... against me!
5 Everyone is plotting ...               e ... against everything her mother represented.
6 There was a time when she rebelled ... f ... against a knee injury.
7 The government has decided ...         g ... against high level corruption.

**C** Fill in the gaps in the sentences below using the verbs in this list. Use each verb once.

advise   appeal   protest   race   react   win

1 Mr Drew wanted to take Nancy home, but the doctor ................................. against this.
2 In the quarter-finals, Worcestershire beat Glamorgan, and Somerset ................................. against Middlesex.
3 I've ................................. against champions all over the world and Michael is one of the best.
4 The negative campaigns of the '80s won't work in the '90s because voters will ................................. against them.
5 He has said he will ................................. against the decision in the Supreme Court.
6 Hundreds of people took to the streets to ................................. against the continued detention of political prisoners.

**D** Put the different parts of these sentences in the right order.

1 beat / the rain / against / the windows ................................................................
2 a wall / a glass ornament / against / smashed ................................................................
3 against / you / rebelling / what / are ................................................................
4 stood / against / he / the president / in the 1990 election

................................................................
5 the government / more than forty Conservatives / voted / against

................................................................
6 worth / this / is / against / something / fighting ................................................................
7 its mistress's legs / came / rubbed / and / against / into the room / a cat

................................................................

# Verbs used with *against*: 2

Some verbs are followed by a noun group and a prepositional phrase which consists of *against* and a noun group. For example, in *We insured the house against fire*, the verb *insure* is followed by the noun group *the house*, the preposition *against*, and the noun group *fire*. This pattern is V n *against* n.

## Active pattern

|  | Verb group | noun group | *against* | noun group |
|---|---|---|---|---|
| Your policy | insures | you | against | redundancy. |
| She | pressed | her back | against | the door. |

## Passive pattern

|  | Verb group | *against* | noun group |
|---|---|---|---|
| Children | should be vaccinated | against | measles. |
| My gain | must be balanced | against | your loss. |

(With phrasal verbs, the particle comes either after the noun group or after the verb.)

Verbs with this pattern belong to the following meaning groups:

■ **verbs concerned with protecting someone or something**

| cover | defend | insulate | protect | vaccinate |
|---|---|---|---|---|
| cushion | immunize | insure | spray | |

*We **couldn't protect** ourselves against attack.*

*In normal times, the federal government has the means to **cushion** the nation against a recession.*

*Record numbers of children **were immunised** against infectious diseases last year.* (passive)

■ **verbs concerned with striking or putting one thing against another**

| bang | lean | press | prop | slam | strike |
|---|---|---|---|---|---|

*The Commissioner **propped** his cane against the bed and sat down.*

*Dean fell and **struck** his head against the bannister.*

■ **verbs concerned with attacking someone or being hostile towards someone**

| direct | level | perpetrate |
|---|---|---|

*The violence **has been directed** against foreigners who've come to Germany as refugees or guest workers.* (passive)

*He claimed he was not well enough to answer the charges that **have been levelled** against him.* (passive)

■ **verbs concerned with considering or dealing with two or more different things, people, or groups**

| balance | match | play off | set | weigh |
|---|---|---|---|---|

*Union leaders **have been playing off** one bid against another to try to secure the best possible deal.*

*You **have to weigh** the responsibilities against the rewards.*

■ *Turn* and *warn* also have this pattern.

*She feared that he **would turn** her daughter against her.*

In the case of *warn*, the preposition *against* is sometimes followed by an '-ing' clause.

*When this business first started I **warned** him against staying there.*

## Different forms of the pattern

*They are criminals of the worst sort, **against whom** society **must be protected**.*

*Sieg closed the book he **had propped** against his glass.*

**A** Fill in the gaps in the sentences below using the verbs in this list. Use each verb once. The sentences show the pattern **V n *against* n** or its passive, or the pattern **V *against* n** (see Unit 39). Say which pattern is shown in each sentence.

brush    campaign    insulate    insure    lean    play
press    protect    spray    turn    vaccinate    warn

1  One in four homes is not .......*insured*....... against theft, fire or flood. *V n against n (passive)*..

2  She ................................. her bike against a tree. .............................................

3  The two men were arrested frequently as they ................................. against racial segregation.

   .............................................

4  The government has to ................................. its citizens against terrorists. .............................................

5  She ................................. a finger against her lips, signaling him to remain silent. .............................................

6  Hungary were the best team I ................................. against. .............................................

7  Try to see that the living room is well ................................. against draughts. .............................................

8  These new taxes have helped ................................. public opinion against the government.

   .............................................

9  If your bare hand or arm ................................. against one of the stone walls carelessly, the stone

   would draw blood. .............................................

10  It would do no good at all to ................................. this boy against any danger. .............................................

11  They wanted to be sure that everybody was ................................. against cholera. .............................................

12  Mist the foliage twice daily on hot days and ................................. the plants against pests.

    .............................................

**B** Rewrite these sentences using the verb given in brackets with *against* and a noun group or '-ing' clause.

1  She attacked the vice president. (direct)
   *She directed an attack against the vice president.*.............................

2  Regular physical exercise also helps prevent you getting heart disease. (protect)
   .............................................................................

3  You have to compare the advantages and the disadvantages before you begin. (weigh)
   .............................................................................

4  Because of her father's wealth, she did not suffer the effect of several disasters. (cushion)
   .............................................................................

5  Before I set off, Mother would tell me not to go anywhere dangerous. (warn)
   .............................................................................

6  He hit the edge of the desk with his hand. (bang)
   .............................................................................

7  The same criticism can hardly be made about James Baker, the former Secretary of State. (level)
   .............................................................................

# Verbs used with *as*: 1

**1** Some verbs are followed by a prepositional phrase which consists of *as* and a noun group. For example, in *She works as a designer*, the verb *work* is followed by the preposition *as* and the noun group *a designer*. This pattern is **V as n**.

|  | Verb group | *as* | noun group |
|---|---|---|---|
| She | trained | as | a teacher. |
| The scandal | began | as | a family feud. |

Verbs with this pattern belong to the following meaning groups:

■ **verbs concerned with doing a job, getting or leaving a job, or training for a job**

| practise | run | stand | train |
|---|---|---|---|
| qualify | serve | stand down | work |
| resign | sign up | step down | |

He **worked** *as a kitchen assistant* for the Ministry of Defence.

She **has** recently **qualified** *as a doctor* and is hoping to practise in Pakistan.

He intends to **step down** *as chairman* in 1997.

■ **verbs concerned with having a role or a function**

| act | double up | operate |
|---|---|---|
| double | function | serve |

Always breathe through your nose: it **acts** *as a filter*.

The room **had to double up** *as my studio*.

■ **verbs concerned with beginning, continuing, and ending**

| begin | end | finish | remain | start off |
|---|---|---|---|---|
| continue | end up | finish up | start | start out |

The camp **began** *as a maze of tents*, but over 14 years it has grown into a proper village.

Mr. Barker **will continue** *as chairman of the company's corporate finance division*.

When we were together at Liverpool, I never thought Kevin **would end up** *as a manager*.

■ **verbs indicating that someone or something is perceived as a particular thing**

| come across | count | go down | qualify | rate |
|---|---|---|---|---|
| come over | emerge | pass | rank | shape up |

Moving home **ranks** *as one of life's most stressful events*.

The MP **came across** *as a genuine, committed socialist*.

The work barely **qualifies** *as opera* at all.

■ **verbs indicating that someone is trying to be perceived as something they are not, or that something is intended to be perceived as something it is not**

| dress up | masquerade | pose |
|---|---|---|

Jones and his accomplice **posed** *as police officers* to gain entry to the house.

As a youngster he loved **dressing up** *as Superman*.

**Productive use:** Many other verbs are sometimes followed by a prepositional phrase beginning with *as* which indicates the role of the Subject. For example, someone can *compete* as an amateur, *live* as a recluse, or *testify* as a witness.

**2** A few verbs are followed by a prepositional phrase which consists of *as* and an adjective group. For example, in *That counts as old*, the verb *count* is followed by the preposition *as* and the adjective *old*. This pattern is **V as adj**.

|  | Verb group | *as* | adjective group |
|---|---|---|---|
| A large number of plants | qualify | as | medicinal. |

Verbs with this pattern indicate that someone or something is perceived as having a particular quality or status.

| come across | count | pass |
|---|---|---|
| come over | emerge | qualify |

I'm told that I **come across** *as hard and intimidating* but I don't feel hard and intimidating.

In Italy, many women **count** *as unemployed* even if they have a perfectly respectable 'black market' job.

**A** Rewrite these sentences using the verb given in brackets with the pattern **V** *as* **n**.

1  In 1976, Harold Wilson announced that he would no longer be Prime Minister. (resign)

*In 1976, Harold Wilson resigned as Prime Minister.*

2  She had to put on men's clothes. (dress up)

..................................................................................................................................

3  She became a chemical engineer. (qualify)

..................................................................................................................................

4  She studied to become a commercial artist. (train)

..................................................................................................................................

5  He was Minister of Agriculture for four years. (serve)

..................................................................................................................................

6  In the early 1960s he was a Labour candidate in local elections. (stand)

..................................................................................................................................

7  Henry will still be chairman and chief executive officer. (continue)

..................................................................................................................................

8  He was conscripted into the German army and eventually became a prisoner of war. (end up)

..................................................................................................................................

**B** Fill in the gaps in the sentences below using the noun groups in this list. Use each noun group once.

| | | | |
|---|---|---|---|
| a great cricketer | females | a lawyer | a lorry driver |
| an office | a single person | women | a world power |

1  He took two degrees and practised as ................................... in Durham.
2  My brother had two or three odd jobs and he finished up as ...................................
3  These men are said to have masqueraded as ...................................
4  The grant is quite good as I'm not married and so I count as ...................................
5  There are lots and lots of fish that change gender. Mostly they start off as ................................... and later they become males.
6  Like Japan, China has emerged as ...................................
7  We met in her comfortable North London home, which doubles as ...................................
8  I believe he will go down as ...................................

**C** In the sentences below, put a dotted line under the verb used with *as* and an adjective group. Then underline each of the other parts of the pattern.

1  In many of the books science comes across as interesting, exciting, fun.
2  These works emerge as more complex and more interesting than you might expect.
3  A train has to be one hour behind schedule to count as late compared with five minutes in 1986.
4  13 percent of American households qualify as poor.
5  They come over as nice but characterless.

83

# Verbs used with *as*: 2

Some verbs are followed by a noun group and a prepositional phrase which consists of *as* and a noun group. For example, in *They chose her as their representative*, the verb *choose* is followed by the noun group *her*, the preposition *as*, and the noun group *their representative*. This pattern is **V n *as* n**. With some verbs, the preposition is sometimes followed by an '-ing' clause.

## Active pattern

|  | Verb group | noun group | *as* | noun group/-ing |
|---|---|---|---|---|
| They | regard | him | as | a real friend. |
| She | perceived | Jean | as | being ungrateful. |
| She | began | her career | as | a model. |

## Passive pattern

|  | Verb group | *as* | noun group/-ing |
|---|---|---|---|
| A life sentence | is defined | as | being twenty-five years. |
| Ellen | was chosen | as | a tour leader. |

(With phrasal verbs, the particle comes either after the noun group or after the verb.)

Verbs with this pattern belong to the following meaning groups:

■ **verbs concerned with labelling or describing someone or something in a particular way**

| | | | | |
|---|---|---|---|---|
| address | classify | denounce | identify | mention |
| attack | condemn | describe | know | name |
| cite | define | dismiss | label | |

*A Home Office spokesman **has described** reports of deaths inside the prison **as speculation**.*

*Do you want to **be labelled** as a woman playwright?* (passive)

■ **verbs concerned with having a particular idea regarding someone or something**

| | | | | |
|---|---|---|---|---|
| accept | fancy | put down | regard | write off |
| acknowledge | intend | rank | remember | |
| consider | interpret | rate | see | |
| count | perceive | recognize | view | |

*Like most exporters, it **regards** China **as the next great target in Asia**.*

*Carter **is remembered** as the president who wore a heavy wool sweater in the White House.* (passive)

*I think it's too easy for bands to **be written off** as sounding like other people.* (passive)

In the case of *fancy*, the noun group following the verb is always a reflexive pronoun.

*Like most joyriders, Stuart **fancied himself** as an expert driver and a match for the police.*

■ **verbs concerned with nominating or choosing someone for a particular position**

| | | | | |
|---|---|---|---|---|
| adopt | cast | elect | name | proclaim |
| appoint | choose | install | nominate | select |

*The president is likely to **appoint** a woman **as secretary of the navy**.*

■ **verbs concerned with representing or presenting someone or something in a particular way**

| | | | |
|---|---|---|---|
| express | pass off | present | promote |
| market | portray | project | represent |

*The group tended to **represent** its interests **as those of society as a whole**.*

■ **verbs concerned with showing someone or something to be a particular thing**

| | | | | |
|---|---|---|---|---|
| confirm | establish | expose | mark out | reveal |

*In 1876 he **had been exposed** as a fraud and jailed.* (passive)

■ **verbs concerned with using or treating someone or something in a particular way**

| | | | | |
|---|---|---|---|---|
| employ | keep | train | treat | use |

*He **could use** his shirt **as a rope**, and tie one end to the branch.*

*Men need to **treat** women **as equals**.*

■ **verbs concerned with beginning, continuing, or ending something**

| | | | | |
|---|---|---|---|---|
| begin | continue | end | finish | start |

*Lloyd Wright **began** his career **as a landscape architect**.*

■ *Strike* also has this pattern.

*He **struck** me **as being a very healthy young man**.*

## Different forms of the pattern

*It had become obvious that Mrs Thatcher and **the man** she **had appointed** as her deputy did not see eye to eye.*

*He **dismissed** as scare stories reports that teachers were being sacked because schools couldn't pay them.*

*Journalists have expressed concern at **what** they **see** as a sinister new development.*

**A** In the sentences below, put a dotted line under the verb used with *as*. Then underline each of the other parts of the pattern.

1  The board named Allan Gilmour as vice chairman for financial services.
2  When he reached the back porch, he met an officer, whom he addressed as captain.
3  His views have been widely denounced as being racist.
4  We should not dismiss as lies the incredible stories that children may tell us about themselves.
5  In 1960, John Fitzgerald Kennedy was elected as the 37th US President.
6  He had been cast as the king in Shaw's 'The Apple Cart'.
7  Manchester United are the team that have the best chance of finishing the season as Premier League champions.
8  He regarded Harry as being still solidly part of the family.
9  It was a long time before anyone recognised him as the great driver he is.
10  Top executives around the country have rated Atlanta as the nation's best city for business.

**B** Rewrite these sentences using the verb given in brackets with the pattern **V n as n** or its passive.

1  He seemed to me a serious but friendly person. (strike)
*He struck me as a serious but friendly person.*

2  Joe thought his stress was an inevitable part of his job. (perceive)

3  His peers said he was the best rider Australia had produced. (acknowledge)

4  The refugees were called 'vagabonds and escaped prisoners'. (label)

5  His irreverence for authority indicates that he is a troublemaker. (mark out)

6  Tilefish is a beautifully colored fish which is often sold under the name golden bass. (market)

7  The market became flooded with fake watches. People pretended they were originals. (pass off)

8  I often wondered why this band wanted me to be their singer. (choose)

9  He declared that the tape was a fake. (denounce)

10  The documentary suggests that Los Angeles is a city about to explode. (portray)

# Verbs used with *as*: 3

Some verbs are followed by a noun group and a prepositional phrase which consists of *as* and an adjective group. For example, in *I saw the question as crucial*, the verb *see* is followed by the noun group *the question*, the preposition *as*, and the adjective *crucial*. This pattern is **V n *as* adj**.

## Active pattern

|  | Verb group | noun group | *as* | adjective group |
|---|---|---|---|---|
| We | can't dismiss | it | as | trivial. |
| She | perceived | him | as | stupid. |

## Passive pattern

|  | Verb group | *as* | adjective group |
|---|---|---|---|
| The talks | were described | as | frank and friendly. |
| The area | can be considered | as | safe from attack. |

(With phrasal verbs, the particle comes either after the noun group or after the verb.)

Verbs with this pattern belong to the following meaning groups:

■ **verbs concerned with labelling or describing someone or something in a particular way**

| | | | |
|---|---|---|---|
| attack | condemn | describe | label |
| cite | denounce | dismiss | |

*Eyewitnesses* **described** *the attack as savage.*

*He* **attacked** *the governors' decision as 'ludicrous'.*

*The Australian government* **has condemned** *the killings as outrageous and cowardly.*

■ **verbs concerned with having a particular view of someone or something**

| | | | | |
|---|---|---|---|---|
| accept | interpret | rate | remember | write off |
| acknowledge | perceive | recognize | see | |
| consider | rank | regard | view | |

*He refused to* **accept** *the judgement as final.*

*Depending upon your circumstances, you* **might interpret** *redundancy as welcome or unwelcome.*

*One man* **regards** *a glass of water as half full while another* **views** *it as half empty.*

*The state* **was** *still* **recognized** *as independent in 1925.* (passive)

■ **verbs concerned with representing or presenting someone or something in a particular way**

| | | | |
|---|---|---|---|
| pass off | portray | present | represent |

*The four denied trying to* **pass** *the notes* **off** *as genuine.*

*Abraham's death* **is presented** *as good.* (passive)

■ **verbs concerned with showing someone or something to have a particular characteristic or quality**

| | | |
|---|---|---|
| confirm | expose | mark out | reveal |

*The whole idea* **was exposed** *as stupid and naive.* (passive)

*Her diamond rings* **marked** *her* **out** *as seriously rich.*

■ *Strike* also has this pattern.

*The answering machine wasn't on and that* **struck** *her as strange.*

## Different forms of the pattern

*I do not intend to cause distress to its members by publishing the texts of rituals* **which** *they* **perceive** *as sacred.*

*Dr Cato* **described** *as 'disgusting' a proposal to build a restaurant in the park.*

**A** In the sentences below, put a dotted line under the verb used with *as*. Then underline each of the other parts of the pattern.

1  They rate themselves as ambitious and strong-willed.
2  The doctors wrote him off as incurable eight years ago, but he is still alive.
3  The separation and eventual divorce were presented as amicable.
4  Adorno set out to expose as false all claims that the 'good' or 'just' society had been achieved.
5  The demonstrators were trying to draw attention to the export of live sheep to France, which they denounced as cruel.
6  With healthy self-esteem we perceive ourselves as lovable and capable.
7  In the UK all babies who weigh less than 5lb 8oz (2.5kg) at birth are labelled as premature.
8  It's a suggestion that officials dismiss as misleading.
9  The company admitted to re-finishing surplus airplane parts and then passing them off as new.

**B** These sentences show the pattern **V n *as* n** or its passive. Rewrite them using the pattern **V n *as* adj** or its passive.

1  He remembers her as an exceptional beauty.
   *He remembers her as exceptionally beautiful.*
2  The book was condemned as blasphemy by many people.
   ..............................................................................................................................................
3  The atmosphere inside the House of Commons was described as absolute chaos.
   ..............................................................................................................................................
4  Her story was beginning to be widely accepted as the truth.
   ..............................................................................................................................................
5  He denied that he was trying to portray himself as a madman.
   ..............................................................................................................................................

**C** Fill in the gaps in the sentences below using the adjective groups in this list. Use each adjective group once.

   dead    more important    satisfactory    timid and tearful    too violent    unfair

1  The British Airways pilot is today recovering at Southampton General Hospital. His condition is described as ..................................
2  The movie has been attacked by many critics as ..................................
3  This tax was regarded as .................................. because it meant millions of people made no direct financial contribution to local services.
4  We rank pets as .................................. to us than issues like the British economy, our personal hobbies and exercise, and holidays.
5  Then he'd been noble and heroic and now he was revealed as ..................................
6  Six government soldiers are confirmed as .................................. after the six hour battle.

# Verbs used with *at*: 1

Some verbs are followed by a prepositional phrase which consists of *at* and a noun group. For example, in *They swore at him*, the verb *swear* is followed by the preposition *at* and the noun group *him*. This pattern is **V *at* n.**

|  | Verb group | *at* | noun group |
|---|---|---|---|
| The rivals | shouted | at | each other. |
| He | glanced | at | his watch. |

Verbs with this pattern belong to the following meaning groups:

■ verbs indicating that one person speaks loudly or unpleasantly to someone else, or laughs at them

| go on | scream | snap |
|---|---|---|
| laugh | shout | swear |

He **used to shout** at people *and sometimes even hit his assistants.*

Most of these verbs are sometimes used in the passive.

*I didn't want him to look foolish and* **be laughed** *at.*

*Go on, scream* and *shout* are sometimes followed by a prepositional phrase beginning with *at*, and a to-infinitive clause.

*They were firing. I* **screamed** *at them to stop.*

■ verbs indicating that someone communicates using a facial expression or a gesture

| grin | smile | wave | wink |
|---|---|---|---|

*Michael just* **grinned** *at her, maddeningly.*

*I saw my parents* **waving** *at me through the window.*

■ verbs indicating that someone looks at something or someone

| glance | glare | look | stare |
|---|---|---|---|

**Look at the holes in the walls!**

*Betty* **glared** *at her in disgust.*

These verbs are sometimes used in the passive.

*I often realise I* **am being stared** *at just because my clothes are unusual.*

■ verbs indicating that someone expresses a bad opinion of something

| grumble | lash out | protest |
|---|---|---|
| hit out | laugh | scoff |

*They* **scoffed** *at my suggestion.*

*They* **are protesting** *at conditions in the jail.*

■ verbs indicating that someone hits or touches something or tries to do so

| beat | hack away | pull | stab | tap |
|---|---|---|---|---|
| grab | knock | slash | swing | tear |

*I* **knocked** *at the front door.*

*'Maria?' he said again and* **pulled** *at her wrist.*

■ verbs indicating that a person or animal bites, eats, or drinks something

| chew | nibble | peck | sip | suck |
|---|---|---|---|---|
| gnaw | nip | pick | snap | |

*He* **chewed** *at the end of his pencil, thinking out the next problem.*

*Near the garden gate a hen and her chicks* **peck** *at corn.*

■ verbs indicating that someone attacks someone else

| aim | fire | rush |
|---|---|---|
| come | fly | shoot |

*The soldiers* **were shooting** *at anything that moved now.*

■ verbs used when indicating the size, level, weight, or price of something

| average out | level off | run | stand |
|---|---|---|---|
| bottom out | peak | sell | work out |

*The cost of the fighter programme now* **stands** *at more than four thousand million dollars.*

*The average rise* **works out** *at 6.5 per cent.*

■ other common verbs

| aim | guess | hint | point |
|---|---|---|---|

*The girl* **pointed** *at the blackboard on the wall.*

In the case of *aim* and *hint*, the preposition *at* is sometimes followed by an '-ing' clause.

*The Government* **must aim** *at getting Britain back to work.*

## Different forms of the pattern

*What* **are** *you* **looking** *at?*

*He looked for some clue about **what** the doctor* **was hinting** *at.*

*She set **a standard of excellence** for me to* **aim** *at.*

**A** In the sentences below, put a dotted line under the verb used with *at*. Then underline each of the other parts of the pattern.

1 He nibbled at his bottom lip and shook his head slowly.
2 It's hoped that the game will sell at less than a pound.
3 People complained they'd been sworn at for failing to park according to the rules.
4 Then he gave a cry and the two officers turned to see what he was staring at.
5 They sped off, firing at random at people in the streets.
6 If you can't laugh at yourself, who can you laugh at?
7 Skylark is a temperamental horse and doesn't like being shouted at.
8 Provide interesting pictures, books and mobiles to look at.

**B** Rewrite these sentences using the pattern **V** *at* **n**.

1 Mahoney gave him an angry look.
*Mahoney looked at him angrily.*
2 Arnold took a few sips of his beer.
.................................................................................................................
3 She turned to Frank and gave him a triumphant grin.
.................................................................................................................
4 The police can only make a guess about the scale of the problem.
.................................................................................................................
5 I gave Sandy a casual wave.
.................................................................................................................

**C** Complete the questions below using the words given in brackets with *at*. Then rewrite them as reported questions, starting with the words provided.

1 a) What ............... *are they pointing at?* ............................... (they / are / pointing)
   b) I asked someone ............... *what they were pointing at.* ...............................
2 a) What .......................................................................... ? (you / are / looking)
   b) I asked him ..........................................................................
3 a) Who .......................................................................... ? (you / are / waving)
   b) I asked her ..........................................................................
4 a) Who .......................................................................... ? (they / are / shooting)
   b) I asked him ..........................................................................
6 a) What .......................................................................... ? (you / are / hinting)
   b) I asked her ..........................................................................
7 a) Who .......................................................................... ? (he / was / shouting)
   b) I asked someone ..........................................................................

# Verbs used with *at*: 2

Some verbs are followed by a noun group and a prepositional phrase which consists of *at* and a noun group. For example, in *She shouted insults at him*, the verb *shout* is followed by the noun group *insults*, the preposition *at*, and the noun group *him*. This pattern is **V n *at* n**.

## Active pattern

|  | Verb group | noun group | *at* | noun group |
|---|---|---|---|---|
| I | shook | my fist | at | him. |
| Estimates | put the | death toll | at | about 200. |

## Passive pattern

|  | Verb group | *at* | noun group |
|---|---|---|---|
| Bombs | were thrown | at | shops in the capital. |
| The share price | was set | at | £1.75. |

Verbs with this pattern belong to the following meaning groups:

■ **verbs indicating that someone points or aims something at someone or something**

| aim | point | stab |
|---|---|---|
| direct | shake | swing |

*She **pointed** the gun at him.*

*He **swung** a hammer at her head but missed.*

■ **verbs indicating that someone throws an object at someone or something**

| chuck | fling | hurl | throw |
|---|---|---|---|

*She **threw** a pillow at him.*

*A gang who nearly killed a policeman by **hurling** a brick at his car have been jailed for a total of sixty years.*

■ **verbs indicating that someone speaks to someone, often in a hostile way**

| aim | direct | hurl | scream | shout |
|---|---|---|---|---|

*They stood there and **shouted** abuse at me as I walked down the street.*

*Accusations about stealing money **were hurled** at her by her husband.* (passive)

■ **verbs indicating that someone looks or smiles at someone or something**

| direct | flash | shoot | throw |
|---|---|---|---|

*He turns to **flash** a loving smile at his new bride.*

*The maid backed out, **throwing** one last cautionary look at her mistress.*

■ **verbs indicating that someone buys, sells, or puts a value on some property**

| buy | price | quote | sell | value |
|---|---|---|---|---|

*Estates **may sell** property at a discount to raise money quickly for taxes.*

*One day Carret **was able to buy** some bonds at $89, which he then sold at a profit.*

■ **verbs indicating that someone estimates, fixes, or maintains a number or amount**

| estimate | maintain | put | reckon | set |
|---|---|---|---|---|

*The number of child workers **was put** at more than 4.8 million.* (passive)

*The cost **is estimated** at more than twelve thousand million dollars.* (passive)

*In winter, **maintain** the temperature at 36 degrees F or higher.*

## Different forms of the pattern

*But his words clearly carry no weight at all with those at whom they **were directed**.*

*The authorities now **put** at twenty the number of dead in the recent unrest.*

*His suit was spattered with the eggs that students **had thrown** at him.*

**A** In the sentences below, put a dotted line under the verb used with *at*. Then underline each of the other parts of the pattern.

1 Norma aimed the gun at them.

2 After a few moments I realised that her question was directed at me.

3 Angrily, the woman shook her fist at Bragg's departing back.

4 Michael shot a quick glance at him, then turned back to Miss Treves.

5 He flashed a handsome smile at the television cameras.

6 In early trading in Hong Kong, gold was quoted at $366.50 an ounce.

7 Casualties were estimated at over 1,000.

8 Groups of people threw stones at us throughout the journey.

9 In the end I couldn't take the violence and the insults she would hurl at me.

10 The bombs hit the targets they were aimed at about 25 percent of the time.


**B** Fill in the gaps in these sentences. For each pair, one verb from this Unit goes in both sentences.

1 I had abuse .................................. at me by supporters of the hunt.

Rocks were .................................. at the police.

2 A procession of haughty and accusing looks were .................................. at the interviewer.

The Blackburn manager is alleged to have .................................. improper comments at Stockport referee William Flood.

3 He .................................. his rifle at me.

But he denied his comments were .................................. at Liberal Party colleagues.

4 For some reason I just cracked and .................................. my drink at this guy.

One reporter noted the angry glares Desiree .................................. at Tyson yesterday.


**C** Write sentences about these amounts, using the verb given in brackets with the passive of the pattern **V n *at* n**.

1 The number of birds: one billion. (estimate)
   *The number of birds was estimated at one billion.*

2 The number of people out of work: more than thirty-eight thousand. (put)
   ..................................................................................................

3 The cost of repairs: £1 million. (estimate)
   ..................................................................................................

4 The turnout in the election: sixty percent. (put)
   ..................................................................................................

5 The number of victims: around three percent of the population. (reckon)
   ..................................................................................................

6 The dividend: 9.2 pence. (maintain)
   ..................................................................................................

7 The exchange rate: 39 pesos to the US dollar. (set)
   ..................................................................................................

# Verbs used with *between* or *among*

**1** Some verbs are followed by a prepositional phrase which consists of *between* and a **plural noun group**. For example, in *She alternated between anger and depression*, the verb *alternate* is followed by the preposition *between* and the plural noun group *anger and depression*. This pattern is **V *between* pl-n**.

| | Verb group | *between* | plural noun group |
|---|---|---|---|
| I | liaise | between | these groups. |
| They | can't distinguish | between | right and wrong. |

Verbs with this pattern belong to the following meaning groups:

■ **verbs indicating that someone sorts out or helps the relationship between two people or groups**

| adjudicate | arbitrate | liaise | mediate |
|---|---|---|---|

*I've been instructed to **liaise** between my chief and the Branch and to assist where I can.*

■ **verbs concerned with recognizing the difference between two or more things**

| differentiate | discriminate | distinguish |
|---|---|---|

*It's difficult to **differentiate** between chemical weapons and chemicals for peaceful industrial use.*

■ **verbs concerned with doing, being, or using two things alternately**

| alternate | oscillate | vacillate | waver |
|---|---|---|---|

*In the winter he started to have constant back pain. He **had to alternate** between work and lying down.*

*She **oscillated** between anger and guilt.*

■ **verbs indicating that something has a range of values**

| hover | oscillate | range | vary |
|---|---|---|---|

*Prices **range** between $30 and $50.*

■ *Choose* also has this pattern.

*Why **should** women **have to choose** between a job and a family?*

**2** Some verbs are followed by a noun group and a prepositional phrase which consists of *between* or *among* and a **plural noun group**. For example, in *He divided his money among his children*, the verb *divide* is followed by the noun group *his money*, the preposition *among* and the plural noun group *his children*. This pattern is **V**

**n *between/among* pl-n**. With phrasal verbs, the particle comes either after the noun group or after the verb.

## Active pattern

| | Verb group | noun group | *between/ among* | pl. noun group |
|---|---|---|---|---|
| I | Split | the wages | between | you. |
| | would rate | him | among | the top players. |

## Passive pattern

| | Verb group | *between/ among* | pl. noun group |
|---|---|---|---|
| The cash | will be shared | between | the two charities. |
| The food | was distributed | among | the refugees. |

Verbs with this pattern belong to the following meaning groups:

■ **verbs concerned with dividing something between two or more people or groups**

| distribute | divide up | share out | split up |
|---|---|---|---|
| divide | share | split | |

When only two people or groups are involved, the preposition is usually *between* rather than *among*. When more than two people or groups are involved, you can use either *between* or *among*.

*Drain the noodles and **divide** them among the individual serving bowls.*

*The tips **are divided up** equally between the staff, and then added on to their wage packet.* (passive)

■ **verbs indicating that someone considers someone or something to be in a particular group**

| number | rank | rate |
|---|---|---|

Only the preposition *among* is used with these verbs.

*He **numbered** several Americans among his friends.*

*Rank* is sometimes used with an ordinal number in this pattern, as shown below.

*One survey **ranked** her fifth among preferred presidential candidates.*

## Different forms of the pattern

*He even **numbered** among his connections certain lords.*

*Heads of schools that improved would be given cash bonuses to **distribute** among teaching staff.*

## Practice

**A** In the sentences below, put a dotted line under the verb used with a pattern described in this Unit. Then underline each of the other parts of the pattern.

1 A prominent government supporter has promised to mediate between the two sides.

2 Always try and alternate between two or three tasks.

3 The sheep farmers have 120 million dollars of government hand-outs to share out between them.

4 For general daylight use, these two cameras are difficult to choose between.

5 With album releases of this quality he'll soon be rated among the top reggae producers.

6 The group numbers among its members some of the most influential women in Sweden.

7 Last year they raised £22,000, which was split between several charities.

8 The money will be split up between the three of them.

**B** Fill in the gaps in these sentences using *between* or *among*.

1 Temperatures on the coast vary ...................... 25 and 30 degrees Celsius all year round.

2 Eskimo hunters are trained to discriminate ...................... dozens of types of snow.

3 My school is ranked ...................... the high achievers in Brisbane.

4 Payments are expected to range ...................... $9 billion and $12 billion this year.

5 He vacillated ...................... republican and monarchist sentiments.

6 The new president numbers building and joinery ...................... his hobbies.

**C** Fill in the gaps in the sentences below using the nouns in this list. Use each noun once.

death   doubt   family   football   women

1 As a youngster he'd had to choose between athletics and ...................................

2 The whole question is about how we divide our lives between work and ...................................

3 He was in intensive care, hovering between life and ...................................

4 The Koran does not discriminate between men and ...................................

5 She stood there worrying, vacillating between happiness and ...................................

**D** Rewrite these sentences using the verb given in brackets with *between* or *among*.

1 Her brown eyes were sometimes amused and sometimes embarrassed. (waver)
*Her brown eyes wavered between amusement and embarrassment.*

2 The President thinks that economic and political refugees are different. (distinguish)

3 He was willing to help the government and the workers come to an agreement. (arbitrate)

4 He gave pennies to all the neighbourhood children. (distribute)

5 I think he is one of the fastest bowlers in the world. (rate)

**1** Some verbs are followed by a prepositional phrase which consists of *by* and an '-ing' clause. For example, in *They responded by ordering him to go home*, the verb *respond* is followed by the preposition *by* and the '-ing' clause *ordering him to go home*. This pattern is **V *by* -ing**.

|  | Verb group | *by* | -ing clause |
|---|---|---|---|
| He | began | by | asking me about my house. |
| Protesters | retaliated | by | throwing stones. |

Verbs with this pattern belong to the following meaning groups:

■ **verbs concerned with starting or finishing a task, session, or period of time in a particular way**

| begin | end | finish off | start | start out |
|---|---|---|---|---|
| close | finish | finish up | start off | |

*Start off by exercising for five to ten minutes every day.*

*She **ended** by inviting her listeners to send their own experiences to her.*

■ **verbs concerned with responding to something that has been done, or compensating for it**

| atone | counter | reciprocate | respond |
|---|---|---|---|
| compensate | react | reply | retaliate |

*Pollack **responded** by calling the police.*

*The company tried to **compensate** by expanding sales at home.*

**Productive use:** Many other verbs which involve a response to an action or situation sometimes have this pattern.

**2** Some verbs are followed by a noun group and a prepositional phrase which consists of *by* and an '-ing' clause. For example, in *He ended his speech by saying that there would be elections soon*, the verb *end* is followed by the noun group *his speech*, the preposition *by*, and the clause *saying that there would be elections soon*. This pattern is **V n *by* -ing**. With phrasal verbs, the particle comes either after the noun group or after the verb.

|  | Verb group | noun group | *by* | -ing clause |
|---|---|---|---|---|
| They | started | the day | by | having a cup of coffee. |
| He | opened | the session | by | calling for reforms. |

Verbs with this pattern are concerned with beginning or ending a session, career, or period of time in a particular way.

| begin | end | finish up | preface | start off |
|---|---|---|---|---|
| close | finish | open | start | start out |

*When my father's education finished, he **began** his engineering career by building ice factories.*

*The South Korean president **has ended** his visit to Japan by inviting Emperor Akihito to pay a return visit to South Korea.*

*He **started off** this particular interview by saying, 'Yes, I think you're on to a good idea.'*

**Productive use:** You can use this pattern with a wide range of verbs. The prepositional phrase indicates the means by which something is done, as in *He escaped the law by fleeing the country*.

**3** Some verbs are followed by a noun group and a prepositional phrase which consists of *by* and a noun group. For example, in *He took her by the arm*, the verb *take* is followed by the noun group *her*, the preposition *by*, and the noun group *the arm*. This pattern is **V n *by* n**.

|  | Verb group | noun group | *by* | noun group |
|---|---|---|---|---|
| He | grabbed | me | by | the hair. |
| I | held | her | by | the waist. |

Verbs with this pattern indicate that someone holds or takes hold of part of someone's body.

| catch | grab | have | hold | take |
|---|---|---|---|---|

The noun group after *by* usually begins with *the*.

*He **grabbed** Rivers by the shoulders and dragged him out of the car.*

# UNIT 47 Practice

**A** In the sentences below, put a dotted line under the verb used with a pattern described in this Unit. Then underline each of the other parts of the pattern.

1 He started his career by shortening his name.
2 She started off by accusing him of blackmail but he just ignored her.
3 I'd like to begin by asking about the system of management in the school and how you fit into that.
4 They finished the day by reaching the final of the Queen Mother Challenge Cup.
5 Bake the pudding in the oven for 7 minutes. Finish by browning it under a grill.
6 He opened the meeting by quoting lyrics from Bob Dylan's 'The Times They Are A-Changin'.'

**B** Rewrite the second sentence in each pair using the verb given in brackets with the pattern **V by -ing**.

1 Furness shivered and stepped closer to Mace. He put an arm around her. (respond)
   *He responded by putting an arm around her.*

2 He stepped on the cat. The cat scratched his leg. (react)

3 Again the police charged to separate rival groups. The fans pelted them with plastic chairs. (retaliate)

4 When Caroline was five she scribbled on a wall. Her father threw her toys on the fire. (respond)

5 I told them I could not possibly pay the sum demanded. They reduced the demand to £730. (reply)

**C** Rewrite these sentences using the verb given in brackets with the pattern **V n by n**.

1 Shelley took hold of his ankles and dragged him down. (grab)
   *Shelley grabbed him by the ankles and dragged him down.*

2 He took hold of my hair and pushed me roughly up the trailer steps. (grab)

3 Then she stepped toward the door, but George took hold of her wrist. (catch)

4 He took her hand and led her into the next room. (take)

5 I was holding his ears and I was beating his head against the pavement. (have)

6 She stood there, holding Sofia's hand but not looking her in the face. (hold)

# Verbs used with *by*: 2

**1** Some verbs are followed by a prepositional phrase which consists of *by* and a noun group indicating an amount. For example, in *Their incomes have dropped by 30 per cent*, the verb *drop* is followed by the preposition *by* and the noun group *30 per cent*. This pattern is **V *by* amount**.

|  | Verb group | *by* | amount |
|---|---|---|---|
| The overall number of jobs | decreased | by | 1000. |
| The Reds | were leading | by | two runs. |

Verbs with this pattern belong to the following meaning groups:

■ **verbs indicating that a quantity or level increases or decreases.** The prepositional phrase indicates the size of the increase or decrease.

| | | | | |
|---|---|---|---|---|
| climb | dive | increase | shoot up | slump |
| come down | drop | jump | shrink | soar |
| decline | fall | plummet | sink | tumble |
| decrease | go down | plunge | slide | |
| dip | go up | rise | slip | |

*Queensland's population **has increased by 13 percent** in that period.*

*The price of petrol at Shell garages **is coming down by more than four pence a gallon**.*

*Sales **went up by 0.1 per cent** last month as consumers began to shop early for Christmas.*

■ **verbs concerned with winning and losing.** The prepositional phrase indicates either the difference in the scores, or the actual scores.

| | | |
|---|---|---|
| lead | lose | win |

*In the event, Cambridge **won by fifteen points**.*

*The government **lost by one vote**.*

*Popov **is leading by 11 points to nine**.*

■ **verbs indicating that an amount that was set is exceeded**

| | |
|---|---|
| overrun | overspend |

*The reception **overran by forty-five minutes**.*

*Guy's hospital and Lewisham hospital **have** already **overspent by £800,000**.*

**2** Some verbs are followed by a noun group and a prepositional phrase which consists of *by* and a noun group indicating an amount. For example, in *It is cutting its prices by a third*, the verb *cut* is followed by the noun group *its prices*, the preposition *by*, and the noun group *a third*. This pattern is **V n *by* amount**.

## Active pattern

|  | Verb group | noun group | *by* | amount |
|---|---|---|---|---|
| The company | has cut | its workforce | by | 3,000. |
|  | Multiply | each figure | by | five. |

## Passive pattern

|  | Verb group | *by* | amount |
|---|---|---|---|
| Fares | were raised | by | 10 per cent. |

Verbs with this pattern are concerned with increasing or decreasing an amount.

| | | | | |
|---|---|---|---|---|
| cut | devalue | increase | multiply | reduce |
| decrease | divide | lower | raise | |

*The government plans to **raise** petrol prices **by thirty six per cent**.*

*You need to **divide** the total **by six** to work out your income.*

### Different forms of the pattern

*He announced that France **will cut by half** the rate of interest it charges on loans to most countries in Africa.*

**A** In the sentences below, put a dotted line under the verb used with a pattern described in this Unit. Then underline each of the other parts of the pattern.

1 Beer prices have shot up by 10 per cent or so over the past 12 months.

2 Its shares slumped by a third after the crash of BCCI.

3 Economists have forecast that employment will fall by between 10,000 and 30,000.

4 Sterling has been devalued by some 17 per cent and interest rates have been cut by four points.

5 The World Health Organisation says the number of cases of cholera reported worldwide has increased by ten per cent.

6 This historic treaty will reduce by two-thirds current nuclear arsenals.

7 The Argentine Agriculture Minister rejected EC proposals to cut farm subsidies by thirty percent as totally unacceptable.

8 The average family spent a third of its budget on food back then, so the cost of the diet was multiplied by three to determine the poverty line.

**B** Divide the list of verbs beginning with *climb* into two smaller groups:

1 verbs indicating that a quantity or level increases

..................................................................................................................................

2 verbs indicating that a quantity or level decreases

..................................................................................................................................

..................................................................................................................................

**C** Fill in the replies using the pattern **V** *by amount*.

1 Who won the Test match? (Pakistan scored 217 runs. New Zealand scored 150 runs.)
*Pakistan won by 217 runs to 150.* or *Pakistan won by 67 runs.*

2 Who won the rugby? (Ireland scored nine points. France scored 25 points.)

..................................................................................................................................

3 Who's winning? (Fiji have 13 points. England have 17 points.)

..................................................................................................................................

4 Who's leading at the moment? (Edberg has won two sets. Krickstein hasn't won any sets.)

..................................................................................................................................

5 How many votes did he lose by? (He got 34 votes. His opponent got 46 votes.)

..................................................................................................................................

6 Are Manchester winning or losing? (Manchester United have scored one goal. Aston Villa have scored three goals.)

..................................................................................................................................

# Verbs used with *for*: 1

Some verbs are followed by a prepositional phrase which consists of *for* and a noun group. For example, in *He asked for a pay rise*, the verb *ask* is followed by the preposition *for* and the noun group *a pay rise*. This pattern is **V for n**.

|  | Verb group | *for* | noun group |
|---|---|---|---|
| He | pleaded | for | mercy. |
| We | are hoping | for | a happy ending. |

Verbs with this pattern belong to the following meaning groups:

■ **verbs indicating that someone asks for something or tries to get something**

| advertise | call | fish | push | send off |
|---|---|---|---|---|
| aim | campaign | hold out | put in | shout |
| appeal | claim | lobby | register | stand |
| apply | compete | negotiate | ring | strike |
| ask | demonstrate | plead | run | try |
| beg | fight | pray | scream | vote |
| bid | file | press | send | wish |

*I'm asking for your protection.*

*They are campaigning for multi-party democracy.*

*Send off for your free tickets now!*

*Michel Rocard first stood for the presidency in 1969.*

Some of these verbs, especially *apply* and *send*, are sometimes used in the passive.

*The doctor was sent for and arrived surprisingly quickly.*

■ **verbs indicating that someone looks for something or is alert for something**

| check | feel | listen out | search | watch out |
|---|---|---|---|---|
| dig | hunt | look | shop |  |
| explore | listen | look out | watch |  |

*Always look for other ways of managing difficult situations.*

*Meanwhile, the band are searching for an appropriate venue for a special festive show.*

*Watch out for pests and disease.*

With many of these verbs, the prepositional phrase beginning with *for* can come after or before another prepositional phrase, or an adverb, which indicates where someone is searching.

*He felt in his pockets for a coin.*

*I've been looking for you everywhere.*

■ **verbs indicating that someone wants something**

| be dying | hope | long | pray | wish |
|---|---|---|---|---|

*I'm dying for a breath of fresh air.*

*Hope* and *pray* are sometimes used in the passive.

*It's probably the best that can be hoped for in the circumstances.*

■ **verbs indicating that someone chooses something**

| go | opt | plump | settle |
|---|---|---|---|

*None of the children has opted for farming as a career.*

*Go for products with the lowest amount of fat.*

The preposition *for* is sometimes followed by an '-ing' clause.

*I wanted to be a dancer but my father said I couldn't possibly do that, so instead I settled for getting married and having children.*

■ **verbs indicating that someone goes towards a particular destination**

| depart | head | leave | make | run |
|---|---|---|---|---|

*He spun around and headed for the door.*

*My wife and I are leaving for Mexico next month.*

**A** In the sentences below, put a dotted line under the verb used with *for*. Then underline each of the other parts of the pattern. (For different forms of the pattern, see Unit 50.)

1 The Socialist Democrats are still pressing for a boycott of the elections.
2 What level of responsibility are you aiming for?
3 Ingrid tried to file for a Swedish divorce, but the technical difficulties made it impossible.
4 He persuaded the Duchess to hold out for the best deal possible.
5 She doubted he really checked the instruments or even really knew what to check for.
6 These are all good points to look for.
7 You can send off for the competition details by cutting the coupon.

**B** Fill in the gaps in the sentences below using the verbs in this list. Use each verb once.

aim   feel   fight   listen   plead   pray   run   scream   search   shop

1 Shop fronts were smashed and tourists ................................. for cover as a short, sharp street battle erupted.
2 For weeks she lay in her hospital bed as her devoted husband ................................. for a miracle.
3 We should unite and ................................. for our rights.
4 While he ................................. for his own apartment they were roommates.
5 The major was alert in a second, ................................. for his revolver deep inside his fur pocket.
6 Every fifty meters, he'd stop and ................................. for those behind him.
7 Women ................................. for them and run to the stage and kiss them and hand them flowers.
8 In its original targets Euro Disney ................................. for an average daily attendance of 30,000.
9 Relief workers are ................................. for further international help to alleviate the conditions.
10 When you ................................. for food, how frequently do you go to a large supermarket?

**C** Rewrite these sentences using the verb given in brackets with the pattern **V** *for* **n**.

1 Cross saw Brown come through the door and move towards the bed. (head)
  *Cross saw Brown come through the door and head for the bed.*
2 Most university students choose the straight three-year course. (opt)
  ................................................................................................
3 The officials said two of them have requested political asylum. (ask)
  ................................................................................................
4 His father, Tony, told him not to be satisfied with second best. (settle)
  ................................................................................................
5 I'm not sure that the people demanding this change have thought through its implications. (push)
  ................................................................................................
6 First, the police must be asked to come. (send)
  ................................................................................................

#  Verbs used with *for*: 2

**1** Here are some more groups of verbs which are followed by the preposition *for* and a noun group or an '-ing' clause:

■ **verbs indicating that someone works for someone or does something for them**

| | | | |
|---|---|---|---|
| act | fight | play | work |
| cover | fill in | speak | write |
| cover up | model | stand in | |

He **works** *for a local heavy engineering firm.*

*I'm always* **having to cover up** *for her and lie to my father.*

*Then someone rang and asked if I* **would stand in** *for Frank Bough and do the Sunday cricket on BBC2.*

■ **verbs indicating that someone is training or preparing for something**

| | | | | |
|---|---|---|---|---|
| gear up | prepare | revise | study | train |

*The crew of the space shuttle Atlantis* **is preparing** *for the ride back to Earth tomorrow.*

*Janet* **has been revising** *for her exams this week.*

■ **verbs concerned with compensating for an action or situation in some way**

| | | | |
|---|---|---|---|
| apologize | compensate | make up | pay |

*The government has always said that it will raise salaries to try to* **compensate** *for the price increases.*

The preposition *for* is sometimes followed by an '-ing' clause.

*I* **apologized** *for wasting his time.*

■ **other common verbs**

| | | | | |
|---|---|---|---|---|
| care | go | live | qualify | sell |
| enter | last | pay | save up | wait |

*Come on, Frank, let's* **go** *for a walk.*

*This effect* **can last** *for several days after the treatment session.*

*They want us to* **pay** *for services we don't use.*

*I* **was waiting** *for you at the crossroads.*

*Care* and *pay* are sometimes used in the passive.

*For some weeks the baby* **was cared** *for in the Convent of St Sulpice.*

## Different forms of the pattern

*What* **are** *you* **waiting** *for?*

*She showed no surprise when he explained* **what** *he* **was looking** *for.*

*The concessions it* **has asked** *for would cost us money.*

*I have* **nothing** *to* **apologize** *for.*

*The new atmosphere of spontaneity was exactly* **what** *we* **had hoped** *for.*

Some verbs are sometimes used in a pattern with *than*.

*They are giving us much more than we* **have asked** *for.*

**2** Some verbs are followed by a prepositional phrase beginning with *for*, and a to-infinitive clause. This pattern is **V** *for* **n to-inf.**

| | Verb group | *for* | noun group | to-infinitive clause |
|---|---|---|---|---|
| The director | asked | for | him | to be removed. |
| She | 's longing | for | Mark | to come home. |

Verbs with this pattern belong to the following meaning groups:

■ **verbs indicating that someone asks for something to be done or to happen**

| | | | | |
|---|---|---|---|---|
| appeal | call | plead | press | shout |
| ask | campaign | pray | push | |

*The CBI* **is pressing** *for firms to invest more cash in training.*

In the case of *ask* and *campaign*, the to-infinitive is usually passive.

*They* **asked** *for their identities to be kept secret.*

■ **verbs indicating that someone wants something to happen or be done**

| | | |
|---|---|---|
| be dying | long | pray |

*All the women* **will be dying** *for you to make a mistake.*

*He* **longed** *for the winter to be over.*

■ *Arrange* and *wait* also have this pattern.

*We* **can arrange** *for you to be picked up at the airport and transferred to your hotel.*

*I don't want to sit around* **waiting** *for the phone to ring.*

**A** Match up the two halves of each sentence.

| | |
|---|---|
| 1 At 15 she was modelling ... | a ... for letting him escape. |
| 2 I was filling in ... | b ... for my bike. |
| 3 It's taken me a year to save up ... | c ... for $2,000 each. |
| 4 The demonstrators were calling ... | d ... for it in enthusiasm and charm. |
| 5 He decided to begin studying ... | e ... for the tournament. |
| 6 Nine teams entered ... | f ... for the injured Graham Gooch. |
| 7 You'll never know how very much I longed ... | g ... for him to resign. |
| 8 They will pay ... | h ... for us to be friends. |
| 9 He wasn't very handsome, but he made up ... | i ... for Elle magazine. |
| 10 His photographs sell ... | j ... for the Vermont bar exams. |

**B** In each of the sentences below, one of the verbs from this list is missing. Mark where it goes and say what it is. Use each verb once.

apologize   care   fight   last   live   pay   stand in   train   wait   work

1 Her future husband will be/for her at Sydney. ......*waiting*..............

2 Teresa has been for the 2.7km walk by walking the 1.5km to her local shop. .................................

3 The rainy season has just begun and will for several more months. .................................

4 She has been for the company for 16 years and says that she is still learning. .................................

5 Can we afford the luxury of what you propose? Who will for it? .................................

6 The baby is for from 9.30 to 6.30 by an extremely capable 27-year-old trained nanny.

.................................

7 He for his work and he would have gone on for ever if he could. .................................

8 I have done nothing for which I should. .................................

9 His big break come when he for another dentist who had been taken ill. .................................

10 He went on to say he was proud that he had for his country. .................................

**C** These sentences show the pattern **V *for* n to-inf**. Fill in the first gap using the verbs in this list. Then think of a way to fill in the second gap.

campaign   plead   pray   press   shout   wait

1 For four years he had ......*campaigned*...... for disabled athletes *to be allowed to compete in* *the Games.*

2 The father of a girl who disappeared from her home a month ago ................................. for her to

.............................................

3 We'll ......................... for somebody to ............................................., then grab him before he can close the door behind him.

4 She eyed the phone, ......................... for it to .............................................

5 The hostages' relatives have been ......................... for more action to

.............................................

6 Graham hurried after the porter, ......................... for him to .............................................

# Verbs used with *for*: 3

Some verbs are followed by a noun group and a prepositional phrase which consists of *for* and a noun group. For example, in *He asked his father for the money*, the verb *ask* is followed by the noun group *his father*, the preposition *for*, and the noun group *the money*. This pattern is **V n *for* n**. With some verbs, the preposition is sometimes followed by an '-ing' clause.

## Active pattern

|  | Verb group | noun group | *for* | noun group/-ing |
|---|---|---|---|---|
| She | has brought | a nice present | for | you. |
| I | don't blame | you | for | being upset. |

## Passive pattern

|  | Verb group | *for* | noun group/-ing |
|---|---|---|---|
| A room | has been booked | for | him. |
| He | was arrested | for | stealing a car. |

(With phrasal verbs, the particle comes either after the noun group or after the verb.)

Verbs with this pattern belong to the following meaning groups:

■ **verbs indicating that someone does something for someone else**

| book | cook | find | leave | play |
|---|---|---|---|---|
| bring | do | fix | make | pour |
| buy | fetch | get | order | prepare |

*I followed her to the kitchen where she **was making** coffee for all of them.*

*My father took me into town one day and **bought** the record for me.*

In the case of *do*, the noun group following the verb is often an **amount**.

*The nurses **can't do** much for her, apart from make her comfortable.*

**Productive use:** Any verb concerned with doing something for someone can be used with this pattern.

■ **verbs concerned with exchanging one thing for another**

| barter | substitute | trade |
|---|---|---|
| exchange | swap | trade in |

*Someone **swapped** the blank for a real bullet. He is lucky to be alive.*

■ **verbs indicating that someone asks someone for something**

| ask | beg | press |
|---|---|---|

*They **asked** me for fresh ideas, but I had none.*

■ **verbs indicating that someone has or expresses a good or bad opinion of someone else.** The prepositional phrase indicates the reason.

| admire | blame | congratulate | (cannot) fault | tell off |
|---|---|---|---|---|
| attack | condemn | criticize | praise | tick off |

*I **admire** them for their independent attitudes.*

*The whole world seems to **condemn** you for being overweight.*

*Adam **ticked** him **off** for smoking too much.*

*The air force and navy **are being praised** for the rescue operation.* (passive)

■ **verbs concerned with treating someone in a particular way because of what they have done**

| arrest | forgive | punish | sue | want |
|---|---|---|---|---|
| compensate | pay back | report | thank |  |
| execute | prosecute | reward | try |  |

*I **had** generously **rewarded** her for her services, which had delighted her.*

*They **could sue** him for breach of contract.*

*I **must thank** you for being so kind to me.*

*He told officers he wanted to **pay** them **back** for locking him up three weeks earlier.*

*He's **wanted** for murder.* (passive)

**Productive use:** Any verb concerned with treating someone in a particular way can be used with this pattern.

**A** In the sentences below, put a dotted line under the verb used with *for* (see this Unit and Units 49 and 50). Then underline each of the other parts of the pattern.

1  I admire him tremendously for his efforts.

2  He listened for sounds inside as he climbed the stairs.

3  He studied engineering and went to work for the telephone company.

4  I ordered a birthday gift for my mother last month.

5  We'll trade in the Buick for another car.

6  They made a home for him in the nursery.

7  Was he covering up for Grace? Or was he telling the truth?

8  Some day I'll pay you back for this!

9  He was warmly congratulated by his five colleagues for hosting the first meeting.


**B** Rewrite each of the following pairs of sentences as one sentence, using *for* and a noun group or '-ing' clause.

1  Her daughter had taken control of her own finances. Sissie had never forgiven her.
   *Sissie had never forgiven her daughter for taking control of her own finances.*

2  I just want some money from Gil. I've begged him again and again.
   ......................................................................................................

3  He was drunk on duty. A crew member reported him.
   ......................................................................................................

4  He wanted hot water. I picked up a bucket to fetch some.
   ......................................................................................................

5  Both leaders were wanted in France. They were to be questioned in connection with an alleged plot.
   ......................................................................................................


**C** These sentences show the pattern **V n n** (see Units 8 and 9). Rewrite them using the pattern **V n *for* n**, if possible. If it is not possible, leave the space blank.

1  Perhaps you might cook him dinner.
   *Perhaps you might cook dinner for him.*

2  She forgave Lisette her deception because she knew what a desperate position she was in.
   ......................................................................................................

3  We will send you a letter which will tell you the day you are expected to come into hospital.
   ......................................................................................................

4  I always wondered why they named him Stanley.
   ......................................................................................................

5  Shirley had bought him a double espresso to thank him for taking her to Baton Rouge.
   ......................................................................................................

6  They asked me some sensible questions.
   ......................................................................................................

7  Devlin got him his coat and took him out to the car.
   ......................................................................................................

# Verbs used with *for*: 4

Here are some more groups of verbs which are followed by a noun group and a prepositional phrase beginning with *for*:

■ **verbs concerned with preparing someone or something for a particular task, purpose, or situation**

| | | | | |
|---|---|---|---|---|
| equip | intend | prepare | qualify | train |

*We're **preparing** our children for the 21st century.*

*The course is designed to **equip** students for a career in radio or magazines.*

■ **verbs concerned with considering or choosing someone or something for a particular role or purpose**

| | | | |
|---|---|---|---|
| choose | nominate | recruit | select |
| interview | recommend | seek | |

*President Clinton **had** originally **nominated** Ms Guinier for the job.*

*Amanda Saranah and Michelle Taylor **have been chosen** for the regional netball team.* (passive)

*This remedy is toxic in large doses and **is not recommended** for use by untrained persons.* (passive)

■ **verbs indicating that someone pays or charges for something**

| | |
|---|---|
| charge | pay |

The noun group following the verb may indicate the person who is paid or charged money, or the amount paid.

***Pay** the gentleman for his services, please.*

*A collector **has paid** many thousands of pounds for a pistol used by Winston Churchill.*

There is sometimes an **amount** between the noun group and the prepositional phrase.

*He was shocked when the bank **charged** him £110 for the manager's time.*

■ **verbs concerned with searching somewhere for something**

| | | | | |
|---|---|---|---|---|
| comb | explore | scan | scour | search |

*Police **searched** the area for other bombs.*

*Seventy officers and a police helicopter **combed** the streets for seven-year-old Maria.*

■ **other common verbs**

| | | | | |
|---|---|---|---|---|
| enter | pay | say | sell | treat |
| hold | put down | schedule | test | wait |

*The President **has scheduled** a news conference for this afternoon.*

*They deserve to **pay** the penalty for their crimes.*

*The truck driver **was treated** for shock.* (passive)

*Passengers **had to wait** 40 minutes for another train.*

*Rough streets **hold** no fears for her.*

In the case of *say*, the noun group following the verb is always an **amount**.

*The fact that she had the full support of her husband **says** much for his courage.*

## Different forms of the pattern

*What **can** I **do** for you?*

*I was trying to work out **what** to **buy** for my mother.*

*She was wearing a dress **that** her mother **had made** for her.*

*This is a real opportunity to go and do the job **that** we've **been trained** for.*

*I **chose** for these interviews Roger de Grey, Lawrence Gowing, and John Piper.*

# Practice

**A** **Fill in the gaps in the sentences below using the verbs in this list. Use each verb once.**

charge   interview   prepare   say   scan   select   test

1 He ................................. the horizon anxiously for his camera crew.
2 Flasks are ................................. for their ability to keep liquid hot or cold.
3 They never doubted that they had done their best to ................................. the country for war.
4 That the Escort is still the nation's bestselling car ................................. a lot for the power of Ford's marketing people.
5 Space engineers meet today to ................................. a launch date for the next space mission.
6 They ................................. high prices for admission and keep details of the venues secret until the last minute.
7 If you are being ................................. for an executive position, a dark suit and a conservative shirt and tie are essential.

**B** **Rewrite these sentences, using the verb given in brackets with the pattern V n *for* n or its passive. In some cases the beginning of the sentence is provided.**

1 The car probably cost him about £7,900. (pay)
He *probably paid about £7,900 for the car.*

2 The course did not give her the skills needed for a new career. (equip)
.................................................................................................

3 Ashton decided that Diana Adams should dance the ballerina role. (choose)
.................................................................................................

4 A child's admission is $4 and an adult admission is $7 at all of our local cinemas. (charge)
All of our local cinemas .................................................................

5 I think we should go all over the house, looking for clues. (search)
.................................................................................................

6 She was not interested in the magazine. (hold)
The magazine .................................................................................

7 It has been decided that the next meeting will be held on Monday. (schedule)
The next meeting .............................................................................

**C** **Put the different parts of these sentences in the right order.**

1 an ambulance / waited / for / 53 minutes / she .......................................
2 I / for / interesting pieces of clothing / scour / second-hand shops .......................................
3 was nominated / for / Ingrid / an Academy Award as best actress .......................................
4 this product / I / for / don't recommend / long hair .......................................
5 my doctor / wants / for / me / diabetes / to be tested .......................................
6 for / this is / what / not / was intended / the grant .......................................

105

# Verbs used with *from*: 1

**1** Some verbs are followed by a prepositional phrase which consists of *from* and a noun group. For example, in *We will all benefit from this change*, the verb *benefit* is followed by the preposition *from* and the noun group *this change*. This pattern is **V** *from* **n**. With some verbs, the preposition is sometimes followed by an '-ing' clause.

|  | Verb group | *from* | noun group/-ing clause |
|---|---|---|---|
| They | could not escape | from | the country. |
| Fitness | comes | from | working against gravity. |
| She | could borrow | from | her family. |

Verbs with this pattern belong to the following meaning groups:

- **verbs indicating that someone or something leaves or comes from a place, thing, or person**

| | | | | |
|---|---|---|---|---|
| back away | emerge | issue | run away | vanish |
| break away | escape | return | separate | withdraw |
| depart | fall | rise | split off | |
| drain | get away | rise up | transfer | |

*The last bus **will depart** from the stadium at 9.30pm.*

*She's going to destroy me. I **have to get away** from her.*

- **verbs used when indicating the cause, source, or origin of something**

| | | | | |
|---|---|---|---|---|
| arise | derive | flow | result | stem |
| come | develop | follow | spring | |

*Heavy drinking often **results** from feeling stressed or overworked.*

*They will enjoy the sense of security which **stems** from knowing how to deal with emergencies when they occur.*

In the case of *arise*, *come*, and *result*, the preposition *from* is sometimes followed by a noun group and an '-ing' clause.

*Conflict **results** from A trying to grab something belonging to B.*

- **verbs indicating that someone gets something from a source.** The thing that is obtained is not explicitly mentioned.

| | | |
|---|---|---|
| borrow | import | quote |

*That's why it's so expensive to **borrow** from finance companies.*

- **verbs indicating that someone gets a benefit of some kind from something**

| | | |
|---|---|---|
| benefit | gain | learn |

*Many areas of the world **would** actually **gain** from global warming.*

*I'm sure our players **would benefit** from having fewer matches.*

- **verbs concerned with not doing something, stopping doing something, or not wanting to do something**

| | | |
|---|---|---|
| keep | retire | shy away |
| refrain | shrink | withdraw |

*But he stressed he had no intention of **retiring** from politics yet.*

*He never **shrank** from a fight, and he actively sought new challenges.*

*We **refrain** from giving advice unless it is asked for.*

With *keep*, the preposition *from* is always followed by an '-ing' clause.

*She bit her lip to **keep** from crying out.*

- **verbs concerned with having something such as an illness or a shock**

| | | |
|---|---|---|
| die | recover | suffer |

*He **is suffering** from cancer.*

- **verbs concerned with being or becoming different**

| | | |
|---|---|---|
| differ | evolve | stand out |

*The culture of the south **differs** from that of the north in many ways.*

## Different forms of the pattern

*They are sure that the illness **from which** they **are suffering** is a purely physical illness.*

**Practice**

**A** Match up the two halves of each sentence.

1  It is good to be able to learn ...
2  The hydrogen, being light, will escape ...
3  Most of these settlements developed ...
4  In 1975, John Lennon withdrew ...
5  They can't borrow ...
6  Each year 35,000 British smokers die ...
7  Whales evolved ...
8  I saw Andrew emerge ...

a  ... from heart disease.
b  ... from the doorway.
c  ... from his career altogether.
d  ... from banks any more.
e  ... from agricultural centres.
f  ... from a crisis.
g  ... from the atmosphere.
h  ... from four-legged mammals.

**B** Fill in the gaps in the sentences below using the verbs in this list. Use each verb once.

benefit   come   flow   import   keep   recover   refrain   retire   stand out   vanish

1  She is going to have to work hard to ................................... from the crowd.
2  All grief and despair ................................... from her face as quickly as a summer rain.
3  She may never fully ................................... from her horrific burn injuries.
4  We ................................... from a major manufacturer in America, the home of the mountain bike.
5  Ten years from now I expect I will ................................... from politics.
6  She fell against his shoulder and held on to him to ................................... from falling.
7  Mrs Hardie ................................... from making any comment.
8  Most applications ................................... from people seeking money to cover their rent or mortgages.
9  Large revenue gains ................................... from relatively modest increases in taxes.
10  It was announced that Kenya will ................................... from a sixty million dollar grant from Washington.

**C** Rewrite each of the following pairs of sentences as one sentence, using a relative clause as shown.

1  There was a huge crack in the floor. Puffs of steam issued from it.
   *There was a huge crack in the floor, from which puffs of steam issued.*
2  Our hero sustained wounds in battle. He later died from them.
   ...................................................................................................
3  They are in the grip of a dreadful power. They cannot escape from it.
   ...................................................................................................
4  Richard has recently had a bad bout of flu. He needs to recover from it.
   ...................................................................................................
5  Education is an investment. Everyone benefits from it.
   ...................................................................................................
6  She has been staying with her husband. She separated from him five months ago.
   ...................................................................................................

# Verbs used with *from*: 2

**1** Here are some more common verbs which are followed by the preposition *from* and a noun group:

| choose | date | deviate | hear | take over |
|---|---|---|---|---|

You **will** also **be able to choose** from a range of topics such as Business Language, Language in the Media, and Grammar.

The building **dates** from the middle of the last century.

Lady Thatcher **will take over** from the university's first chancellor, Lord Hailsham.

Hear is sometimes used in the passive.

They **have not been heard** from since.

Choose often has the following form of the pattern.

There are **plenty of designs** to **choose** from.

**2** Some verbs are followed by a prepositional phrase beginning with *from* and another prepositional phrase beginning with *to*. This pattern is **V *from* n *to* n**.

Verbs with this pattern belong to the following meaning groups:

■ verbs indicating that someone stops doing or using one thing and starts doing or using another

| change | change over | move | switch | turn |
|---|---|---|---|---|

I find it easy to **switch** from one role to the other.

Health is another reason for **turning** from tap water to mineral water.

■ verbs indicating that someone or something becomes different

| change | turn |
|---|---|

Her attitude to the town **had changed** from resentment to a feeling of belonging and involvement.

With both these verbs, the second preposition is sometimes *into* instead of *to*.

I watched little Molly **turn** from a baby into a child.

■ verbs used when indicating a range

| range | vary |
|---|---|

Hundreds of them were given expert advice on problems **ranging** from debt to credit card management.

The cost **varies** from £25 to £85 per session.

■ Last and pass also have this pattern.

It has appeared very difficult for such diseases to **pass** from one species to another.

We are now in the peak hay fever season, which **lasts** from May to July.

**3** Some verbs are followed by a prepositional phrase which consists of *from* and a noun group referring to an amount, and another prepositional phrase which consists of *to* and a noun group referring to an amount. This pattern is **V *from* amount *to* amount**.

Verbs with this pattern indicate that a quantity or level increases or decreases.

| climb | drop | jump | shrink | soar |
|---|---|---|---|---|
| come down | fall | plummet | sink | tumble |
| decline | go down | plunge | slide | widen |
| dip | go up | rise | slip | |
| dive | increase | shoot up | slump | |

Inflation **has increased** from 8.9 per cent to 9 per cent.

My wages **will come down** from just under £270 a week to about £210.

**A** Match up the two halves of each sentence.

1 Guests may choose ...
2 Most ancient fossils date ...
3 It is forbidden to deviate ...
4 I would like to hear ...
5 Civilian leaders took over ...

a ... from about six-hundred-and-fifty-million years ago.
b ... from the military a dozen years ago.
c ... from these rules.
d ... from ten hot dishes and twenty cold dishes.
e ... from boys and girls aged 14-16.

**B** In the sentences below, put a dotted line under the verb used with *from* and *to*. Then underline each of the other parts of the pattern.

1 OPEC has seen its share of the the world oil market drop from two thirds to one third.
2 What were the most difficult things about changing over from the one school to the other?
3 Now the labs are attempting to turn from weapons of mass destruction to more peaceful industries.
4 The Multi-Cultural Programmes Department makes a wide range of programmes varying from topical current affairs to popular entertainment.
5 The 93-day event will last from August 7 to November 7.

**C** Think of a way to complete each sentence.

1 What is required is a job structure in which people can move from part-time to ...............................
2 The exhibited artists range from established names to ......................................................
3 The beach barbecues last from dusk to ....................................................................
4 Our experience of life can change from something approaching hell to ..........................................
5 In the past two weeks, the British have switched from red meat to ..........................................

**D** Complete these sentences using the verb and figures given in brackets and the pattern **V** *from amount to amount*.

1 Despite improved sales, Densitron International's pre-tax profits
   *slipped from £550,000 to £376,000* ....................................... (slip / £376,000 / £550,000)
2 Next year, Elland Road Stadium's capacity will temporarily
   ........................................................................ (fall / 30,000 / 32,728)
3 With imports continuing to rise, the trade deficit has
   ........................................................................ (widen / $5 billion / $9.3 billion)
4 For the past 25 years, the business has seen its workforce
   ........................................................................ (shrink / nine / 16 people)
5 Truck production is likely to
   ........................................................................ (decline / 260,000 / 276,000)
6 Weekly production of Range Rovers
   ........................................................................ (go up / 350 / 370)
7 Pre-tax profits are expected to
   ........................................................................ (climb / £98 million / £105 million)
8 Unemployment has
   ........................................................................ (soar / over 300,000 / near zero)

# Verbs used with *from*: 3

Some verbs are followed by a noun group and a prepositional phrase which consists of *from* and a noun group. For example, in *I borrowed the money from my father*, the verb *borrow* is followed by the noun group *the money*, the preposition *from*, and the noun group *my father*. This pattern is **V n *from* n**. With some verbs, the preposition is sometimes followed by an '-ing' clause.

## Active pattern

|  | Verb group | noun group | *from* | noun group/-ing clause |
|---|---|---|---|---|
| He | borrowed | money | from | friends. |
| He | saved | her | from | having a breakdown. |

## Passive pattern

|  | Verb group | *from* | noun group/-ing clause |
|---|---|---|---|
| Egypt | has been eliminated | from | the World Cup. |
| They | were spared | from | watching England lose. |

(With phrasal verbs, the particle comes either after the noun group or after the verb.)

Verbs with this pattern belong to the following meaning groups:

■ **verbs indicating that someone gets something from someone or somewhere, or tries to get it**

| | | | | |
|---|---|---|---|---|
| acquire | collect | draw | inherit | seek |
| borrow | demand | gain | learn | select |
| choose | derive | get | obtain | steal |

*Often they just **cannot get** money from anyone.*

*He says he **has been demanding** more support from the other agencies.*

*A number of documents **were stolen** from the building.* (passive)

In the case of *learn*, the noun group following the verb is often an **amount**.

*I **learned** a lot from him.*

■ **verbs concerned with removing someone or something from somewhere**

| | | | | |
|---|---|---|---|---|
| chase | divert | pull | take | wipe |
| clear | drain | remove | take away | withdraw |
| dismiss | eliminate | strip | tear away | |

*He's in a stable condition after having surgery to **remove a blood clot** from the brain.*

*He **wiped** the sweat from his forehead.*

*She **couldn't tear herself away** from the radio.*

*She **had been dismissed** from her job at the university a year earlier.* (passive)

■ **verbs concerned with not including someone or something**

| | |
|---|---|
| exclude | omit |

*Their names **had been omitted** from the voting lists.* (passive)

■ **verbs concerned with separating someone or something from something, physically or metaphorically**

| | | | |
|---|---|---|---|
| distinguish | isolate | mark out | set apart |
| divide | mark off | separate | |

*Unfortunately, he appears unable to **distinguish** fantasy from reality.*

***Should** the offender **be separated** from her children and sent to prison?* (passive)

■ **verbs indicating that someone frees or rescues someone from a dangerous or unpleasant situation**

| | | |
|---|---|---|
| deliver | release | save |
| free | rescue | spare |

*The band are currently trying to **free** themselves from their contract with their record company.*

*Fire-fighting ships are still trying to **save a Norwegian supertanker** from sinking off the coast of Texas.*

*Three other people **were rescued** from the sea by defence force officers.* (passive)

**A** In the sentences below, put a dotted line under the verb used with *from* (see this Unit and Unit 53). Then underline each of the other parts of the pattern. (For different forms of the pattern, see Unit 56.)

1  The Netherlands differs from other EC states in that there are many English speaking companies.
2  Who did you learn your chess from?
3  Mark has separated from Annette, so he and I will be sharing a place in Studio City.
4  I must watch carefully, and learn from my father's example.
5  The shock was so profound that it seemed to drain all strength from her.
6  You have to choose your basic design from a few previously drawn by the computer.
7  Think about the word RELAX and let the tension drain from your stomach.
8  With the commander's help we separated the police from the journalists.
9  Apart from her professor's salary, she had money that she had inherited from her father.
10  Fired by this motivation, we are likely to eliminate from our behaviour all that is socially unacceptable.

**B** Fill in the gaps in the sentences below using the verbs in this list. Use each verb once.

borrow   collect   divide   exclude   get   pull   save   take away

1  Many people cease to have migraine attacks if they ................................. certain foodstuffs from their diets.
2  Ian, from Manchester, was ................................. unconscious from the water and is now recovering.
3  You can now ................................. your boarding pass from the domestic Executive Club Lounge.
4  They worked side by side to help ................................. dolphins from being killed by tuna fishermen.
5  President Juarez ................................. the Church from the government to reduce its power.
6  The family raised half the price itself and ................................. the rest from the bank.
7  In a bid to beat the terrorists, litter bins have been ................................. from airport terminals.
8  He said that he'd ................................. my name from a newspaper article.

**C** Rewrite the following sentences using the verb given in brackets with the pattern **V n *from* n** or its passive.

1  Dr. Brandon began to take the fossils out of the trunk. (remove)
   *Dr. Brandon began to remove the fossils from the trunk.* ...........................................................
2  They need to think of ways in which they can keep the good guys and the bad guys apart. (separate)
   ...........................................................................................................................................
3  He was let out of prison this afternoon after £19,000 bail was paid over. (free)
   ...........................................................................................................................................
4  He was charged with using his influence to take out loans with two government-owned banks. (acquire)
   ...........................................................................................................................................
5  He got the recorder out of his shirt and adjusted it. (take)
   ...........................................................................................................................................

# UNIT 56 Verbs used with *from*: 4

**1** Here are some more groups of verbs which are followed by a noun group and a prepositional phrase beginning with *from*:

■ **verbs concerned with stopping someone from doing something**

| | | | |
|---|---|---|---|
| ban | discourage | prevent | restrict |
| bar | keep | prohibit | stop |

The preposition *from* is usually followed by an '-ing' clause rather than a noun group.

*The doctors tried to **stop me from going in** but I ignored them.*

*He **was banned from driving** for three years.* (passive)

■ **verbs indicating that someone hides or keeps something, usually information, from someone**

| | | |
|---|---|---|
| conceal | hide | keep |

*She quickly realized that it was virtually impossible to **conceal** her family background **from** her fellow students.*

■ **verbs indicating that someone makes something from a particular material or thing**

| | | | |
|---|---|---|---|
| carve | create | make | produce |
| construct | fashion | manufacture | |

*Father explained how to **make glass from sand**.*

■ *Protect* also has this pattern.

*You **can protect yourself from attack** by using an insect repellent.*

## Different forms of the pattern

*Where **did** you **get** that idea **from**?*

*He knew that he could not pay back **the money** he **had stolen from** his companies.*

*Their idea is to **exclude from** the election any group that breaks the ceasefire.*

**2** Some verbs are followed by a noun group and two prepositional phrases, the first beginning with *from* and the second beginning with *to*. This pattern is **V n *from* n *to* n**.

Verbs with this pattern belong to the following meaning groups:

■ **verbs concerned with moving someone or something from one place or level to another**

| | | | | |
|---|---|---|---|---|
| divert | pass | promote | send | transfer |

*A colleague tried to **send** a parcel **from Cardiff to London**.*

*He **was promoted from eighth to third place**.* (passive)

With these verbs, the second preposition is sometimes *into*.

*We can even arrange for your bank to **transfer** funds **from your account into the trust account** each month.*

■ **verbs indicating that someone increases or lowers an amount**

| | | | |
|---|---|---|---|
| increase | lower | raise | reduce |

*The bank **lowered** its discount rate **from 3.75 per cent to 3.25 per cent**.*

*The pensionable age for men and women **was raised from 60 to 65**.* (passive)

■ **verbs concerned with changing something from one thing to another**

| | | | |
|---|---|---|---|
| change | transform | translate | turn |

*She **changed** her name **from Blanca to Bianca**.*

With these verbs, the second preposition is sometimes *into*.

*They are attempting to **transform** their country **from a totalitarian state into a democracy**.*

With *translate*, the second preposition is always *into*.

*His grandfather **translated** science books **from German into English**.*

**A** Rewrite these sentences, starting with the words provided. Use the verb given in brackets with *from* and an '-ing' clause.

1 Large crowds surrounded polling booths and people were unable to vote. (prevent)
Large crowds *surrounded polling booths and prevented people from voting.*

2 People are not allowed to ask for money on the city streets at night. (prohibit)
People ...............................................................................................................................................

3 Because of his good manners, he did not tell her what he really thought. (kept)
His good manners ...........................................................................................................................

4 Some couples don't marry because of the tax and social security laws. (discourage)
The tax and social security laws ...................................................................................................

5 Renaissance artists were highly original, despite the conservative environment. (stop)
The conservative environment .......................................................................................................

6 Shell Australia will not allow its customers to use mobile phones at its service stations. (ban)
Shell Australia's customers ............................................................................................................

**B** Rewrite these sentences, starting with the words provided. Use the pattern **V n *from* n *to* n**.

1 Nuclear Electric's workforce will fall from 12,394 to just 9,000 over the next three years. (reduce)
Nuclear Electric *will reduce its workforce from 12,394 to just 9,000 over the next three years.*

2 Under the administration plan, the grant would go up from $2,400 to $3,700. (raise)
The administration plan ..................................................................................................................

3 The Conservative majority rose from one to thirty-five. (increase)
The Conservatives ...........................................................................................................................

4 The price has gone down from $115 to $90. (lower)
Wine merchants ...............................................................................................................................

**C** Put the different parts of these sentences in the right order.

1 Joey / tried / to hide / she / from / her despondency .................................................................

2 their children / are supposed / harm / from / parents / to protect
..............................................................................................................................................................

3 plants / from / are able to manufacture / water / their own food
..............................................................................................................................................................

4 from / delegates / entering the hall / were barred .....................................................................

5 sheep's teeth / necklaces / Stone Age settlers / fashioned / from
..............................................................................................................................................................

6 will pass / to / twenty-six small satellites / simple digital messages / from / place / place
..............................................................................................................................................................

7 the president / the highest tax rate / 31 per cent / 28 per cent / is prepared / to increase / from / to
..............................................................................................................................................................

8 French / Rachid Boudjedra / translated / Arabic / into / from / his novels
..............................................................................................................................................................

# Verbs used with *in*: 1

Some verbs are followed by a prepositional phrase which consists of *in* and a noun group. For example, in *They believe in democracy*, the verb *believe* is followed by the preposition *in* and the noun group *democracy*. This pattern is **V** *in* **n**. With some verbs, the preposition is sometimes followed by an '-ing' clause.

|  | Verb group | *in* | noun group/-ing clause |
|---|---|---|---|
| She | lectures | in | economics. |
| Drugs | can help | in | lowering the level of cholesterol. |

Verbs with this pattern belong to the following meaning groups:

■ **verbs concerned with being in or entering a thing, group, or situation**

| appear | go | lie | rank | sit |
|---|---|---|---|---|
| belong | land | move | ride | |

*Over the past few years, he **has sat** in Parliament as an independent Social Democrat.*

*Fifty-year-olds **don't** really **belong** in the same category as their mothers of 70.*

*World champion Lance Armstrong **is** currently **lying** in third place.*

■ **verbs indicating that someone has a feeling or thought.** The feeling or thought is the Subject.

| live | live on | rise | stick | stir |
|---|---|---|---|---|

*Panic started to **rise** in my throat.*

*It is something that **will live** in my memory for the rest of my life.*

■ **verbs concerned with being involved in something or taking part in an activity**

| act | compete | help | join | star |
|---|---|---|---|---|
| aid | engage | interfere | participate | |
| appear | feature | intervene | share | |
| assist | figure | invest | stand | |

*The job gave her a chance to **participate** in sales and product development.*

*The sales staff **can assist** in making selections.*

*He has not yet announced whether he **will stand** in the election.*

*You do not have the right to **interfere** in our internal affairs.*

■ **verbs indicating that someone is successful or unsuccessful**

| fail | succeed |
|---|---|

*Local residents **had failed** in an attempt to have the march banned.*

In the case of *succeed*, the preposition *in* is often followed by an '-ing' clause.

*I finally **succeeded** in getting him out of the room.*

■ **verbs concerned with learning or teaching a subject**

| graduate | lecture | major | qualify | train |
|---|---|---|---|---|

*He now **lectures** in crime prevention at various London colleges.*

*He went to a junior college and **majored** in computer programming.*

■ **verbs concerned with trading or work**

| deal | specialize | trade |
|---|---|---|

*He **specializes** in treating epileptics and schizophrenics.*

*He **deals** in antiques and fine art.*

# Practice

**A** In the sentences below, put a dotted line under the verb used with *in*. Then underline each of the other parts of the pattern. (For different forms of the pattern, see Unit 58.)

1 Brought up in the Midlands, she graduated in English and Drama from Manchester University.

2 The negotiators say environmental protection does not belong in a trade agreement.

3 In my feverish state, one image stuck in my mind.

4 Sainsbury's, Tesco and Safeway have between them £1.4 billion of equity capital to assist in their development programmes.

5 He had been warned in writing not to deal in shares between January and March.

6 Okay, so you know what you want out of a fund and what type of fund you want to invest in.

7 The author suggests that this is the area in which future development lies.

**B** Fill in the gaps in these sentences using *in* or *with* (see Unit 83). Sometimes both are possible.

1 Kendall called me into his office to put together a plan to deal ........................ the crisis.

2 He had interfered ........................ the country's internal affairs by criticizing the conduct of local elections.

3 Johnson will be unable to compete ........................ the world junior championships next year because of her age.

4 She hired two consultants to help ........................ the search for a new school superintendent.

5 California and Florida were the only states to rank ........................ the top ten in all three categories.

6 I had ideas and information that belonged ........................ police hands.

**C** Rewrite the sentences below using the verbs in this list. Use each verb once. Use *in* with a noun group or an '-ing' clause.

aid    figure    lecture    star    stick    succeed    trade

1 Piloo was a professor of English Literature at the universities of Bombay and Delhi.
*Piloo lectured in English Literature at the universities of Bombay and Delhi.*

2 Fred Astaire and Jack Buchanan take the lead roles in this tale of a song-and-dance man.
........................................................................................

3 He buys and sells vintage posters, brochures, and other memorabilia.
........................................................................................

4 He did not manage to publish his book.
........................................................................................

5 Yoga can be helpful in the prevention, cure and management of many diseases.
........................................................................................

6 Their plans don't include marriage.
Marriage ........................................................................................

7 I have remembered that incident all these years, and now I know why.
That incident ........................................................................................

# Verbs used with *in*: 2

Here are some more groups of verbs which are followed by the preposition *in* and a noun group or an '-ing' clause:

■ **verbs concerned with enjoying something or feeling good about something**

| bask | delight | exult | rejoice | revel |

*Soviet journalists **revelled** in their new freedom to probe and to criticize.*

*He **delights** in stirring up controversy and strife.*

■ **verbs concerned with belief**

| believe | trust |

*I **don't believe** in coincidences.*

■ **verbs indicating what something abstract consists of or involves**

| consist | lie |

*Most people think that happiness **consists** in experiencing pleasure.*

*As with so many other aspects of a relationship, the solution **lies** in communication.*

■ **verbs indicating that something or someone suddenly starts to be in a different state**

| break out | come out | go up |

The range of noun groups used after *in* is quite restricted. *Break out* and *come out* are followed by phrases such as *in spots* and *in a sweat*; *go up* is followed by *in flames* and *in smoke*.

*They either **come out** in spots, grow too much hair where they don't want it or go bald!*

*The whole place **went up** in flames.*

■ **verbs concerned with beginning and ending. The** prepositional phrase indicates the situation or event at the beginning or end of something.

| begin | culminate | end |

*His tenure of office **began** in confusion when his predecessor refused to go.*

*Andrew's first marriage **ended** in disaster.*

In the case of *culminate* and *end*, the preposition *in* is sometimes followed by a noun group and an '-ing' clause.

*They had an argument, which **culminated** in Tom getting drunk and beating her in front of all the customers.*

■ **verbs indicating that something increases, decreases, or is different in some way**

| change | decrease | drop | go down | rise |
| come down | differ | fall | go up | shrink |
| decline | double | gain | increase | vary |

*Gasoline, for instance, **has gone up** in price in the last week.*

*This frees manufacturers from relying on natural supplies, which **can vary** in quality.*

■ **other common verbs**

| come | dress | persist |
| confide | dress up | result |

*The badges **come** in 20 different colours and shapes.*

*I wish she **would confide** in me.*

*She always **dresses** in black.*

*It was too beautiful a day to **persist** in such efforts.*

*The operation **resulted** in the arrest of one alleged kidnapper and the death of another from gunshot wounds.*

In the case of *persist*, the preposition *in* is sometimes followed by an '-ing' clause.

*Even though he's happy with her weight, she **persists** in dieting.*

In the case of *result*, the preposition *in* is sometimes followed by a noun group and an '-ing' clause.

*These circumstances **may result** in a child being taken away from its family for good.*

## Different forms of the pattern

*What events **did** you **specialize** in?*

*People should be prepared to stand up for **the things** they **believe** in.*

**A** Fill in the gaps in the sentences below using the verbs in this list. Use each verb once.

believe   consist   double   dress up   end   go up   rejoice   result

1 Thieves watched thousands of pounds ................................. in smoke after accidentally setting fire to the contents of a shop safe.
2 An international conference on global warming has ................................. in controversy.
3 Dr. Spock cautioned that a lack of vitamins could ................................. in reduced body size.
4 Do you ................................. in love at first sight?
5 The next task ................................. in listing the questions to be answered.
6 High-street store The Gap intends to ................................. in size over the next four years.
7 She asked a group of students to ................................. in different costumes and wigs so that they all looked different from each other.
8 I ................................. in the simple pleasures that are available all the time.

**B** Fill in the gaps in these sentences using *in* or *from* (see Unit 54).

1 The Chinese yuan has fallen ....................... value by 25 per cent this month.
2 Detached houses, however, went up ....................... price by a multiple of 14.9.
3 The number of horses in his care has risen ....................... eight to 20.
4 The US dollar has gone down ....................... value recently and that makes US goods more attractive to foreigners.
5 Wage inflation fell ....................... 15 to less than four per cent, but unemployment still rose.
6 A course of treatment varies ....................... length as it depends on your body's needs.
7 The temperature had dropped ....................... 20 degrees to four, on the coldest May day on record.
8 The response of the audience varied ....................... outright rejection to warm hospitality.

**C** Complete the second of each pair of sentences using the information contained in the first sentence. Use the verb with *in*, a noun group, and an '-ing' clause.

1 He left her.
Rumours of problems culminated in ...*him leaving her.*..........................................................
2 People will have several occupations during their lifetimes.
These changes will eventually result in ......................................................................................
3 She was removed from power.
Her policies led to a growing anger against her, which ended in ................................................
4 He took an overdose of sleeping tablets.
He went through a rebellious phase which culminated in ..........................................................
5 He was sued for libel.
His fearless campaigning for racial justice resulted in .............................................................
6 She was attacked by robbers.
He persuaded her to take the trip to Egypt which ended in .......................................................

# Verbs used with *in*: 3

Some verbs are followed by a noun group and a prepositional phrase which consists of *in* and a noun group. For example, in *He dipped a biscuit in his tea*, the verb *dip* is followed by the noun group *a biscuit*, the preposition *in*, and the noun group *his tea*. This pattern is **V n *in* n**.

## Active pattern

|  | Verb group | noun group | *in* | noun group |
|---|---|---|---|---|
| They | threw | him | in | jail. |
| She | covered | his car | in | paint. |
|  | Include | your partner | in | your activities. |

## Passive pattern

|  | Verb group | *in* | noun group |
|---|---|---|---|
| The machine | will be encased | in | concrete. |
| The biscuits | were packed | in | airtight tins. |

Verbs with this pattern belong to the following meaning groups:

■ **verbs concerned with putting, moving, or keeping something somewhere, either physically or metaphorically**

| | | | | |
|---|---|---|---|---|
| concentrate | immerse | keep | place | stick |
| dip | include | land | put | throw |
| enter | insert | lock | settle | |
| fix | invest | pack | shut | |

*Wash the fish fillets and dry them, then **dip them in the beaten egg**.*

*We **locked** her in the bathroom.*

*Several of them **could be placed** in the category of 'high flyer'. (passive)*

*More than 100 stitches **were inserted** in her head during the surgery. (passive)*

■ **verbs concerned with covering or enclosing something in something**

| | | | | |
|---|---|---|---|---|
| coat | cover | encase | enclose | wrap |

***Wrap the chicken in foil** and bake for 2 hours.*

■ **verbs concerned with someone becoming involved in an activity**

| | | | | |
|---|---|---|---|---|
| be caught up | employ | engage | include | involve |

*He has already started to **involve** himself **in the country's domestic political issues**.*

*I went and **engaged** her **in conversation**.*

The preposition *in* is sometimes followed by an '-ing' clause.

*Riding in the car offers a wonderful opportunity to **engage** your child **in observing the surroundings**.*

■ **verbs indicating that someone takes part in an activity along with someone else**

| | | | |
|---|---|---|---|
| assist | help | join | lead |

*We **assist** students **in their search for employment**.*

*Why **do** you **not join** your friends **in the fight against Fascism**?*

The preposition *in* is sometimes followed by an '-ing' clause.

*The leader strikes a bell three times and **leads** the others **in chanting** something in a foreign language.*

■ **verbs indicating that someone concentrates very hard on something**

| | | |
|---|---|---|
| bury | immerse | lose |

The noun group following the verb is always a reflexive pronoun.

*I **immersed** myself **in the writings** of this remarkable Japanese writer.*

*Imaginative children **lose** themselves **in fantasy worlds** through stories.*

**A** Match up the two halves of each sentence.

1  Eden returned to Cairo to join the others ...
2  Please don't keep us ...
3  They covered the armchairs ...
4  The police should throw them ...
5  He packed papers ...
6  These factories employ disabled people ...
7  He said he included his name ...

a  ... in prison.
b  ... in the bottom of the case and shirts on top.
c  ... in the message so he could be contacted.
d  ... in keeping an eye on the situation.
e  ... in a turquoise-and-white striped material.
f  ... in suspense.
g  ... in productive work.

**B** In the sentences below, put a dotted line under the verb used with *in*. Then underline each of the other parts of the pattern. (For different forms of the pattern, see Unit 60.)

1  One delegate said it was important to involve members in policy making.
2  Since her divorce last year, she has buried herself in charity work.
3  The children will be caught up in the excitement.
4  Tommy began carefully folding up the brown paper in which the painting had been wrapped.
5  Maybe she could just shut him in his room while Robert was visiting.
6  Similar devices had been placed in several hotels in the area.
7  The 50,000 brochures we inserted in Cycling Weekly in February were well received.
8  I assisted Phil in getting control of his own life situation.
9  Some recipes tell you to coat the meat in flour first.
10  I would include in this category organizing social events such as the Christmas party.

**C** Rewrite the sentences using the verb given in brackets with *in* and an '-ing' clause.

1  We must reverse this process if we want the students to learn. (engage)
   *We must reverse this process if we want to engage the students in learning.*

2  I'm concentrating on writing music. (bury)
   ............................................................................................................

3  She admits helping her boss to shred important documents. (assist)
   ............................................................................................................

4  He and Franklin issued radio messages together. (join)
   ............................................................................................................

5  Some 500 people are currently building the dam. (be employed)
   ............................................................................................................

6  Irving Berlin sang 'God Bless America' and the audience sang with him. (lead)
   ............................................................................................................

Here are some more groups of verbs which are followed by a noun group and a prepositional phrase beginning with *in*:

■ **verbs indicating that someone hits or injures someone else.** The prepositional phrase indicates the part of the body that is harmed.

| | | | |
|---|---|---|---|
| bite | kick | shoot | stab |
| hit | punch | smash | strike |

The noun group after *in* usually begins with *the*.

He **was stabbed** in the back. (passive)

The fiery actress punched him on the nose and **kicked** him **in the shins**.

■ **verbs concerned with making a hole in something**

| | | | |
|---|---|---|---|
| bore | drill | gouge | punch |

The researchers **drilled small holes in the pipes** at 1-metre intervals.

■ **verbs concerned with dividing something into pieces**

| | | | |
|---|---|---|---|
| break | cut | slice | split |
| chop | divide | snap | tear |

I **tore the letter in pieces**.

The preposition *in* is sometimes followed by a fraction or number.

**Divide the pastry in half**.

■ **verbs indicating that someone has a particular feeling or attitude with regard to something**

| | | | | |
|---|---|---|---|---|
| find | hold | place | put | take |

*Her parents **will find** comfort in the fact that they have been blessed with a large family.*

*He said he **was placing** his faith in prayer.*

The preposition *in* is sometimes followed by an '-ing' clause.

*How **could** anyone **find** pleasure in hunting and killing this beautiful creature?*

With the verb *hold*, the prepositional phrase indicates the person's attitude.

*Little by little you'll come to hate me and **hold** me in contempt.*

■ **verbs indicating that someone or something causes someone to feel an emotion**

| | |
|---|---|
| arouse | stir |

*He urged people to avoid any action which **could arouse** fear or passion in others.*

■ **other common verbs**

| | | |
|---|---|---|
| interest | be ranked | tie |
| lead | see | train |

*Australia **leads** the world in modern winemaking techniques.*

*Throughout the Seventies she **was ranked** in Britain's top ten. (passive)*

*It **was tied** in a knot. (passive)*

In the case of *interest*, *lead*, *see*, and *train*, the preposition *in* is sometimes followed by an '-ing' clause.

*Some salesmen tried to **interest** me in buying property here.*

*The militants **see** no contradiction in using violence to bring about a religious state.*

The verb *be ranked* is often followed by an ordinal and a prepositional phrase beginning with *in*.

*Gul **is ranked** eighth in the world.*

## Different forms of the pattern

*They could probably get back some of **the money** they'**d invested** in the album.*

*The thought **aroused** in Isaacs a sense of excitement.*

**A** **Fill in the gaps in the sentences below using the verbs in this list. Use each verb once.**

divide   drill   hold   be ranked   see   shoot   stir   take

1 The New Yorkers ................................. delight in explaining the intricacies of their city.

2 Although she ................................. in the top five, she was relatively little known.

3 It is very difficult to ................................. somebody in the arm.

4 Soccer can ................................. great passions in men from all walks of life.

5 The Port Authority wants to ................................. a hole in the roof above this parking garage.

6 She ................................. no point in visiting the school now Martin had settled down.

7 They both ................................. him in great affection and respect.

8 The food is so plentiful you can ................................. a lunch in two and save half for dinner.

**B** **Rewrite these sentences using the pattern V n *in* n.**

1 He took a knife from his car and stabbed her neck.
   *He took a knife from his car and stabbed her in the neck.*

2 So I took my lunch box and tried to hit Rab's face with it.
   ................................................................................

3 Get off my property before I come out there and punch your nose.
   ................................................................................

4 Nicky, the singer, tried to kick his face.
   ................................................................................

5 A consultant yesterday admitted he had struck his fiancee's face with a bunch of flowers.
   ................................................................................

6 Dewey's chest was bitten twice by two rattlesnakes.
   ................................................................................

**C** **Rewrite these sentences using the verb and noun group given in brackets. Sometimes the noun group follows the verb and sometimes it follows *in*.**

1 They talked a lot and enjoyed each other's company. (find / pleasure)
   *They talked a lot and found pleasure in each other's company.*

2 We may despise him, but he might be the only viable president. (hold / contempt)
   ................................................................................

3 From the outset he had trusted me, the son of his old friend. (put / his trust)
   ................................................................................

4 The public tend to have little respect for architects. (hold / low esteem)
   ................................................................................

5 I am comforted by the fact that earnings are up this year. (find / comfort)
   ................................................................................

6 I always enjoy giving photographers my most radiant smile. (take / delight)
   ................................................................................

# Verbs used with *into*: 1

Some verbs are followed by a prepositional phrase which consists of *into* and a noun group. For example, in *He bumped into a chair*, the verb *bump* is followed by the preposition *into* and the noun group *a chair*. This pattern is **V into n**.

|  | Verb group | *into* | noun group |
|---|---|---|---|
| The plane | broke | into | pieces. |
| Mike | sank | into | suicidal depression. |

Verbs with this pattern belong to the following meaning groups:

■ **verbs indicating that something becomes something else**

| change | develop | evolve | grow | turn |
|---|---|---|---|---|
| convert | escalate | form | merge | |

*With her care, he **grew** into a normal, healthy child.*

*Caterpillars **turn** into butterflies.*

■ **verbs indicating that something breaks or divides into pieces or groups**

| break | divide | shatter | split |
|---|---|---|---|
| crumble | separate | smash | |

*The plane hit the ground and **broke** into three pieces.*

■ **verbs indicating that one person or thing collides with another**

| bang | crash | slam |
|---|---|---|
| bump | run | smash |

*The spokesman said both vehicles **crashed** into a burned-out car.*

■ **verbs concerned with someone entering a place**

| book | check | crowd | move | pile |
|---|---|---|---|---|
| break | cram | dive | pack | push |

*We drove back to Lichfield and **booked** into a hotel.*

*Then we all **crowded** into a small restaurant and ordered a meal.*

*I want you to **move** into my apartment.*

*Break* is sometimes used in the passive.

*Our house **was broken** into earlier this year.*

■ **verbs indicating that someone or something disappears or is not noticeable**

| blend | fade away | merge |
|---|---|---|
| fade | melt | vanish |

***Does** the new housing stick out like a sore thumb or **blend into its surroundings**?*

■ **verbs concerned with pressing something or making a hole in something**

| bite | dig | drill | eat | sink |
|---|---|---|---|---|

*He **bit** into the bread and chewed slowly.*

■ **verbs indicating that someone investigates something**

| dig | inquire | look | probe | research |
|---|---|---|---|---|

*The team **has been researching** into the genetic cause of the disease for more than six years.*

*Look* is sometimes used in the passive.

*He said that the matter **was being looked** into.*

■ **verbs indicating that someone becomes involved in something**

| break | get | plunge | tumble | walk |
|---|---|---|---|---|
| enter | go | rush | venture | |

*Always seek professional legal advice before **entering** into any agreement.*

*I'd like to **get** into management.*

■ **verbs indicating that someone or something starts being in a different state or starts doing something**

| break | descend | fly | plunge | slip |
|---|---|---|---|---|
| burst | dissolve | get | retreat | |
| burst out | erupt | lapse | sink | |
| come | fall | launch | slide | |

*She **burst** into tears.*

*Three days later he **slipped** into a coma and died.*

■ **verbs indicating that someone puts on different clothes**

| change | slip |
|---|---|

*I **changed** into my suit.*

■ *Fit* and *tap* also have this pattern.

*It's hard to see how he **would fit** into the team.*

*We'll help you **tap** into your creative energy.*

**A** Here are some pairs of sentences showing a verb used with the pattern **V _into_ n** with two different meanings. Write down what each sentence means, using a verb with a different pattern.

1 a) She changed into her nightgown. _She put on her nightgown._

   b) She changed into a snake. ....................................................................................

2 a) He broke into song. ...........................................................................................

   b) Someone had broken into my house. ........................................................................

3 a) Her fingers dug into his arm. ...............................................................................

   b) I've been digging into Laura's past. ........................................................................

4 a) He slipped into his bathrobe. ...............................................................................

   b) He slipped into a fitful doze. ...............................................................................

5 a) The plate smashed into pieces. .............................................................................

   b) His car smashed into a garden fence at 75 mph. ..........................................................

6 a) How did our schools get into this state? ..................................................................

   b) The Malloy twins got into the business at age 17. ........................................................

**B** Fill in the gaps in the sentences below using the verbs in this list. Use each verb once.

bite   dissolve   fly   get   look   melt   pile   run   turn

1 You don't want to .................................. into trouble again, do you?

2 The nylon rope .................................. into his wrists.

3 The crew .................................. into their vehicle.

4 She .................................. into tears at the mention of Munya's name.

5 'She wants to be able to .................................. into the background,' one royal source said.

6 The two countries are sure that their border clashes will not .................................. into full-scale war.

7 35 people died after a commuter train .................................. into the back of a stationary one at about 56 kilometres per hour.

8 In the meantime, Dorset police are .................................. into allegations of corruption in the Metropolitan Police in London.

9 One night he plucked up the courage to ask her about it and she .................................. into a terrible rage.

**C** Match up the two halves of each sentence.

1 At San Antonio, our destination, we checked ...      a ... into a wider war.
2 The fighting could escalate ...                        b ... into several pieces.
3 Sue wants to research ...                              c ... into the jungles south of Jaffna.
4 The camera separated ...                               d ... into the hotel.
5 Companies are now tapping ...                          e ... into the huge potential for advertising.
6 The guerillas vanished ...                             f ... into his family background.

# Verbs used with *into*: 2

Some verbs are followed by a noun group and a prepositional phrase which consists of *into* and an '-ing' clause. For example, in *He talked me into going with him,* the verb *talk* is followed by the noun group *me,* the preposition *into,* and the clause *going with him.* This pattern is **V n into -ing**. The preposition is sometimes followed by a noun group instead of an '-ing' clause.

## Active pattern

|      | Verb group | noun group | into | -ing clause/noun group |
|------|------------|------------|------|------------------------|
| They | pushed     | her        | into | resigning.             |
| I    | provoked   | him        | into | a fight.               |

## Passive pattern

|      | Verb group             | into | -ing clause/noun group |
|------|------------------------|------|------------------------|
| They | should not be pressed  | into | making hasty decisions. |
| She  | was lured              | into | a trap.                |

Verbs with this pattern belong to the following meaning groups:

- **verbs concerned with making someone do something or get involved in something by using force or pressure**

| blackmail | force      | panic    | rush      |
|-----------|------------|----------|-----------|
| bully     | frighten   | press    | scare     |
| coerce    | intimidate | pressure | shame     |
| drag      | manipulate | provoke  | be sucked |
| embarrass | nag        | push     | terrify   |

*He tried to **frighten** people into doing what he wanted.*

*I **bullied** him into taking two days off and coming with me to Paris.*

*The Communist government **forced** Michael into exile in 1947.*

*The intention was to **shame young drivers into better behaviour on the roads** with the threat of a return to L-plates.*

*The British and the French have been very careful not to **be sucked** into the conflict.* (passive)

*They **will not be panicked** into making premature decisions about their tax policy.* (passive)

- **verbs concerned with making someone do something by tricking or deceiving them**

| con     | fool | lure | trick |
|---------|------|------|-------|
| deceive | lull | trap |       |

*You **trapped** my son into marriage because you wanted a father for your child!*

*They had hidden the money and then **fooled** people into thinking it has been lost for ever.*

*He **may have been tricked** into carrying the explosives onto the plane.* (passive)

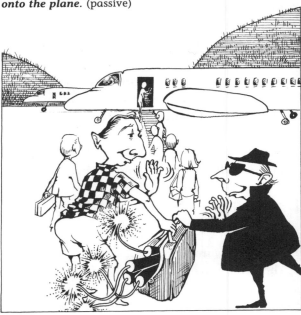

- **verbs concerned with making someone do something by being nice to them in some way or by saying something that pleases them**

| charm | coax | sweet talk |
|-------|------|------------|

*He **has charmed** the local authorities into letting him buy back another family property.*

*Eileen **could be coaxed** into babysitting.* (passive)

- **verbs concerned with persuading someone to do something, or motivating them to do it**

| lure     | spur  | stir | tempt |
|----------|-------|------|-------|
| persuade | steer | talk |       |

*He **talked** me into studying philosophy rather than history.*

*They fear that higher prices for wood **may tempt** builders into using substitute materials.*

*Gerald Smith **was spurred** into action by a dramatic television news broadcast earlier this month.* (passive)

**A** In the sentences below, put a dotted line under the verb used with *into*. Then underline each of the other parts of the pattern.

1 He remained motionless, fearful that any sudden movement might provoke Graham into pulling the trigger.

2 What they did not realise was that they were being lured into a trap.

3 You're not going to trick me into saying things I don't want to.

4 He was so shaken by the heavy lorries roaring past his home he was stirred into action to stop them.

5 For a start, people want to be lulled into a sense of security, false or not.

6 They scramble aboard with knives between their teeth and terrify the crew into surrender.

**B** These sentences show *make* used with the pattern **V n inf**. Rewrite them using the verb given in brackets with the pattern **V n *into* -ing**.

1 Janet made Ian move house. (nag)
*Janet nagged Ian into moving house.*

2 Parents should not make kids take sides. (force)

3 I've just got to make my dad let me have a season ticket now. (persuade)

4 He made my parents get him a watch when he was seven. (pressure)

5 The government was trying to make him testify against my father. (coerce)

6 We made him tell us everything he knew about the robbery. (pressure)

7 He sees it as a way to make children take up the guitar. (tempt)

8 They found out about the magistrate's own wrongdoings and made him step down. (blackmail)

**C** These sentences say what someone did or does. Using the passive form of the verb given in brackets, write a sentence saying why they did it or do it.

1 He had changed his mind. (frighten)
*He had been frightened into changing his mind.*

2 He renounced his throne after Franco chose Juan Carlos to be his successor. (talk)

3 The Government has been trying to do something about the problem. (embarrass)

4 Chinese tourists have been staying home. (scare)

5 So how did you get involved? (con)

6 Don't buy stuff just for the sake of it. (rush)

# Verbs used with *into*: 3

Some verbs are followed by a noun group and a prepositional phrase which consists of *into* and a noun group. For example, in *He rolled his socks into a ball*, the verb *roll* is followed by the noun group *his socks*, the preposition *into*, and the noun group *a ball*. This pattern is **V n *into* n**. (With phrasal verbs, the particle comes either after the noun group or after the verb.)

## Active pattern

|  | Verb group | noun group | *into* | noun group |
|---|---|---|---|---|
| His first album | Shape sent | the dough critics | into into | an oblong. fits of rapture. |

## Passive pattern

|  | Verb group | *into* | noun group |
|---|---|---|---|
| Intent Toxins | has to be translated are absorbed | into into | action. the blood. |

Verbs with this pattern belong to the following meaning groups:

■ **verbs concerned with changing something into something new, or changing its form or shape**

| | | | |
|---|---|---|---|
| change | make | shape | turn |
| convert | process | transform | weave |
| form | roll | translate | |

*Music has the power to **change** one mood into another.*

*Some of my books **have been made** into movies.* (passive)

■ **verbs concerned with breaking or dividing something into smaller pieces or groups**

| | | | | |
|---|---|---|---|---|
| break | chop | divide up | slice | split |
| break down | chop up | resolve | slice up | split up |
| break up | cut | rip | smash | tear |
| carve | cut up | separate | smash up | |
| carve up | divide | shatter | sort | |

*The impact **broke** the truck into three pieces.*

*Then I take the sausages out and **cut** them **up** into pieces.*

*The basic causes of disease **can be divided** into three groups.* (passive)

■ **verbs concerned with putting something or someone into something, either physically or metaphorically**

| | | | | |
|---|---|---|---|---|
| be absorbed | feed | lock | pump | throw |
| book | inject | pack | put | |
| dip | insert | pay | sink | |
| draw | introduce | plunge | stick | |
| enter | load | pour | stir | |

*He **had booked** both of us into the local hotel.*

*Graham handed her the card and she **fed the name into a computer**.*

*The money **was paid** into a special account.* (passive)

■ **verbs concerned with incorporating or absorbing someone or something into a system or organization**

| | | | | |
|---|---|---|---|---|
| absorb | accept | build | incorporate | integrate |

*The decision to **incorporate the students into the army** as a punishment was very much criticised by the independent press.*

*One needs to learn how to **build** enjoyment into what happens day in, day out.*

■ **verbs concerned with causing someone or something to be in a particular state or situation**

| | | | | |
|---|---|---|---|---|
| draw | fling | plunge | talk | work up |
| drive | get | send | throw | |

*The rebels dynamited power lines, **plunging** much of the city into darkness.*

*More complicated events, such as speaking or attending a business meeting, **sent me into a panic**.*

In the case of *fling*, *throw*, and *work up*, the noun group following the verb is always a reflexive pronoun.

*She **flung** herself into anti-racist work.*

*She **worked** herself **up** into a bit of a state.*

■ **verbs concerned with causing something or someone to have a quality or feeling**

| | | |
|---|---|---|
| breathe | inject | strike |

*The massive blast **struck** terror into thousands of innocent office workers and tourists.*

*Grace did her best to **inject** a note of welcome into her voice.*

## Different forms of the pattern

*This created the mould **into which** the molten iron **was poured**.*

*We **must incorporate** into the budgets this possible increase in sales.*

**A** These sentences say what someone or something becomes or is used to make. Rewrite them using the passive form of the verb given in brackets.

1 The remaining part of the building became a chapel. (turn)
   *The remaining part of the building was turned into a chapel.*

2 That area has become a public parking lot. (convert)
   ....................................................................................................

3 Everything is capable of becoming something else. (transform)
   ....................................................................................................

4 A minus can become a plus. (change)
   ....................................................................................................

5 Our country's become a battlefield. (turn)
   ....................................................................................................

6 Its fibres can be used to make rope, fabrics and fine paper. (weave)
   ....................................................................................................

7 Plums and cherries are used to make liqueurs. (make)
   ....................................................................................................

8 There may be potential for the material to be used to make compost. (process)
   ....................................................................................................

**B** Fill in the gaps in the sentences below using the verbs in this list. Use each verb once.

feed   inject   insert   load   pump   stick   stir   throw

1 He threatened to ................................. poison into her veins.
2 He ................................. the bayonets into the ground.
3 ................................. the sugar into the orange juice until it dissolves.
4 Several bags were ................................. into the car.
5 If he took that course he would simply be ................................. into prison.
6 First she ................................. the tape into the player and adjusted a couple of dials.
7 He vowed to ................................. billions of pounds into the health service, education, housing and pensions.
8 This network provides the raw information that the forecasters ................................. into the computers that try to predict the weather.

**C** Match up the two halves of each sentence.

1 This would plunge the country ...          a ... into fits of laughter.
2 My attempt to account for this sent Lawrence ...   b ... into chaos.
3 The recession and hospital bills drove them ...    c ... into defeat.
4 His bluntness got him ...                    d ... into bankruptcy.
6 The Prime Minister talked himself ...        e ... into an ambush.
7 They drew the police ...                     f ... into a fury.
8 He worked himself up ...                     g ... into trouble.

127

# Verbs used with *like, as if,* or *as though*

**1** Some verbs are followed by a prepositional phrase which consists of *like* and a noun group. For example, in *He looked like a policeman*, the verb *look* is followed by the preposition *like* and the noun group *a policeman*. This pattern is **V *like* n**.

|  | Verb group | *like* | noun group |
|---|---|---|---|
| Music | is | like | a living thing. |
| This place | feels | like | a prison. |
| He | didn't act | like | a 13-year-old. |

Verbs with this pattern belong to the following meaning groups:

■ **verbs used to indicate how someone or something seems**

| be | look | smell | taste |
|---|---|---|---|
| feel | seem | sound | |

With all these verbs except *be* and *seem*, you may be saying that one person or thing resembles another, as in *She looks like her mother*, or you may be indicating what you think someone or something is, as in *They look like a good team*.

*He **was** like any other kid any of us knew.*

*From a distance, this **looked** like fields of snow.*

*That **sounds** like a good idea.*

*It **feels** like home already.*

*Feel* sometimes indicates how someone seems to themselves.

*I **feel** like a new person.*

In the case of *be* and *look*, the preposition *like* is sometimes followed by an '-ing' clause. With *look*, the '-ing' clause indicates what someone or something seems likely to do or experience.

*It **was** like being in a dream.*

*He **looks** like being made president for another year.*

■ **verbs concerned with behaviour.** The prepositional phrase indicates whose behaviour it resembles.

| act | behave | dress | live | think |
|---|---|---|---|---|

*If Sid wanted to **behave** like a lunatic, that was his choice.*

*We **lived** like fugitives.*

**Productive use:** Any verb which indicates action or behaviour can be used with this pattern.

■ *Go* also has this pattern. The preposition *like* is always followed by *this*.

*The story **goes** like this.*

■ *Feel* also has this pattern when used to indicate what someone would like to have or do.

*I **feel** like a cup of tea.*

*I **don't** really **feel** like doing any work.*

**2** Some verbs are followed by a finite clause beginning with *as if* or *as though*. For example, in *I felt as if I'd been hit*, the verb *feel* is followed by the clause *as if I'd been hit*. This pattern is **V *as if*/*as though***. In informal English, the clause sometimes begins with *like*, although some people think this is incorrect.

|  | Verb group | *as if*/*as though*-clause |
|---|---|---|
| He | sounds | as though he's enjoying it. |
| He | acted | as if he was expecting me. |

Verbs with this pattern belong to the following meaning groups:

■ **verbs used to indicate how someone or something seems**

| appear | look | smell | taste |
|---|---|---|---|
| feel | seem | sound | |

*Isabel's voice **sounded** as if she had been crying.*

*You **look** like you need a rest.*

*Feel* usually indicates how someone seems to themselves.

*He **felt** as though he had run five miles.*

■ **verbs concerned with behaving or speaking**

| act | behave | speak | talk |
|---|---|---|---|

*Act as if nothing had happened.*

*He **talks** as if he rules the universe.*

**Productive use:** Any verb which indicates action or behaviour can be used with this pattern.

**A** Rewrite the sentences below, changing the verb *be* to one of the verbs in this list.

feel   look   sound   taste

1 It's like a desert. ........................................................................................................................

2 The roar of battle was like thunder. ......................................................................................

3 The young leaves are edible: they are like spinach.

........................................................................................................................................................

4 She was like a film star. .........................................................................................................

5 Your cotton sheets will be like silk. ......................................................................................

6 This is like Russian music. .....................................................................................................

7 The grass beneath your feet is like a cushion.

........................................................................................................................................................

8 This coffee is like washing-up water! ...................................................................................

**B** *Feel* has the pattern **V** *like* **n** with more than one meaning. For each sentence, say whether the noun group after *like* indicates how someone seems to themselves or indicates what someone wants.

1 I feel like a fool. ...*seem*....

2 I feel like an ice cream. ................

3 I feel like a drive. ................

4 I feel like an old man. ................

5 I feel like a sandwich. ................

6 I feel like a caged lion. ................

**C** Fill in the gaps in the sentences below using the verbs in this list. Use each verb once.

act   dress   live   think

1 We were ................................ like outlaws, sleeping in the open, eating on the run.

2 When I started teaching I ................................ like a student and wore jeans and men's jackets.

3 Will you stop ................................ like a baby?

4 I can see you've started ................................ like a politician already.

**D** Match up the two halves of each sentence.

1 She looked ...          a ... as if I have cheated them.
2 This wine tastes ...     b ... as though it was on fire.
3 The air smells ...       c ... as if it cost at least twice the price.
4 I feel ...               d ... as if someone's been frying goats.
5 The house looked ...     e ... as if he was telling the truth.
6 My skin felt ...         f ... as though it was made for the big screen.
7 He sounded ...           g ... as though she might cry.
8 This film looks ...      h ... as if burglars had ransacked it.

129

# Verbs used with *of*: 1

**1** Some verbs are followed by a prepositional phrase which consists of *of* and a noun group. For example, in *She complained of a headache*, the verb *complain* is followed by the preposition *of* and the noun group *a headache*. This pattern is **V of n**. With some verbs, the preposition is sometimes followed by an '-ing' clause.

| | Verb group | *of* | noun group/-ing clause |
|---|---|---|---|
| She | talked | of | killing herself. |
| I | do not approve | of | this change. |

Verbs with this pattern belong to the following meaning groups:

■ **verbs indicating that someone talks about something**

| boast | speak | tell |
|---|---|---|
| complain | talk | warn |

He **complained** of a ringing in his ears.

She **boasted** of knowing all about sailing and fishing.

All these verbs except *tell* are sometimes used in the passive.

A 30 billion dollar deal **is being spoken** of.

■ **verbs indicating that someone thinks about something or has a particular opinion of something**

| approve | | despair | dream |
|---|---|---|---|
| (cannot) conceive | | disapprove | think |

She's not even trying. I **despair** of her!

Peter **is thinking** of giving up teaching to become a full-time politician.

These verbs are sometimes used in the passive.

A recent poll found that the mayor **was approved** of by 55 per cent of people.

■ **verbs indicating that someone gets or has knowledge about something**

| hear | know | learn |
|---|---|---|

They also **knew** of the link between Lathan and the two journalists.

I've **heard** of looking on the bright side of life, but this is ridiculous!

*Hear* is sometimes used in the passive.

They've never **been heard** of again.

■ **verbs indicating that something smells or tastes like something else**

| smell | taste |
|---|---|

The water was refrigerated and **tasted** of metal.

■ **other common verbs**

| come | consist | die | dispose | tire |
|---|---|---|---|---|

Nothing much ever **comes** of his efforts.

The crew **consisted** of pilot, co-pilot, navigator and flight engineer.

It appears he **died** of natural causes.

*Dispose* is sometimes used in the passive.

Toxic waste **should be disposed** of cleanly and efficiently.

In the case of *come*, *consist*, and *tire*, the preposition *of* is sometimes followed by an '-ing' clause.

One of the disembarking passengers **had tired** of waiting for the coach and set off at a smart pace.

## Different forms of the pattern

What **did** he **die** of?

What was the 'price' **of which** he **spoke**?

I have **nothing** to **complain** of.

**2** A number of verbs with the pattern **V of n** are sometimes followed by *of*, a noun group, and an '-ing' clause. They are concerned with talking, thinking, and knowing.

We **talked** of him getting a summer job.

She **disapproves** of me talking to you.

The president admitted that he **did not know** of any rebels having surrendered so far.

**3** Three verbs are followed by a prepositional phrase beginning with *of* and another prepositional phrase which consists of *as* and a noun group, '-ing' clause, or adjective group.

These verbs are concerned with regarding or describing someone or something as a particular thing.

| speak | talk | think |
|---|---|---|

She **speaks** of her family as a 'great support system'.

Some **talk** of her as being arrogant and unfriendly.

I **don't think** of myself as abnormal, just unusual.

## Practice

**A** Match up the two halves of each sentence.

1  Did he die ...
2  61 percent of Americans disapprove ...
3  I dream ...
4  Why does Grandma's house always smell ...
5  I wish I'd thought ...
6  It has become commonplace to talk ...
7  Villagers complained ...
8  I was sorry to learn ...

a  ... of going to law school.
b  ... of suffocation?
c  ... of the death of William Towns.
d  ... of it twenty years ago.
e  ... of the president's handling of the economy.
f  ... of flowers being stolen from the churchyard.
g  ... of America as the sole remaining superpower.
h  ... of cooking?

**B** In the sentences below, put a dotted line under the verb used with a pattern described in this Unit. Then underline each of the other parts of the pattern.

1  Those who know Mick never tire of his singing.
2  The country talked of nothing else and seemed to watch nothing else.
3  They simply cannot conceive of anyone objecting to the way they work.
4  Analysts warn of the risk in releasing a low-budget film during an economic recession.
5  Do you approve of Britain following this path?
6  Glenn's friends speak of him as a man who always wanted to help other people.
7  90 percent of all the poisonous garbage generated in this country is disposed of on site.
8  Do you have to go out and buy a type of saucepan you've never even heard of?

**C** Use the first sentence in each pair to complete the second, so that the verb is followed by *of*, a noun group and an '-ing' clause.

1  Sandra gave up her career.
   Matt approved *of Sandra giving up her career.*
2  Her son was causing noise.
   Neighbours complained .........................................................................................
3  Something was wrong at the football match.
   It was the first I knew ..........................................................................................
4  Children are growing up with breathing difficulties.
   He spoke .................................................................................................................
5  Love was her religion.
   At one point she talked ........................................................................................
6  She had come home.
   She knew others would soon hear ......................................................................
7  Perhaps he'll find me.
   I often dream ........................................................................................................
8  People charge absolutely exorbitant prices.
   I have heard ..........................................................................................................

# Verbs used with *of*: 2

Some verbs are followed by a noun group and a prepositional phrase which consists of *of* and a noun group. For example, in *Mr Goodwin has informed me of your visit*, the verb *inform* is followed by the noun group *me*, the preposition *of*, and the noun group *your visit*. This pattern is **V n** *of* **n**. With some verbs, the preposition is sometimes followed by an '-ing' clause.

## Active pattern

|  | Verb group | noun group | *of* | noun group/-ing clause |
|---|---|---|---|---|
| They | Clear<br>suspected | your mind<br>him | of<br>of | other thoughts.<br>doing away with Beryl. |

## Passive pattern

|  | Verb group | *of* | noun group/-ing clause |
|---|---|---|---|
| People<br>They | were cheated<br>were convicted | of<br>of | their retirement cash.<br>handling explosives. |

Verbs with this pattern belong to the following meaning groups:

■ **verbs concerned with taking something away from someone or something, either physically or metaphorically**

| cheat | cure | free | rid | starve |
|---|---|---|---|---|
| clear | deprive | relieve | rob | strip |

*The Opposition leaders warned that the Bill **might deprive** citizens of fundamental rights.*

*I wish I **could rid** myself of this uneasy feeling.*

*Her brain **was starved** of oxygen for about twenty minutes.* (passive)

*They **were robbed** of their wristwatches and shot during the course of the robbery.* (passive)

■ **verbs indicating that someone talks or writes to someone**

| advise | convince | persuade | remind |
|---|---|---|---|
| assure | inform | reassure | warn |

*It is your duty to **inform** him of the danger to his father's life.*

*He said Western leaders **had assured** him of their commitment to help.*

*He **reminded** voters of the President's 'No new taxes' pledge.*

■ **verbs concerned with declaring or thinking that someone has or has not committed a crime**

| accuse | acquit | clear | convict | suspect |
|---|---|---|---|---|

*They **convicted** Gladys of voluntary manslaughter.*

*He **was cleared** of threatening to kill Holmes's mother.* (passive)

*They **are suspected** of being members of an extreme right-wing organisation.* (passive)

■ **other common verbs**

| ask | expect | make | require | think |
|---|---|---|---|---|
| assure | hear | remind | see | |

*Real Madrid's goalless draw at Valladolid **assured** them of the title for the fifth year running.*

***Make** a feature of glass kitchenware by displaying it on simple, open shelves.*

*You **remind** me of my father.*

In the case of *ask, expect, hear, see,* and *think*, the noun group following the verb is always or often an **amount**.

*I **haven't seen** much of him lately.*

*Little **has been heard** of the plan since then.* (passive)

*Think* and *make* (meaning 'think') often occur in a question or clause beginning with *what*.

*'What **did** you **think** of the video?' 'Well, it's not that bad really.'*

*I asked him what he **made** of the present situation.*

The verb *think* is also sometimes followed by an adverb group and a prepositional phrase beginning with *of*.

*Neil **thinks** very highly of him indeed.*

## Different forms of the pattern

*What **was** he **accused** of?*

*She still could not believe that he had been involved in the murders **of which** he **was suspected**.*

*All these tests, however, **require** of the examinee a moderate command of language.*

*I have a very great favour to **ask** of you.*

# Practice

**A** In the sentences below, put a dotted line under the verb used with *of*. Then underline each of the other parts of the pattern.

1 The naval court <u>acquitted</u> <u>him</u> <u>of</u> <u>the charge of personal dishonesty.</u>
2 It would be too simple to say I was cured of all my symptoms.
3 Manufacturers failed to warn doctors and consumers of the possible side effects.
4 This is a lot to ask of a partner.
5 Three city employees were accused of playing golf while on duty.
6 I assured the president of our intention to maintain only a minimum nuclear strategic force.
7 The government decided to strip the province of its autonomy.
8 What do you make of our neighbours?
9 That means he was not guilty of the crime of which he was accused.
10 Tell me, David, what does the smell remind you of?

**B** Fill in the gaps in the sentences below using *of* or *from* (see Unit 55).

1 That night, someone had robbed him ........................ all his money.
2 His goats strip the leaves ........................ the few sparse trees.
3 We must clear our minds ........................ the other versions.
4 Only the seat belt had saved him ........................ going through the windscreen.
5 A number of documents were stolen ........................ the building.
6 She stretched her neck this way and that to free it ........................ the tension.
7 The young political reformer promised to clear corruption ........................ the halls of government.
8 The World Boxing Association stripped him ........................ his title and his boxing licence.

**C** Rewrite these sentences using the pattern **V n *of* n** or its passive.

1 I'll tell them about your generous offer. (inform)
*I'll inform them of your generous offer.*
....................................................................................................................................

2 I soon made him believe that I was innocent. (convince)
....................................................................................................................................

3 Customs officers are obliged to tell passengers about these rights. (advise)
....................................................................................................................................

4 That story brought to mind one I heard a while ago at college. (remind)
....................................................................................................................................

5 We had been alerted to the danger of pickpockets. (warn)
....................................................................................................................................

6 The authorities have stressed to us their willingness to cooperate. (assure)
....................................................................................................................................

# Verbs used with *on*: 1

Some verbs are followed by a prepositional phrase which consists of *on* and a noun group. For example, in *He remarked on the heat*, the verb *remark* is followed by the preposition *on* and the noun group *the heat*. This pattern is **V *on* n**. With some verbs, the preposition is sometimes followed by an '-ing' clause or a wh-clause.

Sometimes *upon* is used instead of *on*. *Upon* is a more formal or literary word.

## Active pattern

|  | Verb group | *on* | noun group/-ing/wh |
|---|---|---|---|
| They | cannot agree | on | what they want done. |
| Everything | depends | on | the weather. |
| He | is concentrating | on | getting himself re-elected. |

## Passive pattern

|  | Verb group | *on* |
|---|---|---|
| This fault | has been commented | on. |

Verbs with this pattern belong to the following meaning groups:

■ **verbs concerned with speaking, writing, or expressing views**

| | | | |
|---|---|---|---|
| advise | remark | rule | touch |
| comment | report | speak | vote |
| lecture | report back | talk | write |

*The government **has not** yet **commented** on his release.*

*The Parliament is also due to **vote** on lowering the legal voting age from twenty-one to eighteen.*

*Police refused to **comment** on why she had been freed.*

■ **verbs concerned with thought, or the expression of thought**

| | | | |
|---|---|---|---|
| agree | differ | dwell | ponder | speculate |
| brood | disagree | muse | reflect | |

*It gave me a chance to **reflect** on what I was doing.*

*Even the experts **don't** always **agree** on how much sleep we need.*

■ **verbs concerned with depending or relying on something or someone, or hoping to have something**

| | | | | |
|---|---|---|---|---|
| bank | depend | hinge | rest | turn |
| count | hang | rely | ride | |

*I hope we **can count** on your support.*

*A great deal **hangs** on the answer to these questions.*

*People **can** no longer **rely** on doing their chosen job for life.*

*Much **will hinge** on how well the Free Democrats do tonight.*

In the case of *bank, count, depend, hinge,* and *rely*, the preposition is sometimes followed by a noun group and an '-ing' clause.

*In the case of spacecraft such as the Space Shuttle, lives **depend** on such systems working properly.*

In the case of *count, depend,* and *rely*, there is sometimes a second prepositional phrase beginning with *for*, which indicates what is provided or ensured.

*She, too, **relied** upon him for her safety.*

■ **verbs concerned with working**

| | | | |
|---|---|---|---|
| collaborate | experiment | operate | work |

*After his return to Edinburgh, we **collaborated** on a musical version of Kingsley Amis's 'Lucky Jim'.*

*Mr Waldegrave said British diplomats **were working** on solving these problems.*

*He **has been operated** on for cancer.* (passive)

■ **verbs indicating that someone has or starts to have a particular thing as their focus of attention**

| | | | |
|---|---|---|---|
| centre | concentrate | focus | home in |

*Focus on your goal.*

*The film **centres** upon two prisoners: Gerry Conlon and his father Giuseppe.*

*He gave up his party duties to **concentrate** on clearing his name.*

■ **verbs concerned with using something as a basis or exploiting it**

| | | | |
|---|---|---|---|
| act | build | cash in | improve | trade |

*Civil servants, **acting** on government instructions, have started to question the financial management of the society.*

*This year we **are building** upon that success to provide an even better and bigger show.*

# UNIT 67 Practice

**A** In the sentences below, put a dotted line under the verb used with a pattern described in this Unit. Then underline each of the other parts of the pattern. (For different forms of the pattern, see Unit 69.)

1 The Oscar-winning director will collaborate on a series of video-games.
2 She needed to write on what was nearest and most relevant to her life.
3 The accommodation I think could be improved on in many ways.
4 Airlines depend on business travelers for both volume and profit.
5 Computer learning centers focus on teaching children to use computer technology.
6 Many of the papers' lead stories report on the police appeal for help.
7 Even before the agency's first transaction was announced, its every move was speculated on.
8 You're the only person I can count on, Sheppy.
9 Now Paramount is banking on the sequel being another box-office hit.
10 That's what Congress will be voting on.

**B** Fill in the gaps in these sentences using *on* or *that* (see Unit 24).

1 Everyone agreed ........................ commerce was important.
2 Chris had relied ........................ Jeff's knowledge of the movie industry in casting them.
3 Our clients have frequently remarked ........................ the quality of our staff.
4 Some analysts speculate ........................ corn prices won't drop much lower.
5 Nutritionists disagree ........................ whether animal fat is bad for us.
6 I asked if her mother had commented ........................ her lateness.
7 The repairman reported ........................ the computer had a virus.
8 He wants to concentrate ........................ the rehabilitation of his people and the reconstruction of his country.

**C** Rewrite these sentences using the verb given in brackets with the pattern **V on n**.

1 The future of the Republic could be determined by the outcome of these elections. (hinge)
   *The future of the Republic could hinge on the outcome of these elections.*

2 He talked about a variety of social and economic topics. (speak)
   ........................................................................

3 It's fascinating to consider how fashions in the home have changed in the last 15 years. (reflect)
   ........................................................................

4 They take advantage of the generosity of visitors. (cash in)
   ........................................................................

5 Prosecutors in that case didn't mention his fund-raising efforts. (touch)
   ........................................................................

6 The legal dispute is likely to revolve around whether or not commitments were made. (centre)
   ........................................................................

7 The task is not to break new ground, but to develop what has already been accomplished. (build)
   ........................................................................

# Verbs used with *on*: 2

Here are some more groups of verbs which are followed by the preposition *on* (or *upon*) and a noun group:

■ verbs indicating that someone or something hits or touches something

| bear down | knock | pull | stamp | tread |
|-----------|-------|------|-------|-------|
| beat | press | rest | tap | |

She **knocked** *on the door* and waited.

His legs were stretched out and his feet **rested** *upon a sofa*.

■ verbs concerned with going towards or onto something or someone

| bear down | close in | descend | move in | sneak up |
|-----------|----------|---------|---------|----------|
| close | creep up | fall | settle | |

The rebels **are closing in** *on the capital*.

When the news went out that an explosion had occurred, dozens of reporters **descended** *on the campus*.

There was clearly no way to **sneak up** *on the house*.

■ verbs concerned with visiting someone

| call | call in | drop in | look in |
|------|---------|---------|---------|

We**'ll drop in** *on him* after school and take him out.

■ verbs indicating that something affects or begins to affect someone or something, often negatively. The Subject often refers to a worrying thought or situation.

| act | descend | press | tell |
|-----|---------|-------|------|
| creep up | fall | sneak up | weigh |

A gloomy silence once again **descended** *on the room*.

A feeling of responsibility **weighs** *on me*.

■ verbs indicating that someone interrupts or gets involved in something, sometimes when this is unwelcome

| get in | move in | sit in |
|--------|---------|--------|
| intrude | muscle in | walk in |

If you **were to walk in** *on the man you love*, and he was with somebody else, what would you feel?

They wrote him letters from time to time, but **did not intrude** *on his privacy*.

■ verbs indicating that someone attacks or harms someone else, or treats them in a bad or hostile way

| clamp down | gang up | lean | stamp |
|------------|---------|------|-------|
| crack down | hang up | run out | tell |
| dump | inform | set | turn |
| fire | jump | spy | walk out |

They're urging the government to **crack down** *on right-wing extremists*.

One of their leaders had been helping the secret police for 17 years, **informing** *on colleagues*.

His first wife **walked out** *on him*.

I took the short cut, over the fields, and I **was set** *upon* by a gang of boys. (passive)

■ verbs indicating that someone changes their plans or their attitude to something

| back down | cave in | climb down | compromise | go back |
|-----------|---------|------------|------------|---------|

The government **has backed down** *on plans to introduce national tests for seven-year-old children*.

You **can't go back** *on your promise*.

Neither side is prepared to **compromise** *on the issue*.

**A** Match up the two halves of each sentence.

1 She tried to stamp ...
2 They all jumped ...
3 At night, the police crept up ...
4 The journalists will come and sit in ...
5 I will be glad to call ...
6 Her spell fell ...
7 The Government wants to clamp down ...
8 A young man and woman knocked ...

a ... on him like a rugby scrum.
b ... on student unions.
c ... on his feet and push him away.
d ... on you at your office.
e ... on the lobby windows a few feet away.
f ... on the interviews.
g ... on the house and surrounded it.
h ... on everyone who came in contact with her.

**B** Fill in the gaps in the sentences below using the verbs in this list. Use each verb once.

go back   inform   intrude   look in   settle   sneak up   tap   weigh

1 I'm sure he doesn't want to ................................. on his promise for no new taxes, but I guess he's finding that he just can't keep that promise.
2 He eventually admitted that he'd ................................. on four people who were later shot.
3 They had no right to ................................. on my personal life in the way that they did.
4 I stood in a phone booth, holding the receiver, until a guy came by and ................................. on the glass.
5 A pigeon ................................. on the window-sill, eyed him uncertainly, then flew off.
6 He wanted to ................................. on Laura and have another word about Grace.
7 It had ................................. on his conscience and now he decided to repay the money.
8 I managed to ................................. on him when you knocked on the door.

**C** Rewrite the sentences below using the verbs in this list with the pattern **V on n**. Use each verb once.

back down   compromise   descend   drop in   fire   walk in   walk out

1 There are no signs that the republic is prepared to withdraw its declaration of independence.
*There are no signs that the republic is prepared to back down on its declaration of independence.*

2 Eight years ago, my husband abandoned me and our two young children.
.................................................................................................................................

3 Why don't you visit me? I live right next door.
.................................................................................................................................

4 He shot at two people who tried to stop him outside a luxury hotel.
.................................................................................................................................

5 A team of one hundred technicians will arrive at the castle.
.................................................................................................................................

6 They are on record as saying they won't change their stand on the issue of democracy.
.................................................................................................................................

7 Suddenly, she felt as if she had interrupted a private conversation.
.................................................................................................................................

# Verbs used with *on*: 3

**1** Here are some more groups of verbs which are followed by the preposition *on* (or *upon*) and a noun group or an '-ing' clause:

■ verbs indicating that a person or animal eats something

| chew | dine | feast | feed | live |
|------|------|-------|------|------|

He **chewed on his toast**, taking his time.

The adult flies **feed** on nectar.

■ verbs used when indicating what resources someone has which enable them to live

| exist | get by | live | survive |
|-------|--------|------|---------|

They may not look for work once they are accustomed to **living on benefit**.

She **is getting by** on borrowed money.

■ verbs concerned with using less of something or spending less on it

| cut back | cut down | economize | save |
|----------|----------|-----------|------|

Pregnant women are still advised to **cut down on coffee**.

■ other common verbs

| bet | check up | lose out | reflect | start |
|-----|----------|----------|---------|-------|
| catch up | fall | miss out | rub off | stock up |
| check | insist | read up | run | wait |

I'll get somebody to **check** on the luggage.

My 31st birthday **fell on a Friday**.

Every new mother **should read up on the food requirements of her children**.

I mean, even your own personal behavior as a teacher, outside of school hours, **reflects on the school itself**.

A car which **runs on natural gas** has been developed by engineers in Milton Keynes.

We're ready to **start on the runways**.

In the case of *insist* and *miss out*, the preposition *on* is sometimes followed by an '-ing' clause.

Reggae band Inner Circle said they were very upset to **have missed out on performing at the Carnival**.

In the case of *bet* and *insist*, the preposition is sometimes followed by a noun group and an '-ing' clause.

They **insist on three conditions being met**.

## Different forms of the pattern

*What **are** you **working** on at the moment?*

*You're one of **the few people** I **can rely** on absolutely.*

*What the play **concentrates** on is Britten's development as a composer.*

**2** A few verbs are followed by a prepositional phrase beginning with *on* or *upon*, and a to-infinitive clause.

Verbs with this pattern belong to the following meaning groups:

■ verbs indicating that someone hopes or is certain that someone will do something

| bank | count | depend | rely |
|------|-------|--------|------|

One lesson they may have learned is that they **cannot rely on anyone else to fight their battles for them**.

■ verbs indicating that someone asks or persuades someone to do something

| call | prevail |
|------|---------|

So we **call on everyone to seize this opportunity and to look at it positively**.

He **may be prevailed** upon to join the Supreme National Council. (passive)

**3** The verb *look* is followed by a prepositional phrase beginning with *on* or *upon* and another prepositional phrase which consists of *as* and a noun group, '-ing' clause, or adjective group. The second prepositional phrase indicates what someone regards someone or something as being.

**Look on it as a challenge.**

People who put their own pleasure higher up on the list of priorities **are** often **looked** on as selfish or immature. (passive)

# Practice

**A** In the sentences below, put a dotted line under the verb used with a pattern described in this Unit. Then underline each of the other parts of the pattern.

1  I just missed out on getting an Agfa camera.
2  She practically lived on instant breakfasts.
3  They showed they can be relied on to do the job.
4  His team taught residents how to save on their fuel bills by weatherproofing.
5  What I insist on is a totally positive campaign that goes right through the party.
6  For too long the school has had to exist on a limited budget.
7  The main political parties look on these votes as already lost.
8  I always have chocolate and cheese but I also stock up on tons of fruit.

**B** Rewrite these sentences, starting with the words provided. Use a prepositional phrase beginning with *on*, and a to-infinitive clause.

1  They hoped that the President would deliver the speech of his life.
   They were banking *on the President to deliver the speech of his life.*
2  He suggested that richer nations should relieve the suffering of poorer people.
   He called ..................................................................................................................
3  He thought that Elaine would be sure to act out of love for him.
   He thought that he could depend ........................................................................
4  Will you do the same?
   Can I count ..........................................................................................................
5  She persuaded her parents to let her go to London.
   She prevailed ........................................................................................................
6  He was confident his influential friends would get him out of trouble.
   He relied ...............................................................................................................

**C** Rewrite these sentences using the verb given in brackets with one of the patterns in this Unit.

1  I'm going to come back and bring my paperwork up-to-date in peace. (catch up)
   *I'm going to come back and catch up on my paperwork in peace.*
2  If you're starting to gain a bit of weight, reduce the carbohydrates. (cut back)
   ...............................................................................................................................
3  His father has been finding out about the disease. (read up)
   ...............................................................................................................................
4  Once he began telling stories of his time here, we heard the lot. (start)
   ...............................................................................................................................
5  I consider it to be an adventure, something positive we can experience together. (look)
   ...............................................................................................................................
6  The Prime Minister had roast chicken and peas for dinner. (dine)
   ...............................................................................................................................
7  She was firm about paying for the coffee. (insist)
   ...............................................................................................................................

# Verbs used with *on*: 4

Some verbs are followed by a noun group and a prepositional phrase which consists of *on* and a noun group. For example, in *He played a trick on her*, the verb *play* is followed by the noun group *a trick*, the preposition *on*, and the noun group *her*. This pattern is **V n *on* n**. With some verbs, the preposition is sometimes followed by an '-ing' clause or a wh-clause.

Sometimes *upon* is used instead of *on*. *Upon* is a more formal or literary word.

## Active pattern

|  | Verb group | noun group | *on* | noun group/-ing/wh |
|---|---|---|---|---|
| They | advise | governments | on | negotiating. |
| They | questioned | him | on | what he had said. |
| The army | inflicted | heavy losses | on | the rebel forces. |

## Passive pattern

|  | Verb group | *on* | noun group/-ing/wh |
|---|---|---|---|
| They | were not consulted | on | the policy. |
| They | were congratulated | on | acting quickly. |
| Much emphasis | is placed | on | how they perform. |

(With phrasal verbs, the particle comes either after the noun group or after the verb.)

Verbs with this pattern belong to the following meaning groups:

■ **verbs concerned with speaking or writing to someone about something**

| advise | compliment | consult | let in | question |
|---|---|---|---|---|
| brief | congratulate | fill in | press | update |

*This guide **will brief** you **on** sightseeing and shopping.*

*I **congratulated** Katherine **on** her decision to advance her education.*

*I'll **let** you **in on** a little secret.*

*She **complimented** them **on** staying together for such a long time.*

***Consult** your vet **on** how to deal with the problem.*

■ **verbs concerned with giving something unpleasant to someone, or making them undergo an unpleasant experience**

| bring | impose | serve | thrust |
|---|---|---|---|
| dump | inflict | spring | wish |
| force | play | take out | |

*Rob **dumped** his children **on** the grandparents but my family does not live nearby.*

*Rose grieved privately with her immediate family and **did not impose** her grief **on** friends.*

*They **brought** this tragedy **on** themselves.*

*A Home Office spokeswoman said last night: 'We **have served** a writ **on** Central Television** to prevent the programme being screened.'*

*I didn't mean to **take** my anger **out on** him, but I couldn't help myself.*

■ **verbs concerned with giving something to someone**

| bestow | confer |
|---|---|

*An honorary doctorate in criminology **was conferred on** him by the University of Manila in 1968. (passive)*

*The King and Queen **bestowed** their grateful thanks **upon** Lancelot.*

■ **verbs concerned with putting something somewhere metaphorically**

| cast | lay | place | put | set | throw |
|---|---|---|---|---|---|

*Only three EC countries **set** no limit **on** the hours worked.*

*The government have agreed to **place** greater emphasis **on** the rights of individuals.*

*The prosecutors want to **cast** doubt **on** whether Smith has a good character.*

**A** In the sentences below, put a dotted line under the verb used with *on* or *upon*. Then underline each of the other parts of the pattern.

1 I'm not mean enough to wish unemployment on anyone.
2 It dismissed all the evidence that threw doubt on the alleged confession.
3 Through an interpreter, we complimented her on doing an excellent job.
4 The purchase of this object conferred a certain status upon the purchaser.
5 If too much strain is put on the back, a slipped disc may result.
6 I will fill you in on the whole story when I see you.
7 A government spokesman said heavy casualties had been inflicted on the rebels.
8 We'd update people on what's happening around the club.

**B** Rewrite each of the following pairs of sentences as one sentence.

1 They brief interviewers. They tell them about the ground rules.
*They brief interviewers on the ground rules.*
2 They congratulated her. She looked so well just two months after the birth.
3 Mr Stevens was questioned. Where was the money for the project coming from?
4 Could you advise me? I'd like to know how to treat this problem.
5 We'll update you. We have the day's top news stories.
6 He complimented Tania. He admired her cooking.
7 Where did it come from? She consulted the shopkeeper.
8 When I come back, you can fill me in. You can tell me about his plans.

**C** Fill in the gaps in the sentences below using the verbs in this list. Use each verb once.

bestow    bring    congratulate    consult    impose    place    press    serve

1 He told them that they had .................................. disgrace on themselves and their families.
2 There is no more precious gift that can be .................................. upon a child than the gift of education.
3 They are .................................. on important economic decisions.
4 Before anybody could .................................. a warrant on him, he had dropped out of sight.
5 The army immediately .................................. a curfew on the town.
6 I .................................. him on why he would lend his weight to the board of a tobacco company.
7 He .................................. the society on having preserved these important relics.
8 He wasn't a man who .................................. a strong emphasis on personal relationships.

# Verbs used with *on*: 5

Here are some more groups of verbs which are followed by a noun group and a prepositional phrase beginning with *on* (or *upon*):

■ **verbs indicating that someone focuses their attention, feelings, or efforts on someone or something**

| | | | |
|---|---|---|---|
| be centred | direct | focus | turn |
| concentrate | fix | pin | |

*Scientists now **pin** their hopes **on** treatment with combinations of drugs – but these hopes are not high.*

*Firefighters **concentrated** their efforts **on** trying to free people trapped in elevators.*

*The debate **is centred on** whether the country's president should be **elected** directly by the people or by parliament.* (passive)

In the case of *turn*, the feeling you focus on someone is usually aggressive.

*The crowd then **turned** their anger **on** the Prime Minister.*

■ **verbs indicating that someone directs a weapon or camera at someone**

| | | |
|---|---|---|
| pull | train | turn |

*A judge **pulled** a gun **on** an unruly prisoner yesterday and threatened to shoot him dead.*

■ **verbs concerned with striking one thing on another, or catching one thing on another**

| | | | | |
|---|---|---|---|---|
| bang | catch | drum | strike | wipe |

*He shouted out loud in his anger, and **banged** his fists **on** the steering wheel.*

*He **caught** his shirt **on** a nail.*

■ **verbs concerned with writing something somewhere**

| | | | | |
|---|---|---|---|---|
| carve | print | put down | write | write down |

*I wish to thank my friend Theresa King, who encouraged me to develop my ideas and **put** them **down on** paper.*

■ **verbs concerned with basing one thing on another**

| | | |
|---|---|---|
| base | build | model |

*They tried to **build** an empire **on** shaky foundations.*

*As far as their preferences and dislikes are concerned, most children tend to **model** themselves **on** their parents.*

*Our politics **should be based upon** ethical standards.* (passive)

■ **verbs concerned with gambling**

| | | | | |
|---|---|---|---|---|
| bet | lay | place | put | stake |

*She and a friend both **bet** five pounds **on** him.*

The preposition *on* is sometimes followed by a noun group and an '-ing' clause.

*You wouldn't want to **stake** your life **on** the signal being picked up.*

■ **verbs concerned with spending, saving, and wasting time, money, or resources**

| | | | |
|---|---|---|---|
| blow | save | spend | waste |

*'I **do spend** a lot **on** expensive jewelry and clothing,' she admits.*

*She **blew** part of the cash **on** furnishing her flat.*

*How much time and how many resources **have been wasted on** the arms race!* (passive)

■ **other common verbs**

| | | | |
|---|---|---|---|
| blame | feed | pride | urge |
| (not) commit | judge | take up | |

*They made it available to us and we **took** them **up on** the offer.*

*The President **urged** restraint **on** the security forces.*

*That earlier accident **was blamed on** a faulty signal.* (passive)

In the case of *commit* and *pride*, the noun group following the verb is always a reflexive pronoun.

*John Major failed to **commit** himself **on** the issue in the Commons.*

## Different forms of the pattern

*What **are** you **going to spend** it **on**?*

*The material **on which** this book **is based** comes from three distinct sources.*

*They **impose on** the media a duty to report fairly.*

*They have **nothing** to **spend** their money **on**.*

# Practice

**A Rewrite each of the following pairs of sentences as one sentence.**

1 Concentrate your attention. Think about your lower back.
*Concentrate your attention on your lower back.*

2 I wrote his number down. I used that pad of paper by the phone.
......................................................................................................................

3 He had already placed a bet. He had chosen one of the horses.
......................................................................................................................

4 Enough taxpayers' money is wasted already. It goes on propaganda.
......................................................................................................................

5 The Prime Minister failed to commit himself. He avoided the issue.
......................................................................................................................

6 Some nights I would blow £200. I would pay for a meal with it.
......................................................................................................................

7 The man jumped over the counter and pulled out a knife. He threatened the clerk with it.
......................................................................................................................

**B Rewrite these sentences using the verb given in brackets and the pattern V n *on* n.**

1 They are expected to tell the government that caution is necessary. (urge)
*They are expected to urge caution on the government.*

2 Politicians here take pride in their accessibility to the public. (pride)
......................................................................................................................

3 He attributed the job losses to rising production costs. (blame)
......................................................................................................................

4 I wish people would look at my contribution when evaluating me. (judge)
......................................................................................................................

5 I accepted her suggestion. (take up)
......................................................................................................................

6 What do they give the rabbits as food? (feed)
......................................................................................................................

**C Put the different parts of these sentences in the right order.**

1 their cameras / trained / them / on / the foreigners ...................................................

2 on / her name / wrote / the side of the package / she ...............................................

3 his fingers / drummed / the bar / in time to / he / on / the music
......................................................................................................................

4 on / he / getting the treaty through / has staked / his reputation
......................................................................................................................

5 is modelled / much of the clothing / the clothing that will be worn by the European team / on
......................................................................................................................

6 the things / is going to be judged / those are / he / on ...............................................

7 a question / are spending / it's / of / what / on / they / their time
......................................................................................................................

# Verbs used with *out of*: 1

Some verbs are followed by a prepositional phrase which consists of *out of* and a noun group. For example, in *He's pulled out of the deal*, the verb *pull* is followed by the preposition *out of* and the noun group *the deal*. This pattern is **V *out of* n**.

|  | Verb group | *out of* | noun group |
|---|---|---|---|
| Everyone | piled | out of | the car. |
| He | had changed | out of | his work clothes. |

Verbs with this pattern belong to the following meaning groups:

■ **verbs indicating that someone or something comes out of or leaves a place or thing**

| break | clear | go | pile |
|---|---|---|---|
| check | get | move | pull |

On the same day a former police chief **broke** *out of prison* and took over police headquarters.

He **checked** *out of his hotel room* at nine this morning.

'If we ever **move** *out of this house*, we'll sell everything with it,' he resolves.

■ **verbs concerned with not being involved in something, not doing something, or withdrawing from something**

| back | contract | get | pull | walk |
|---|---|---|---|---|
| break | drop | opt | stay | wriggle |

Actress Julia Roberts **has backed** *out of a £1.8 million movie deal*.

He **dropped** *out of school* as early as he could.

The preposition *out of* is sometimes followed by an '-ing' clause.

I found myself trying to scheme how I **could get** *out of taking my kid to the beach*.

America had decided to **pull** *out of financing the proposed construction of the Aswan Dam*.

■ **verbs indicating that someone or something stops being in a particular state**

| fall | get | go | pull | snap |
|---|---|---|---|---|

He **fell** *out of favour* last summer when he supported an anti-government student demonstration.

Big computers **are going** *out of fashion*.

Most economists predict that the economy **will pull** *out of the recession* by mid-year.

■ **verbs indicating that someone takes off their clothes**

| change | slip |
|---|---|

Then she went into the bathroom to get a robe and **change** *out of her wet clothes*.

■ **verbs indicating that one thing develops or results from another**

| arise | develop | grow |
|---|---|---|

Depression and anxiety **may arise** *out of loneliness and isolation*.

This book **grew** *out of three experiences which happened in 1968*.

■ **verbs indicating that someone uses or sells all they have of something**

| run | sell |
|---|---|

After a few months he **ran** *out of money* and needed his job back.

A sign of increased consumer demand is that some retailers **have sold** *out of popular items*.

■ *Grow* also has this pattern when it is used to refer to mental or physical development.

Most girls go through a phase of loving ponies, and most **grow** *out of it*.

I had to have my older sister's clothes when she **grew** *out of them*.

## Different forms of the pattern

Scientific theories are shaped by the shared values of the communities *out of which* they **arise**.

**A** Fill in the gaps in these sentences using *out of* or *into* (see Unit 61).

1 She slipped ....................... the jacket and tossed it on the couch.

2 How are we going to get ....................... this mess?

3 He lived in the farmhouse, which had fallen ....................... disrepair.

4 They piled ....................... the car and ordered: 'Drive!'

5 The London Nursery Campaign developed ....................... these initiatives.

6 We're running ....................... time.

7 Civilians had broken ....................... the building, apparently in the belief that it contained food.

8 The Slovene delegation walked ....................... the debate in protest.

9 Late in the day they checked ....................... a motel in a small town near the state line.

10 Youngsters who lack affection and stability at home are more likely to get ....................... trouble.

**B** Rewrite these sentences using the verb given in brackets, *out of*, and an '-ing' clause.

1 Is he just trying to avoid doing the dishes? (get)
   *Is he just trying to get out of doing the dishes?*
   ....................................................................................................................

2 Russia decided not to aid China's nuclear programme. (back)
   ....................................................................................................................

3 His job in banking brought about several moves and he stopped cycling for a while. (drop)
   ....................................................................................................................

4 She could then avoid doing all the things she did not want to do. (get)
   ....................................................................................................................

5 The Government has largely stopped providing continual care for the elderly. (opt)
   ....................................................................................................................

6 I didn't go through with applying but if I'd got the grant it would have saved a lot of money. (pull)
   ....................................................................................................................

7 But many who lost their jobs complain that insurance firms are now trying to avoid paying up.
   (wriggle)
   ....................................................................................................................

**C** Fill in the gaps in the sentences below using the verbs in this list. Use each verb once.

arise   change   get   move   sell   stay

1 Lesley had ................................. out of her shirt and jeans into a straight white sleeveless dress.

2 I'm 30 now, so I do not think that I will ................................. out of Denmark again.

3 It's amazing what people will do to ................................. out of paying taxes.

4 'Okay,' Nancy murmured, 'I'll try to ................................. out of trouble, because I love you, too.'

5 My local supermarket ................................. out of beef last week for the first time ever.

6 The concept of community schools ................................. out of a push to make education more
   relevant to community needs.

# Verbs used with *out of*: 2

Some verbs are followed by a noun group and a prepositional phrase which consists of *out of* and a noun group. For example, in *I dragged the information out of him*, the verb *drag* is followed by the noun group *the information*, the preposition *out of*, and the noun group *him*. This pattern is **V n *out of* n**.

## Active pattern

|  | Verb group | noun group | *out of* | noun group |
|---|---|---|---|---|
| They | didn't get | any advantage | out of | this. |
| They | kicked | him | out of | the country. |

## Passive pattern

|  | Verb group | *out of* | noun group |
|---|---|---|---|
| They | were conned | out of | several hundred pounds. |
| They | have been driven | out of | their homes. |

Verbs with this pattern belong to the following meaning groups:

■ **verbs concerned with fraudulently taking something, usually money, away from someone.** The prepositional phrase indicates what is taken away.

| cheat | con | do | swindle | trick |
|---|---|---|---|---|

*He feels I **did** him **out of** a profit on some shares.*

■ **verbs concerned with getting something from someone with some difficulty.** The prepositional phrase indicates the person involved.

| charm | drag | screw | wring |
|---|---|---|---|
| con | get | squeeze | |

*The company has a monopoly position that it uses to **screw** more money **out of** people.*

■ **verbs concerned with gaining something from an activity or thing**

| get | make |
|---|---|

*The attempt to **make** money **out of** the historic find has caused outrage.*

The preposition *out of* is sometimes followed by an '-ing' clause.

*You **might get** a lot of pleasure **out of** refurnishing and re-equipping a new home.*

■ **verbs indicating that someone or something forces someone to leave a place, position, activity, or state**

| chase | kick | put | turn |
|---|---|---|---|
| drive | knock | shake | vote |
| force | order | throw | |

*He said he would oppose moves to **force** the president **out of** office.*

*Ivan Lendl **has been knocked** out of the Wimbledon Tennis Championships.* (passive)

■ **verbs concerned with excluding someone or something**

| block | edge | leave | put | squeeze |
|---|---|---|---|---|
| cut | freeze | lock | rule | |

*She **had locked** him **out of** the apartment.*

*You know it can happen but you **have to block** it **out of** your mind*.

*They were concerned that they **were being left** out of the decision-making process.* (passive)

■ **verbs concerned with rescuing someone from a bad situation**

| bail | get | pull | talk |
|---|---|---|---|

*We**'d bail** him **out of** trouble when he owed money.*

In the case of *talk*, the noun group following the preposition is always a reflexive pronoun. This verb sometimes indicates that someone gets themselves out of a good situation rather than a bad one.

*I always have the sense that I **can talk** myself **out of** trouble.*

*He **talked** himself **out of** a job.*

■ **verbs indicating that someone makes something**

| carve | create | fashion | manufacture |
|---|---|---|---|
| construct | cut | make | |

*She **makes** beautiful bowls **out of** red earthenware clay.*

■ *Talk* also has this pattern when it is used to indicate that someone persuades someone not to do something. The preposition *out of* is sometimes followed by an '-ing' clause.

*My mother tried to **talk** me **out of** getting a divorce.*

## Different forms of the pattern

*Proteins are the very large and complex molecules **out of** which living things **are made**.*

*He said his priority was to **force** out of the country the remnants of forces loyal to the former president.*

**A** In the sentences below, put a dotted line under the verb used with *out of* (see this Unit and Unit 72). Then underline each of the other parts of the pattern.

1 Parents often bailed their children out of financial, legal, and emotional difficulties.
2 He had left out of his account something that was crucial.
3 Food markets in the capital were said to have sold out of bread and milk.
4 Soil is the raw material out of which a gardener creates his dreams.
5 If people want to get rid of legislators, then all they have to do is vote them out of office.
6 The thousands of people that she threw out of work are still having a difficult time.
7 The American, Fred Couples, has pulled out of the event with a back injury.
8 They are fighting against the health problems which have arisen out of poor housing.

**B** Fill in the gaps in these sentences using the noun groups given in brackets.

1 He is good at charming .................................................. out of ..............................................
   (money / companies)
2 Jacob cheated ........................................................ out of ..............................................
   (his birthright / his brother Esau)
3 He was jailed for conning ........................................ out of ..............................................
   (their life savings / women)
4 The bank has done ........................................................ out of ..............................................
   and I'm absolutely furious. (thousands of dollars / me)
5 I don't think we'd get ........................................................ out of ..............................................
   (any useful information / him)
6 She didn't come straight out and tell me, I had to drag ..................... out of ..................... (it / her)
7 He had recently discovered that Fisch was a crook who had tricked ..........................................
   out of .................................................. (several thousand dollars / him)
8 They forced him to try to screw .................................................. out of ..............................................
   (some extra concessions / the West)
9 This has become just another way of squeezing ................................. out of ...................................
   (cash / the government)

**C** *Talk* is used with a reflexive pronoun and *out of* with three slightly different meanings. Here are three examples.

a You may realise what is happening but talk yourself out of taking any action.
b He talked himself out of a really good deal.
c If he had done, he might have talked himself out of dismissal that day at Wembley.

**In which of the sentences above does *talk* mean:**

1 get yourself out of a bad situation? ................
2 get yourself out of a good situation? ................
3 persuade yourself not to do something? ................

# Verbs used with *over*

**1** Some verbs are followed by a prepositional phrase which consists of *over* and a noun group. For example, in *They're arguing over details*, the verb *argue* is followed by the preposition *over* and the noun group *details*. This pattern is **V over n**. With some verbs, the preposition is sometimes followed by a wh-clause.

|  | Verb group | *over* | noun group/wh-clause |
|---|---|---|---|
| They | argued | over | whether to extend the deadline. |
| He | ruled | over | a vast kingdom. |

Verbs with this pattern belong to the following meaning groups:

■ **verbs indicating that two or more people argue or disagree about something**

| argue | disagree | haggle | squabble |
|---|---|---|---|
| differ | fight | quarrel | |

*The candidates **differed** over a number of issues, including government, foreign affairs, and the environment.*

*But yesterday Baker said the two sides still **disagree** over when those meetings should be held.*

*We **argued** over household chores.*

■ **verbs indicating that someone changes their plans or their attitude to something**

| back down | climb down | compromise |
|---|---|---|

*The Prime Minister was forced to **back down** over plans to pardon corrupt businessmen and politicians.*

■ **verbs indicating that someone does not discuss or deal with something as thoroughly as they should**

| gloss | skate | skip |
|---|---|---|

*Official histories tend to **gloss** over this state of affairs.*

These verbs are sometimes used in the passive.

*The stories are too long to **be skated** over here.*

■ **verbs concerned with being in a superior or powerful position**

| preside | prevail | rule | triumph | win out |
|---|---|---|---|---|

*Today, Mr. Corry **presides** over a company whose fortunes have changed abruptly.*

*In the end, good **prevailed** over evil.*

*Free-market liberals **have won out** over soft-hearted social democrats.*

■ **other common verbs**

| descend | extend | hang | range | stumble | wash |
|---|---|---|---|---|---|

*As Gascoigne slowly sank to the ground, a deathly hush **descended** over the stadium.*

*A question mark still **hangs** over the future of 3,000 jobs at British Coal.*

*His speech **ranged** over too many issues.*

*She **stumbled** over her words sometimes.*

*A wave of guilt and shame **washed** over me.*

**2** Some verbs are followed by a noun group and a prepositional phrase which consists of *over* and a noun group. For example, in *Pour the sauce over the fish*, the verb *pour* is followed by the noun group *the sauce*, the preposition *over*, and the noun group *the fish*. This pattern is **V n over n**.

## Active pattern

|  | Verb group | noun group | *over* | noun group |
|---|---|---|---|---|
| The youths | poured | kerosene | over | the floor. |

## Passive pattern

|  | Verb group | *over* | noun group |
|---|---|---|---|
| Cooling water | was sprayed | over | the engines. |

Verbs with this pattern are all concerned with pouring or scattering something over something else.

| distribute | pour | scatter | spray | sprinkle |
|---|---|---|---|---|

***Scatter** the basil leaves over the salad.*

**A** In the sentences below, put a dotted line under the verb used with a pattern described in this Unit. Then underline each of the other parts of the pattern.

1 The storm clouds now extend over much of the planet.
2 The Financial Times says, in effect, the party has chosen to compromise over reform.
3 Water is being sprayed over the cargo holds in an attempt to keep them cool.
4 Nicola, a violinist, triumphed over more than 500 entrants in television's most popular music event.
5 The pain and the psychological upheavals were ignored or glossed over.
6 Economists disagree over how to measure real interest rates.
7 Pour the water into the dish, and pour the apple juice over the apple.
8 He also wrote scores of articles on matters ranging over the whole history of Welsh literature.

**B** Fill in the gaps in these sentences using *over* or *from*.

1 a) A crystal chandelier hung ........................ the high old-fashioned ceiling.
  b) A surreal calm hung ........................ the airport.
2 a) Michael could feel their eyes on him as he climbed down ........................ the bus.
  b) Britain has had to climb down ........................ the status of Hong Kong's negotiators in the British team.
3 a) Inevitably, liberals and conservatives differ ........................ the causes of homelessness.
  b) In what respect would your policies differ ........................ those of the Prime Minister?
4 a) The sun's energy is distributed ........................ the entire surface of the earth.
  b) Food is being distributed ........................ a truck at one end of the port.
5 a) A mood of national mourning descended ........................ Zambia as worldwide condolences poured in.
  b) Drenching rain descended ........................ grey skies on the opening day of the Festival.

**C** Fill in the gaps in the sentences below using the verbs in this list. Use each verb once.

back down   fight   preside   rule   skate   sprinkle   wash   win out

1 It's time the general public learnt that mankind does not ........................ over this natural environment.
2 A mixture of various seeds is ........................ over the fruits.
3 We would rush to the mailbox and ........................ over who got to read the magazine first.
4 Relief ........................ over her beautiful features.
5 Denver hopes to ........................ over other cities for a $1 billion United Airlines maintenance facility.
6 In March 1976, he ........................ over a major international conference on terrorism in Washington.
7 The government has ........................ over plans to change the fire brigades' pay formula.
8 Clever scientists have tended to ........................ over the difficulties of explaining dreams.

# Verbs used with *through*

Some verbs are followed by a prepositional phrase which consists of *through* and a noun group. For example, in *She was looking through a magazine*, the verb *look* is followed by the preposition *through* and the noun group *a magazine*. This pattern is **V *through* n**.

| | Verb group | *through* | noun group |
|---|---|---|---|
| She | sailed | through | her exams. |
| Lloyd | sorted | through | the entire batch. |

Verbs with this pattern belong to the following meaning groups:

■ **verbs concerned with experiencing something or coping with something in a particular way**

| | | | |
|---|---|---|---|
| battle | go | pull | sit |
| come | live | sail | sleep |
| get | pass | scrape | |

'*I **wouldn't go** through that again,*' says Gill with feeling.

*Some patients fail to **live** through the surgery.*

*He **slept** through the entire performance.*

■ **verbs concerned with reading or searching**

| | | | | |
|---|---|---|---|---|
| browse | glance | look | skim | wade |
| flick | go | read | sort | |
| flip | leaf | sift | thumb | |

*I've been **looking** through this handbook, but it doesn't mention anything that fits the description.*

*Police **have been sifting** through the rubble to find out what kind of device it was.*

*It was evident that someone **had gone** through my possessions.*

■ **verbs concerned with making a hole or breaking a barrier**

| | | | | | |
|---|---|---|---|---|---|
| bore | break | cut | dig | drill | smash |

***Drill** through the joint from below.*

*Demonstrators scrambled over walls or used trucks to **smash** through the embassy gates.*

■ **verbs concerned with moving or travelling through a place, thing, or group of things**

| | | | |
|---|---|---|---|
| cut | filter | plough | sweep |

*The boys **cut** through an alley, crossed a street, and turned at the next corner.*

*Only a little sunlight **filtered** through the single dirty window.*

■ **verbs indicating that someone has a thought or feeling, usually briefly. The Subject indicates the thought or feeling.**

| | | | | |
|---|---|---|---|---|
| flash | go | race | run | surge |

*Several possibilities **flashed** through my mind.*

*A convulsive shudder **ran** through his body.*

## Different forms of the pattern

*It will make everything I've **gone** through worthwhile.*

# Practice

**A** In the sentences below, put a dotted line under the verb used with *through*. Then underline each of the other parts of the pattern.

1 I sat through a long interview with the minister for tourism.

2 At least three local rescue teams are on the scene digging through a wall of coal and rock.

3 She was flicking through some magazines when Harry Penrose came into the room.

4 He is a strong man, and he will pull through this operation.

5 Do you have any questions about what we've just read through?

6 A fire officer's car was destroyed as a lorry ploughed through a hedge.

7 He listed the wars he's lived through.


**B** Put the different parts of these sentences in the right order.

1 my father / surgery / through / came / without difficulty

.................................................................................................................................

2 of / raced / her mind / bits and pieces / the past / through

.................................................................................................................................

3 our seats / through / glanced / took / and / the menu / we

.................................................................................................................................

4 of / a fire engine siren / have been known / I / through / to sleep / the wailing

.................................................................................................................................


**C** Fill in the gaps in the sentences below using the verbs in this list. Use each verb once.

break   drill   flash   get   sail   scrape   skim   sweep

1 I went back to our room and ................................. through the newspapers.

2 He helped his son ................................. through a serious crisis.

3 Democratic fervor was ................................. through eastern Europe.

4 The crowd moved back and did not try to ................................. through the police chain.

5 Wilkinson was a gifted psychology student who ................................. through college exams.

6 Many kitchen and bathroom fittings must be screwed to the wall, and this may mean ................................. through a tile.

7 I flushed bright red as a spurt of anger ................................. through me.

8 I became one of the worst students ever to ................................. through the botany school at Oxford.


**D** Fill in the gaps in these sentences. For each pair, one verb from this Unit goes in both sentences.

1 a) Raiders ................................. through padlocks and chains to get into the warehouse.

   b) Soon the little sail had caught the breeze, and the boat began to ................................. through the water.

2 a) I thought you'd be tired after ................................. through so many photos.

   b) All the parties agree the country cannot ................................. through another gruelling and costly election.

# Verbs used with *to*: 1

Some verbs are followed by a prepositional phrase which consists of *to* and a noun group. For example, in *I apologized to him*, the verb *apologize* is followed by the preposition *to* and the noun group *him*. This pattern is **V *to* n**. With some verbs, the preposition is sometimes followed by an '-ing' clause.

|  | Verb group | *to* | noun group/-ing clause |
|---|---|---|---|
| Daniel | had moved | to | Los Angeles. |
| He | admits | to | having self-doubts. |

Verbs with this pattern belong to the following meaning groups:

■ **verbs indicating that someone goes to or reaches a place**

| | | | | |
|---|---|---|---|---|
| come | escape | go round | return | withdraw |
| come round | get | move | run away | |
| cross | go | retire | transfer | |

*Our next door neighbour's moved to New Zealand.*

*As soon as I heard this I went round to his mother's house to give what comfort I could.*

■ **verbs indicating that something comes to someone or that someone gets something**

| | | | |
|---|---|---|---|
| come | fall | occur | transfer |
| come back | go | pass | |

*The attention they deserve will come to them quite naturally.*

*I had rather forgotten what the garden looked like, but as Patty described it, it all came back to me.*

■ **verbs used to indicate that something extends to a particular point, lasts until a particular time, or began at a particular time**

| | | |
|---|---|---|
| date back | go back | reach |
| extend | live | stretch |

*The cornfields stretch to the horizon in every direction.*

*I may live to a ripe old age, but who knows.*

*Parts of the church date back to the seventh century.*

■ **verbs indicating that someone speaks or writes to someone else**

| | | | | |
|---|---|---|---|---|
| apologize | lie | reply | speak | write |
| boast | pray | report | talk | write back |
| complain | propose | report back | talk down | write in |
| confess | read | sing | whisper | write off |

*He needed to talk to someone.*

*'Don't lie to me,' she shouted.*

*She was certain that in the next few months he would propose to her.*

Some of these verbs, particularly *lie*, *speak*, and *talk*, are sometimes used in the passive.

*We're being lied to every day.*

With verbs in this meaning group, a prepositional phrase beginning with *about* is sometimes used after or before the other prepositional phrase to indicate the topic of the speech or writing.

*She says when she complained to her supervisor about the behaviour, no action was taken.*

■ **verbs concerned with admitting something**

| | | |
|---|---|---|
| admit | confess | own up |

*Within a week two young men had confessed to the crime and been arrested.*

*He admitted to liking all the attention.*

■ **verbs concerned with saying or showing that something happened, exists, or is true**

| | | |
|---|---|---|
| point | swear | testify |

*She can't remember committing the murder, although all the evidence points to her guilt.*

*It was him, Sergei. I'd swear to it.*

*One witness testified to hearing the words: 'Don't do it, Peter!'*

■ **verbs indicating that someone communicates by means of a gesture or movement**

| | | |
|---|---|---|
| bow | nod | signal | wave |

*She nodded to Jarvis as he came in.*

**A** In the sentences below, put a dotted line under the verb used with a pattern described in this Unit. Then underline each of the other parts of the pattern. (For different forms of the pattern, see Unit 78.)

1 They just wanted to make a quick fortune so they could retire to the Spanish coast.
2 Many of your best ideas may occur to you at odd moments during the day or night.
3 They realised one day that they had to have a place to escape to.
4 Where are you going to move to?
5 Your child needs to learn that owning up to making a mistake isn't the end of the world.
6 I think you'll find him rather difficult to talk to.
7 Ginny became the friend to whom she could talk about every aspect of her life.
8 I don't know where everyone has gone to.
9 The blown-out church tower testifies to the severity of mortar attacks which have been launched against the small village.
10 Dunne waved to her, indicating there was space beside him on the sofa.

**B** These sentences show the pattern **V that**. Rewrite them using the verb with *to* and an '-ing' clause.

1 Despite the recession, seven out of ten adults admit that they spend money on activities like horse-racing and lotteries.

......................................................................................................................................................

2 Red also confessed that he had driven the getaway car.

......................................................................................................................................................

3 Why had Martin sworn that he'd seen Grace on the July 3rd?

......................................................................................................................................................

4 Eva testified that she had seen Herndon with his gun on the stairs.

......................................................................................................................................................

**C** Fill in the gaps in the sentences below using the verbs in this list. Use each verb once.

cross    date back    lie    pass    reach    report back    signal    withdraw

1 I'll appoint somebody to take notes on what you're saying and ................................ to the class.
2 'Would you please ................................ to the other side of the street,' he said.
3 When he died in 1971, control of the business ................................ to his sons.
4 Federal troops have ................................ to barracks and a ceasefire is in place.
5 Teddy Bears ................................ to 1902 when Theodore 'Teddy' Roosevelt, the US President, could not bring himself to shoot a cub.
6 Bedspreads that ................................ to the floor are generally a nuisance.
7 Margaret ................................ to the waiter, who came at once.
8 It's terrible to know your dad has been ................................ to you all your life about his past.

Here are some more groups of verbs which are followed by the preposition *to* and a noun group or an '-ing' clause:

■ **verbs concerned with doing what someone else wants you to do.** The prepositional phrase indicates that person or their demands.

| bend | cave in | give in | submit | surrender |
|------|---------|---------|--------|-----------|
| bow | defer | sell out | suck up | yield |

The Government **will not bow** to pressure from the Right.

The President is showing no signs that he **will give in** to union demands.

■ **verbs concerned with starting to do something different or starting to be in a different situation**

| change | get back | move over | shoot |
|--------|----------|-----------|-------|
| change over | go over | progress | switch |
| come | move | return | switch over |
| get | move on | revert | turn |

**Switch** to low-fat, wholemeal foods wherever possible.

In various interviews with the media today, he explained why he agreed to **return** to his old job as foreign minister.

She **shot to fame** as a 16-year-old in the film 'Wish You Were Here'.

At first she used a shopping trolley for support, then she **progressed** to walking with a stick.

■ **verbs indicating that someone starts to talk about a different topic**

| come | get back | move | switch | turn |
|------|----------|------|--------|------|
| come back | go back | return | switch over | |

Let us now **turn** to the problem of compensating the population for higher food prices.

**Going back** to the school, how many members of staff are there?

■ **verbs concerned with starting or resuming a task**

| get back | get round | return |
|----------|-----------|--------|
| get down | go back | turn |

Right, lads, let's **get down** to work.

If you'll excuse me, I really **have to get back** to work.

She ignored him and **returned** to painting her nails.

■ **verbs indicating that someone keeps to a belief, agreement, or course of action**

| adhere | cling | hold | keep | stick |
|--------|-------|------|------|-------|

As long as you **stick** to your diet you will lose weight.

They still **cling** to their belief in democracy.

■ **verbs concerned with responding to an event or situation**

| adapt | adjust | react | respond |
|-------|--------|-------|---------|

One of the first world leaders to **react** to the news from Moscow was the British Prime Minister.

At first Maria **could not adjust** to life in London.

■ **verbs indicating that someone dies**

| bleed | choke | freeze | starve |
|-------|-------|--------|--------|

Reports say he **bled to death** after a bullet severed a main artery in his leg.

*Freeze* and *starve* may be used with this pattern to indicate that someone is very cold or very hungry.

Please open the door – I**'m freezing to death** out here.

■ **verbs indicating that someone goes to sleep**

| drift off | drop off | go | nod off |
|-----------|----------|-----|---------|

She **drifted off** to sleep before he could reply.

■ **verbs concerned with dealing with something or serving someone**

| attend | see | tend |
|--------|-----|------|

He added that the President had left the meeting early to **attend** to other matters.

He told me, 'Well, don't worry about it, I**'ll see** to it.'

These verbs are sometimes used in the passive.

Lamy **was attended** to by medics and then airlifted by helicopter to Northampton General Hospital.

■ **verbs concerned with giving, lending, or selling something to someone.** The thing given or sold is not explicitly mentioned.

| contribute | give | hand over | lend | pass | sell |
|------------|------|-----------|------|------|------|

The survey shows that Americans **are** still **giving to charity** despite hard economic times.

In this climate, banks were eager to **lend** to anybody with **a good business idea**.

**A** Fill in the gaps in the sentences below using the verbs in this list. Use each verb once.

adapt   change   contribute   go   keep   return   surrender   tend

1 Her talk kept ................................. to the subject of the decline of the younger generation.
2 About twenty prisoners are still refusing to ................................. to the authorities at Strangeways jail in Manchester.
3 When I came home, I ................................. to sleep because I was so tired.
4 He told me that Communism was not working and they needed to ................................. to a new economic policy.
5 I'm afraid I didn't ................................. to our bargain – I'm sorry.
6 You must be flexible, able to ................................. to any problem or change of circumstance.
7 He won't run in the election because he has to ................................. to his sick wife.
8 Do you want to ................................. to the school fund?

**B** Fill in the gaps in the sentences below using the noun groups in this list. Use each noun group once.

my belief   some business   change   charity   death   pressure   sleep

1 A survey asked 1,245 college professors how much they gave to ................................. each year.
2 He returned late last week to Italy to attend to .................................
3 The company is slow to respond to .................................
4 Scientists believe the Iceman froze to ................................. and was covered by a blanket of snow.
5 The thunder started just as we were nodding off to .................................
6 I still hold to ................................. that people should be allowed to have private lives.
7 The government will not submit to .................................

**C** Match up the two halves of each sentence.

1 We must now move on ...
2 The president will temporarily hand over ...
3 I woke up and couldn't get back ...
4 I am disabled and she sees ...
5 It took him some moments for his eyes to adjust ...

a ... to sleep.
b ... to the darkness of the interior.
c ... to all my needs.
d ... to the next phase of development.
e ... to the vice-president.

**D** Fill in the gaps in the sentences below with the correct particle.

1 I must have dropped ................. to sleep.
2 Alex has fought such a battle to get ................. to a normal life.
3 The Government will not cave ................. to terrorism.
4 The intelligence people switched ................. to more regular duties.
5 As I set off, it occurred to me that I had never got ................. to making a will.
6 His former allies in the nationalist movement had, he said, sold ................. to the communists.
7 To go ................. to what you were saying, there's actually nothing to touch it when it goes well.
8 Handing ................. to his co-pilot, Pegg took Davies into one of the cabins.

**1** Here are some more groups of verbs which are followed by the preposition *to* and a noun group or an '-ing' clause:

■ **verbs indicating that one thing is similar to or the same as another, or is related to it in some way**

| | | | | |
|---|---|---|---|---|
| amount | apply | correspond | measure up | relate |

*That number **corresponds** to a telephone number on this list he gave me.*

*The subject of quality and how it **relates** to school work would be discussed with students.*

■ **verbs indicating that something changes to something else**

| | | | | | |
|---|---|---|---|---|---|
| change | convert | drop | rise | sink | turn |

*Stir until the mixture **changes** to a smooth paste.*

*Before long, the crowd's amusement **turned** to anger.*

*Her voice **dropped** to a whisper.*

■ **verbs indicating that a quantity, level, or thing increases or decreases.** The prepositional phrase indicates the final quantity or level.

| | | | | |
|---|---|---|---|---|
| build | decrease | go down | plunge | slide |
| build up | dip | go up | rise | slip |
| climb | dive | increase | shoot up | slump |
| come down | drop | jump | shrink | soar |
| decline | fall | plummet | sink | tumble |

*The number of people injured **has increased** to almost a thousand.*

*My weight **went down** to seventy pounds.*

■ **verbs used when indicating a total or the result of a calculation**

| | | | |
|---|---|---|---|
| add up | amount | average out | come |

*He said defence spending **amounted** to 17,600 million rupees this year.*

*In 1894 Hamilton scored 196 runs, which **averaged out** to slightly more than 1 per game.*

■ **other common verbs**

| | | | |
|---|---|---|---|
| add | dance | listen | resort |
| agree | extend | lose out | sing along |
| appeal | fall | (not) matter | stand up |
| belong | get through | object | tune in |
| come round | happen | rally | turn |
| contribute | lead | refer | warm |

*This is money which **belongs** to me.*

*What **happened** to James?*

*The poorer nations **objected** to this plan.*

*Agree, listen, object, refer,* and *resort* are sometimes used in the passive.

*Voters rejected the plan even though it **had been agreed** to by all of Canada's political leaders.*

In the case of *object* and *resort*, the preposition *to* is sometimes followed by an '-ing' clause.

*This law was prompted by fears that poor people **might resort** to selling their body parts for hard cash.*

In the case of *lead* and *object*, the preposition *to* is sometimes followed by a noun group and an '-ing' clause.

*The popularity of the fax **has led** to large sums being invested in its development.*

In the case of *refer*, the prepositional phrase is sometimes followed by another prepositional phrase beginning with *as* which indicates what someone or something is called.

*She always **referred** to the murder as 'that business'.*

## Different forms of the pattern

*Who **did** you **talk** to when you were there?*

*We have got to try and find out **who** this **belongs** to.*

*Let us consider first the paintings **to which** Foucault **refers**.*

***The music** is not quite loud enough to **dance** to.*

*I have **some business** to **attend** to.*

*He does not call it capitalism, but that is **what** it **amounts** to.*

**2** A few verbs are followed by two prepositional phrases, the first beginning with *to* and the second beginning with *for*. This pattern is **V *to* n *for* n**.

Most verbs with this pattern are concerned with asking someone for something.

| | | | | |
|---|---|---|---|---|
| appeal | apply | pray | turn | write |

*Detectives **have appealed** to the public for information on the missing girl.*

*Write to the appropriate tourist office for details.*

*Apologize* also has this pattern. The prepositional phrase beginning with *for* indicates why someone apologizes.

*She **apologized** to them for the delay.*

**A** In the sentences below, put a dotted line under the verb used with a pattern described in this Unit. Then underline each of the other parts of the pattern.

1  Something must have happened to him.

2  In response, some people have resorted to carrying guns.

3  But he is prepared to stand up to the critics.

4  They have a right to be listened to by adults.

5  I will not accept the disappearance of the European civilisation to which I belong!

6  There was immediate public concern about what this might lead to.

7  Shortly afterwards he found himself homeless and applied to the council for accommodation.

8  Just knowing that you have someone to turn to can be very helpful.

9  Most people do not object to their records being used for medical research.

10  She steadfastly maintained that her grandsons, whom she always refers to as 'the boys', were innocent.


**B** Rewrite each of the following pairs of sentences as one sentence.

1  In the same month Canada's jobless rate increased. By the end of the month it was 9.3 per cent.
*In the same month Canada's jobless rate increased to 9.3 per cent.*

2  His voice rose. It became a scream.

3  The average monthly wage has fallen. It's now about £19.

4  Her expression changed. It became one of horror.

5  The tax on fuel will go up next spring. It will then be 17.5 per cent.

6  By the 1970s, the number of political clubs had declined. There were only 300.


**C** Rewrite these sentences using the verb given in brackets with the pattern **V** *to* n *for* n.

1  He asked the United States for help in stopping the war. (appeal)

2  I asked God to give me some guidance. (pray)

3  Nicoll was unsure of his ground and sent a letter to Waite asking for advice. (write)

4  I told Fraiser I regretted my treatment of him. (apologize)


157

# Verbs used with *to*: 4

Some verbs are followed by a noun group and a prepositional phrase which consists of *to* and a noun group. For example, in *I lent some money to my father*, the verb *lend* is followed by the noun group *some money*, the preposition *to*, and the noun group *my father*. This pattern is **V n *to* n**. (With phrasal verbs, the particle comes either after the noun group or after the verb.)

## Active pattern

|  | Verb group | noun group | to | noun group |
|---|---|---|---|---|
| We | explained | the situation | to | him. |
| I | showed | the sketches | to | my producer. |

## Passive pattern

|  | Verb group | to | noun group |
|---|---|---|---|
| The car | must be restored | to | its rightful owner. |
| Your findings | should be reported | to | the police. |

Verbs with this pattern belong to the following meaning groups:

■ **verbs concerned with giving, selling, or transferring something to someone**

| | | | | |
|---|---|---|---|---|
| accord | distribute | hand back | pass on | supply |
| assign | donate | hand on | pay | surrender |
| award | export | hand over | present | transfer |
| bring | extend | introduce | rent | transmit |
| commit | feed | lease | restore | turn over |
| concede | give | leave | sell | |
| contribute | give back | lend | serve | |
| dedicate | grant | let | slip | |
| deliver | hand | pass | submit | |

*I **gave** the cards to Helen.*

*The president **assigned** this task to Vice President Al Gore.*

*The building **was leased** to International Creative Management.* (passive)

*The fear is that the disease **could be transmitted** to humans who eat beef.* (passive)

■ **verbs concerned with communicating something to someone**

| | | | |
|---|---|---|---|
| address | describe | pass on | reveal |
| admit | dictate | present | say |
| announce | disclose | put | suggest |
| bid | explain | read | teach |
| break | express | recommend | tell |
| call out | give | relate | wave |
| communicate | introduce | remember | write |
| confess | leak | repeat | |
| deliver | mention | report | |

*She turned and **addressed** her next remarks to Mary Ann.*

*Police **were** last night **breaking** the news of the tragedy to Faye's parents, who were away on holiday.*

*Please **don't** ever **mention** this to Frank.*

*She **wrote** a letter to her parents.*

■ **verbs indicating that someone offers or promises something to someone**

| | | |
|---|---|---|
| offer | pledge | promise |

*Travel companies yesterday **offered** cheap deals to holidaymakers who book next year's break early.*

*He **promised** grants to landowners and farmers.*

■ **verbs indicating that someone shows something to someone**

| | | |
|---|---|---|
| demonstrate | display | show |

*He promised me I'd admire this part of the country, wanted to **show** it to me.*

■ **verbs indicating that someone tells people in authority that someone has done something wrong**

| | | | |
|---|---|---|---|
| betray | denounce | report | turn in |

*The few who challenged him disappeared or **were betrayed** to the police.* (passive)

In the case of *turn in*, the noun group following the verb is often a reflexive pronoun.

*The third suspect **turned** himself **in** to the police department later that afternoon.*

**A** In the sentences below, put a dotted line under the verb used with *to*. Then underline each of the other parts of the pattern. (For different forms of the pattern, see Unit 81.)

1  We never displayed emotion to each other.
2  The gallery director surrendered his keys to the building manager.
3  The guest house had been recommended to me by a friend.
4  Over the past five years, offices in the city have been rented to the public sector.
5  You've never been able to pledge your loyalty to me.
6  He announced that Egypt had presented proposals to the United Nations.
7  In the end, Newman reports to the police an attack on him and a neighbour by the local gang.
8  It's a tragedy he may not be able to pass the company on to his children.

**B** Rewrite these sentences using the pattern **V n *to* n**.

1  She convinced her husband to lend their son $1,200 to start his own business.
   *She convinced her husband to lend $1,200 to their son to start his own business.*

2  She also taught university students English.
   ............................................................................................................................................................

3  I handed Eleanor the letter.
   ............................................................................................................................................................

4  In 1979, only 8 per cent of British firms awarded managers annual bonuses.
   ............................................................................................................................................................

5  When I told my doctor this, he looked worried.
   ............................................................................................................................................................

6  A widower has left a dogs' home £60,000.
   ............................................................................................................................................................

7  He had sold Paramount the film rights in 1926.
   ............................................................................................................................................................

8  He gave the President a message from his kidnappers.
   ............................................................................................................................................................

**C** Fill in the gaps in the sentences below using the verbs in this list. Use each verb once.

admit     break     deliver     demonstrate     denounce
describe     dictate     present     promise     suggest

1  I was a little doubtful when this project was ................................ to me by the Editor.
2  He ................................ a speech to the Rio summit yesterday.
3  Italy has ................................ economic aid to Albania to discourage migration.
4  The award was ................................ to her by the Rt. Honourable Lord Dennis Howell.
5  The bank ................................ its error to the Clarkes and offered to rectify the situation.
6  If he ................................ Evans to the police, none of them would ever keep the money.
7  The news was ................................ to Diana late on Tuesday night.
8  Get a picture in your head and ................................ that person to me.
9  This technique was ................................ to me by my friend, Ellen Zariodis.
10  The Story of Art was ................................ to a typist three mornings a week entirely from memory.

# Verbs used with *to*: 5

Here are some more groups of verbs which are followed by a noun group and a prepositional phrase beginning with *to*:

■ verbs concerned with **adding something to something else** or **connecting one thing to another**, either physically or metaphorically

| | | | |
|---|---|---|---|
| add | compare | lend | relate |
| attach | connect | link | stick |
| bring | join | match | tie |

*This herb **adds** a lovely flavour to the food.*

*The optic nerve **connects** the eye to the brain.*

*The government **has attached** conditions to its peace proposals which are unacceptable to the rebels.*

*The President appeared to **link** a solution to the Gulf crisis to talks on other Middle East disputes.*

*George Orwell **compared** writing a book to having an illness.*

■ verbs concerned with **attributing a particular thing, event, or quality to someone or something**

| | | | |
|---|---|---|---|
| ascribe | attach | attribute | put down |

*He said their success **could be put down** to their simplicity and their clean image.* (passive)

The preposition *to* is sometimes followed by an '-ing' clause.

*Kelly **attributes** her coping ability to growing up in a big family.*

The preposition *to* is sometimes followed by a noun group and an '-ing' clause.

*Some officials **attribute** this to people not knowing where to go.*

■ verbs concerned with **sending or taking someone or something to a place**, or allowing them into a place or organization

| | | | |
|---|---|---|---|
| admit | drive | post | send | transmit |
| commit | lead | refer | take | |
| direct | mail | return | transfer | |

*He **directed** them to a classroom and dashed off.*

*He borrowed heavily to **send** his three sons to the best schools.*

*I **sent** a letter to the hospital, explaining what an exceptional patient she was.*

■ verbs concerned with **appointing someone to a position**, or with **moving them from one job or role to another**

| | | | |
|---|---|---|---|
| appoint | nominate | promote | recruit | transfer |

*The Hungarian Prime Minister **has appointed** two new ministers to his government.*

*The women **were transferred** to other jobs that paid less.* (passive)

■ verbs concerned with **changing something to something else**

| | | | |
|---|---|---|---|
| change | cut down | lower | reduce |
| convert | drop | promote | shorten |
| cut | increase | raise | turn |

*As part of his conversion he **changed** his name to Muhammad Ali.*

*He had a tendency to **drop** his voice to a whisper.*

*Her mother's pension **has** just **been raised** to 16,000 roubles a month.* (passive)

*Kelly **was promoted** to senior vice-president.* (passive)

Many of these verbs are sometimes followed by a noun group and two prepositional phrases, the first beginning with *from*, and the second beginning with *to*.

*The bank **increased** its interest rate from 8 percent to 8.75 per cent.*

*The period for appeal against death sentences **was reduced** from ten days to three.* (passive)

**A** Match up the two halves of each sentence.

1 Why do you compare yourself ...
2 The public no longer attaches any stigma ...
3 Try to relate your child's homework ...
4 You may put this down ...
5 We will then post the leaflets ...
6 The Prime Minister promoted her ...
7 The detector converts the light ...
8 He calmly admitted them ...

a ... to everyday life.
b ... to the house.
c ... to divorce.
d ... to an electrical signal.
e ... to them having no sense of humour.
f ... to you free of charge.
g ... to a Cabinet position.
h ... to your sister all the time?

**B** Put the different parts of these sentences in the right order.

1 to / tie / the ladder / a branch / firmly ..............................................................................
2 six points / have reduced / Arsenal / to / Liverpool's lead ..............................................
3 he / to / in 1968 / Assistant Director / was promoted ..................................................
4 the hospital / referred / to / her / I / for a scan ..........................................................
5 details of the bet / the central computer / were transmitted / to

.....................................................................................................................................................

6 have cut / 9 percent / to / Chase Manhattan and Mellon banks / their lending rates

.....................................................................................................................................................

**C** Fill in the gaps in the sentences below using the nouns in this list. Use each noun once.

accidents   applicants   fires   job   painting   profits   visits

1 As many as 70 per cent of .................................. are attributed to driver error.
2 The captain was informed he had been appointed to another ..................................
3 .................................. will be returned to the United States in dollars.
4 She would like to cut the .................................. down to one a month.
5 They held details of job vacancies and they tried to match .................................. to jobs.
6 So far only one death is attributed to the ..................................
7 Rubens brought a new vitality to ..................................

**D** Rewrite the sentences below using the words or figures given in brackets and the prepositions *from* and *to*.

1 The government computer changed his birthdate. (1917 / 1971)
*The government computer changed his birthdate from 1917 to 1971.*..................................
2 Several of the major banks dropped their interest rates. (7.5 percent / 8 percent)

.....................................................................................................................................................

3 Soon after I arrived, I raised our advertising budget. ($15 million / $100 million)

.....................................................................................................................................................

4 They have rejected plans to lower the voting age. (18 / 20)

.....................................................................................................................................................

5 The Free Democratic Party was able to increase its vote. (9 percent / 11 percent)

.....................................................................................................................................................

# Verbs used with *to*: 6

Here are some more groups of verbs which are followed by a noun group and a prepositional phrase beginning with *to*:

■ **verbs concerned with inviting someone to take part in something**

| | | |
|---|---|---|
| ask | challenge | invite |

*She **invited** us to a lavish party to celebrate her fiftieth birthday.*

■ **verbs concerned with putting someone or something in a particular state, or making them behave in a particular way**

| | | | | |
|---|---|---|---|---|
| drive | move | reduce | restore | put up |

*Atkins admits that the nightmare **has driven** her to thoughts of suicide.*

*She **was reduced** to begging on the streets.* (passive)

■ **verbs concerned with making someone experience something unpleasant**

| | | | | |
|---|---|---|---|---|
| condemn | expose | put | sentence | subject |

*The main aim must be to find these children families and **not condemn** them to institutions.*

In the case of *put*, the prepositional phrase is always *to death*.

*They **were** declared heretics and **put to death**.* (passive)

■ **verbs indicating that someone injures, scares, or bores someone.** The prepositional phrase is used to indicate the result or degree of the action or effect.

| | | | |
|---|---|---|---|
| beat | crush | kick | stab |
| bore | drink | scare | starve |
| burn | frighten | shoot | |

*I wish Alex would take me out, but I'm afraid I **bore** him to death.*

*They were afraid that if they made the slightest mistake they **would be beaten** to a pulp.* (passive)

In the case of *drink*, the noun group following the verb is always a reflexive pronoun. The verb *starve* often has this pattern as well.

*He thought he was a failure and **drank** himself to death.*

■ **verbs concerned with concentrating on or restricting yourself to one particular thing**

| | | | | |
|---|---|---|---|---|
| address | confine | give | pay | turn |
| apply | dedicate | give over | restrict | |
| commit | devote | limit | switch | |

*He wants to **devote** more time to his family.*

*Sean then **turned** his attention to marketing his company's product.*

*I no longer **paid** attention to my lessons.*

With many of these verbs, the noun group following the verb is often a reflexive pronoun. In the case of *address*, it is always a reflexive pronoun.

*The Guardian **addresses** itself to the question of how the Labour opposition should act over the issue.*

*We don't want to **commit** ourselves to doing anything that might require too much strength, endurance, or time.*

*You should try to **limit** yourself to three cups of tea a day.*

■ **other common verbs**

| | | | | |
|---|---|---|---|---|
| apply | expose | introduce | owe | trace back |
| attract | give | leave | postpone | treat |
| do | help | lend | prefer | |
| draw | hold | mean | trace | |

*Gently **apply** the cream to the affected areas.*

*I want to **draw** your attention to some other statistics that were published during the late 1980s.*

*He is a fine sportsman who **has given** pleasure to millions of people.*

*I'm going to **hold** you to your promise, so don't you forget.*

*The goalkeeper seemed to **prefer** dribbling the ball up the field to defending his goal.*

In the case of this sense of *lend*, the noun group following the verb is always a reflexive pronoun. The verb *help* often has this pattern as well.

*The system **did not lend** itself to rapid reform.*

*Do help yourself to another drink.*

In the case of *mean*, the noun group following the verb is always an **amount**.

*Our mothers' approval **means** a lot to us.*

## Different forms of the pattern

*What **did** he **say** to you?*

*Who **did** you **give** the money to?*

*Do you know what she **said** to me today?*

*He was to have been guest of honour at a banquet to which 250 guests **had been invited**.*

*He said he **would hand over** to the police any weapons found in the building that day.*

*I wanted to punish him for what he **did to me**.*

**A** In the sentences below, put a dotted line under the verb used with *to*. Then underline each of the other parts of the pattern.

1 Looking for alternatives, he was attracted to the newspaper business.

2 We have to trace the problem right back to its source.

3 His family will have to take measures to prevent him from drinking himself to death.

4 Why should householders be subjected to the same question year after year?

5 Last week thousands were moved to tears at the sombre memorial service in the town.

6 That was the goal to which she had dedicated herself since Franklin's birth.

7 He told me to just ask you to the dance like a normal person.

8 I split up from a long-term girlfriend and started to apply myself to my work in a really concentrated way.

**B** Fill in the gaps in the sentences below using the verbs in this list. Use each verb once.

bore   challenge   condemn   devote   limit   postpone   prefer   reduce

1 He overheard two women talking about a new children's book that had ................................. them to tears.

2 On March 24, he ................................. Brookes to a fight.

3 He'd really thought he could continue drinking if he ................................. himself to champagne.

4 The hearing has now been ................................. to August 3.

5 Many papers continue to ................................. several pages to the various aspects of events in the Soviet Union.

6 The government ................................. them to a life of poverty.

7 I think I ................................. the snow to this dreary rain.

8 He'll probably ................................. you to death talking about carpentry all day!

**C** Rewrite these sentences using the verb given in brackets with the pattern **V n *to* n** or its passive.

1 I would like to focus your attention on the article overleaf. (draw)
*I would like to draw your attention to the article overleaf.*..................................

2 She could receive the death sentence if she is convicted. (sentence)

..................................................................................

3 Your job is important to you, isn't it? (mean)

..................................................................................

4 Why are we having to suffer all these inconveniences? (expose)

..................................................................................

5 Callwell also dealt with the difficult problem of reprisals. (address)

..................................................................................

6 None of his immediate family were on the guest list for his wedding. (invite)

..................................................................................

7 They would still rather have fish and chips than fruit and fibre. (prefer)

..................................................................................

# UNIT 82 Verbs used with *towards*

**1** Some verbs are followed by a prepositional phrase which consists of *towards* or *toward* and a noun group. For example, in *We are heading towards war*, the verb *head* is followed by the preposition *towards* and the noun group *war*. This pattern is **V *towards* n**. With some verbs, the preposition is sometimes followed by an '-ing' clause.

| | Verb group | *towards* | noun group/-ing clause |
|---|---|---|---|
| We | are racing | towards | complete economic collapse. |
| Bernard | worked | towards | reversing these attitudes. |

Verbs with this pattern belong to the following meaning groups:

■ verbs indicating that someone or something is going to be in a particular state or situation, or is going to do a particular thing

| | | | |
|---|---|---|---|
| drift | head | race | shift |
| edge | move | rush | turn |

*The ruling party seems to **be heading** towards a resounding defeat.*

*The United States **has** apparently **shifted** towards neutrality.*

■ verbs indicating that someone or something is likely to have a particular characteristic or opinion, or to do a particular thing

| | |
|---|---|
| lean | tend |

*They're very anxious, and they **tend** towards depression.*

■ verbs concerned with trying to achieve something

| | |
|---|---|
| strive | work |

*Students participating in the programme are encouraged to **strive** towards a high level of achievement.*

*We need to **work** toward giving women and children the power and resources to protect themselves.*

■ verbs indicating that something or someone is partly responsible for something happening or being achieved

| | | | |
|---|---|---|---|
| contribute | count | help | lead |

*The slowing down of the domestic economy **helped** towards the improvement in exports.*

*People from the neighbourhood **have contributed** towards the cost of the shrine.*

*The document they have drafted **should help** towards finding a solution to the crisis.*

## Different forms of the pattern

*This is **something** we **are** continually **working** towards.*

**2** Some verbs are followed by a noun group and a prepositional phrase which consists of *towards* or *toward* and a noun group. For example, in *She is now directing her talents towards music*, the verb *direct* is followed by the noun group *her talents*, the preposition *towards*, and the noun group *music*. This pattern is **V n *towards* n**. With some verbs, the preposition is sometimes followed by an '-ing' clause.

## Active pattern

| | Verb group | noun group | *towards* | noun group/-ing |
|---|---|---|---|---|
| They | contributed | $3 | towards | costs. |
| He | directed | his efforts | towards | helping people. |

## Passive pattern

| | Verb group | *towards* | noun group/-ing |
|---|---|---|---|
| We | are drawn | towards | a life of simplicity. |
| The savings | were put | towards | reducing the deficit. |

Verbs with this pattern belong to the following meaning groups:

■ verbs concerned with causing someone to do something or be attracted to something

| | |
|---|---|
| draw | push |

*This, coupled with his wife's death, **pushed** him towards resignation in 1983.*

*O'Keeffe **was drawn** towards art from an early age.* (passive)

■ verbs concerned with providing part of a sum of money

| | | |
|---|---|---|
| contribute | give | put |

*The British government **contributed** £50,000 toward the cost of the relief operation.*

*Any spare money **is put** towards buying a flock of sheep.* (passive)

■ *Direct* also has this pattern.

*Planning **is** therefore largely **directed** towards improving or preserving existing living conditions.* (passive)

**Practice**

**A** In the sentences below, put a dotted line under the verb used with a pattern described in this Unit. Then underline each of the other parts of the pattern.

1 Politically I lean towards the right.
2 Marriage was something I believed every girl strove towards.
3 While offering credit, the course would not count toward graduation requirements.
4 We need to pull the British economy out of the recession it now seems to be heading towards.
5 It's a typical political diversion to direct responsibility towards the family.

**B** Put the different parts of these sentences in the right order.

1 is working / he / his Air Transport Pilot's Licence / towards

2 being organised / firms / towards / on a regional basis / are edging

3 inevitably / towards / are pushed / using bank overdraft facilities / they

4 moved / the president / decentralizing his country's rigid state-run economy / towards

**C** Fill in the gaps in these sentences using *towards* or *to* (see Units 77 and 78).

1 We're probably heading ...................... avoiding major choices and major decisions.
2 His debts amounted ...................... over a thousand million dollars.
3 The American healthcare system is shifting ...................... preventive care.
4 The Parliament has agreed ...................... changes in the constitution.
5 The island's banks will not normally lend ...................... small and medium-sized companies.
6 The sleet changed ...................... snow and a blanket of white soon obscured the trail.
7 His £1,000 grant will help ...................... the cost of books, paper and especially postage.
8 Chinese cuisine is 4000 years old and tends ...................... the exotic and spectacular.

**D** Rewrite these sentences using the verb given in brackets with *towards*.

1 It's in their interest to promote whatever encourages greater cooperation. (lead)
   *It's in their interest to promote whatever leads towards greater cooperation.*
2 We are now heading for a terrible war that would be fought with highly destructive bombs. (rush)

3 Small businesses had each donated $3000 for the event. (contribute)

4 It is not surprising that they are trying to have separate identities. (strive)

5 Some of the president's advisers are beginning to favour the use of air attacks. (lean)

6 On the surface, the country is gradually getting closer to democracy. (move)

7 An increasing number of men are interested in facial cosmetic surgery. (turn)

# Verbs used with *with*: 1

Some verbs are followed by a prepositional phrase which consists of *with* and a noun group. For example, in *I couldn't cope with the pressure*, the verb *cope* is followed by the preposition *with* and the noun group *the pressure*. This pattern is **V *with* n**. With some verbs, the preposition is sometimes followed by an '-ing' clause.

|  | Verb group | *with* | noun group/-ing clause |
|---|---|---|---|
| I | can't cope | with | relationships. |
| The volunteers | will help | with | teaching English. |

Many verbs with this pattern are **reciprocal verbs**. These verbs are dealt with in Unit 87, and are not included in the lists in this unit.

Verbs with this pattern belong to the following meaning groups:

■ **verbs concerned with coping or dealing with a problem**

| | | | |
|---|---|---|---|
| battle | deal | grapple | wrestle |
| cope | fight | struggle | |

She **has had to cope** with losing all her previous status and money.

*Deal* is sometimes used in the passive.

The matter **has been dealt** with by the school to our satisfaction.

■ **verbs concerned with continuing to do something, or doing something that has been planned**

| | | | |
|---|---|---|---|
| carry on | go ahead | persevere | proceed |
| continue | go on | persist | push ahead |
| get on | go through | press on | stick |

We **must continue** with the campaign.

In the New Year, the district board will vote on whether to **go ahead** with the plan.

I **couldn't get on** with clearing up in the kitchen because they kept quarrelling.

■ **verbs indicating that someone gets involved with something or someone, sometimes when this is undesirable**

| | | | |
|---|---|---|---|
| (not) bother | interfere | play around | work |
| dabble | mess about | tamper | |
| experiment | play | toy | |

I **didn't experiment** with drugs until I was in my mid-20s.

They say they **will not interfere** with press freedom.

I **played around** with the colour until I got the effect I wanted.

Most of these verbs are sometimes used in the passive.

The vehicle's brakes **had been tampered** with.

■ **verbs concerned with helping someone to do something**

| | | |
|---|---|---|
| assist | help | help out |

She loved **helping out** with amateur dramatic productions.

They **can assist** with organising car hire, ferry tickets, and flights to Geneva.

They **help with feeding the cows.**

■ **verbs concerned with associating with someone, or beginning to have an association with them**

| | | | | |
|---|---|---|---|---|
| associate | get in | go round | keep in | register |
| carry on | get off | integrate | move in | take up |

The point is, I'm not supposed to **associate** with Westerners, except in the way of business.

His wife says she'd have known if he **was carrying on** with any other woman.

Before you **register** with a new doctor, ask around to find one who is good with children.

■ **verbs concerned with speaking to someone**

| | | | |
|---|---|---|---|
| consult | laugh | plead | reason |

I tried to **reason with him.**

In the case of *plead*, the prepositional phrase is sometimes followed by a to-infinitive clause.

I **pleaded** with her to stop but she wouldn't.

**A** In the sentences below, put a dotted line under the verb used with a pattern described in this Unit. Then underline each of the other parts of the pattern. (For different forms of the pattern, see Unit 84.)

1 If you are taking tranquillizers and want to stop, consult with your doctor first.

2 I don't know whether I can go through with this.

3 Do you cope well with stress?

4 I found this quite hard to deal with.

5 We are in a country where nature has been interfered with for a very long time.

6 And on the dressing table sits the clutter of make-up that Nikki loved to experiment with.

7 I pleaded with Frances to get a move on as she dawdled to the car.

**B** Rewrite these sentences using the pattern V *with* n.

1 The President is putting his life at risk by continuing to exercise in a stressful way.
*The President is putting his life at risk by continuing with stressful exercise.*

2 He simply carried on working. ........................................................

3 They had planned to go on investigating. ........................................................

4 Meanwhile, the House of Lords select committees have been pressing on and doing important work.
........................................................

5 The task of a coalition government would be to push ahead and create a market economy.
........................................................

**C** Rewrite each of the following pairs of sentences as one sentence, using *with* and a noun group or '-ing' clause.

1 They carve, sell and demonstrate their products. Their children help.
*Their children help with carving, selling and demonstrating their products.*

2 There may be a major famine in Mozambique. We do not have the resources to cope.
........................................................

3 We are planning the closing ceremonies for October. Volunteers are needed immediately to assist.
........................................................

4 I used to wear expensive jewellery. Now I don't bother.
........................................................

5 Have you considered a softer hair-style? Now is the time to experiment.
........................................................

**D** Fill in the gaps in the sentences below using the verbs in this list. Use each verb once.

deal   integrate   interfere   reason

1 For immigrants there are difficulties in ................................. with the local community.

2 I try to ................................. with him but sometimes he just doesn't listen and I end up shouting at him.

3 He's threatening to use his gun on anyone who tries to ................................. with him.

4 Special police squads were set up to ................................. with the problem of football violence.

Here are some more groups of verbs which are followed by the preposition *with* and a noun group:

■ **verbs indicating that someone does something, or has a particular physical sensation, because of an emotion**

| burn | laugh | scream | sigh |
|------|-------|--------|------|
| cry | roar | shake | tremble |

*The audience **screamed** with delight.*

*She **was trembling** with rage.*

**Productive use:** Any verb which indicates behaviour or a physical feeling can be used with this pattern.

■ **verbs concerned with beginning or ending**

| begin | finish | open | start off |
|-------|--------|------|-----------|
| end | kick off | start | |

*The proceedings **began** with a minute's silence in memory of those who died in the revolution.*

The preposition *with* is sometimes followed by a noun group and an '-ing' clause.

*An earlier attempt by police to remove the demonstrators **ended** with a policeman being shot dead.*

■ **verbs concerned with responding to something that has been done.** The prepositional phrase indicates what someone does in response.

| compensate | counter | reply | respond |
|------------|---------|-------|---------|

*I said hello. Brent **responded** with a glare.*

■ **verbs indicating that something has or contains a lot of something else, or that someone is full of a quality or feeling**

| abound | bulge | be crawling | fill | swarm |
|--------|-------|-------------|------|-------|
| bristle | be bursting | drip | fill up | teem |

*The town **was crawling** with visitors today.*

*Both horse and rider **were dripping** with sweat within five minutes.*

*Fill* and *fill up* indicate that something becomes full of something else.

*Catherine's eyes **filled** with tears.*

■ **verbs indicating that something is compatible with something else, or like something else**

| accord | (not) compare | comply | fit in | tie in |
|--------|---------------|--------|--------|--------|

*Nearly all chores can wait or be organised to **fit in** with a weekly schedule.*

*The emergency lighting system **should comply** with British Standard 5266.*

■ **verbs indicating that someone agrees or disagrees with something such as a plan**

| agree | (not) argue | disagree | fall in | go along |
|-------|-------------|----------|---------|----------|

*I **do not disagree** with this viewpoint.*

*The three main political parties are likely to **go along** with the plan, despite some private reservations.*

■ **verbs concerned with reaching or remaining at a particular level or position**

| catch up | fall behind | keep up |
|----------|-------------|---------|

*If children are removed from their poor environments, they **can catch up** with other children.*

*He faces losing his home after **falling behind** with the payments while in jail.*

■ **other common verbs**

| belong | meet | rest | sympathize |
|--------|------|------|------------|
| check | rank | stock up | |

*You **should** always **check** with your doctor before starting on regular medication.*

*The continuing process of patient negotiation **has met** with limited success.*

*The decision to free him **rests** with the Belgian Justice Minister.*

## Productive uses

1 The prepositional phrase indicates what someone uses to do something. An example is *I **shave** with an old-fashioned Gillette razor.*

2 The prepositional phrase indicates what company someone uses, for example when travelling or investing money. Examples are *We **flew** with British Airways* and *My husband **has banked** with the Co-op since before the war.*

## Different forms of the pattern

*In the cases that we're **dealing** with, they were not sure what their rights were.*

*There are some feelings **which** are hard to **cope** with.*

*Sit him in a highchair with **a toy** to **play** with.*

***What** we **are dealing** with here is pure wickedness.*

## A Fill in the gaps in the sentences below using the nouns in this list. Use each noun once.

despair  exhaustion  joy  laughter  relief  resentment  terror

1 He had his audience of 500 journalists roaring with ................................... at his first joke.
2 Forstmann was a deeply angry man, burning with ...................................
3 She wraps her arms around herself and starts to cry with ...................................
4 Two minutes later he clambered out and stood, shaking with ..................................., at the side of the pool.
5 Crews and sponsors sigh with ................................... when boats reach the finish in one piece.
6 He is so happy that he just laughs with ...................................
7 He remembers screaming with ................................... at being taken away by a stranger.

## B Match up the two halves of each sentence.

1 The ships bristle ...                a ... with tears.
2 His face was dripping ...            b ... with reporters.
3 Our wallets bulge ...                c ... with confidence.
4 The house was swarming ...           d ... with sweat.
5 The priest's eyes filled ...         e ... with fish.
6 I was bursting ...                   f ... with wounded.
7 The rivers and lakes abound ...      g ... with new equipment.
8 Our hospital quickly filled up ...   h ... with credit cards.

## C Fill in the gaps in the sentences below using the verbs in this list. Use each verb once.

check  compare  counter  fall in  fit in  keep up  meet  start  stock up  sympathize

1 Alison ................................... with her employer's wishes.
2 It doesn't ................................... with the real thing, does it?
3 But this plan has ................................... with resistance within the SPD.
4 There was trouble last night that ................................... with a fight in a restaurant.
5 'Where you off to?' he asked Hugh, walking quickly to ................................... with him.
6 I think those who ................................... with the group make up a fairly significant percentage of the population.
7 Women do not enjoy equal status with men. My critics will doubtless ................................... with the argument that men and women cannot be equal because they are different.
8 What the hospitals want ................................... with some of the president's goals for health care reform.
9 He tells me to ................................... with him before I buy any new equipment for the business.
10 I put the answering machine on, ................................... with plenty of food and arrange not to see anyone.

# Verbs used with *with*: 3

Some verbs are followed by a noun group and a prepositional phrase which consists of *with* and a noun group. For example, in *I covered my face with my hands*, the verb *cover* is followed by the noun group *my face*, the preposition *with*, and the noun group *my hands*. This pattern is **V n *with* n**.

## Active pattern

|  | Verb group | noun group | *with* | noun group |
|---|---|---|---|---|
| People | associate<br>Blend | good looks<br>the spinach | with<br>with | good deeds.<br>the egg yolks. |

## Passive pattern

|  | Verb group | *with* | noun group |
|---|---|---|---|
| The paper<br>The cake | will be printed<br>was topped | with<br>with | your own name.<br>chocolate icing. |

(With phrasal verbs, the particle comes either after the noun group or after the verb.)

Verbs with this pattern belong to the following meaning groups:

■ **verbs concerned with considering two people, things, or groups as being the same or connected**

| associate | confuse | identify | match | mix up |
|---|---|---|---|---|
| compare | connect | link | match up | muddle up |

*You have to stop **associating** beauty with gardens or lawns.*

*For most of her long professional life she **was identified** with the theatre.* (passive)

The verb and the preposition *with* are sometimes followed by '-ing' clauses.

*Again and again, we seem to **confuse** talking about an issue with doing something about it.*

■ **verbs concerned with joining or mixing two or more things, physically or metaphorically**

| blend | connect | link | mix |
|---|---|---|---|
| combine | integrate | merge | |

***Mix** the egg yolks with the milk.*

*Heavy consumption of alcohol **is linked** with cancer of the liver.* (passive)

The verb and the preposition *with* are sometimes followed by '-ing' clauses.

*Laura **combines** bringing up a family with buying and selling young horses.*

■ **verbs concerned with giving something to someone or something**

| arm | fit | infect | leave | serve |
|---|---|---|---|---|
| equip | fix up | inject | present | shower |
| feed | furnish | issue | provide | supply |

*He refused to **provide** them with this information.*

*I'll see if I **can fix** you **up** with a job.*

■ **verbs concerned with changing the appearance of something by adding things to it**

| decorate | hang | mark | print | stamp | trim |
|---|---|---|---|---|---|

*The wall facing him **was decorated** with elaborate dark wood carvings.* (passive)

*Each photo **is** automatically **printed** with the date on which it was taken.* (passive)

■ **verbs concerned with putting something around or on top of something, or with covering the surface of something, physically or metaphorically**

| cover | spread | top | wrap up |
|---|---|---|---|
| line | surround | wrap | |

***Cover** the pan with a damp cloth and leave it to cool.*

*Her technique was to **surround** herself with strong women and weak men.*

■ **verbs concerned with filling something, physically or metaphorically**

| cram | fill up | load | pack | soak |
|---|---|---|---|---|
| fill | flood | load up | pile | stuff |

*Then it was time to pack the bags, **load up** the vehicles with bikes and trophies, and make for the airport.*

*I try to **fill** my mind with other things by getting out and about.*

■ **verbs concerned with scattering objects or a liquid on something**

| shower | spray | sprinkle | strew |
|---|---|---|---|

*Firemen **sprayed** the wreckage with foam to prevent the plane catching fire.*

**A** Rewrite these sentences using the pattern **V n _with_ n** or its passive.

1 Spread the rest of the butter on the bread.
*Spread the bread with the rest of the butter.*
..............................................................................................................

2 Paul and the boys have loaded baskets onto a wagon.
..............................................................................................................

3 Sprinkle chopped chives over the fish.
..............................................................................................................

4 Nicotine should be sprayed on the trees about a week after the petals have fallen.
..............................................................................................................

5 I was cramming sausage into my mouth when I heard the news.
..............................................................................................................

6 Fixed entry times will be printed on the tickets to cut unnecessary queuing.
..............................................................................................................

7 As far as he knew, none of the three had supplied any information to the police prior to the raid.
..............................................................................................................

8 The award was to have been presented to Mr Mandela at the concert in his honour on Monday.
..............................................................................................................

9 The band are so noisy that before taking the stage they stuff little bits of foam in their ears.
..............................................................................................................

**B** Rewrite these sentences using the verb given in brackets instead of *give* or *put*.

1 The government has given its troops modern Chinese-made weapons. (equip)
*The government has equipped its troops with modern Chinese-made weapons.*
..............................................................................................................

2 We put balloons and streamers round the dining room. (decorate)
..............................................................................................................

3 Staff will be given new grey-and-yellow designer uniforms. (issue)
..............................................................................................................

4 Put a clean handkerchief over your nose and mouth. (cover)
..............................................................................................................

5 This gave Frances a perfect excuse for leaving home. (provide)
..............................................................................................................

6 We put into carts all the blankets, bandages, and medication we could spare. (load up)
..............................................................................................................

**C** Match up the two halves of each sentence.

1 Certain people are linked in our minds ...     a ... with the painting of Picasso.
2 Envy is often confused ...                      b ... with flower petals, spices, or dried leaves.
3 In 1960 the News Chronicle was merged ...       c ... with jealousy.
4 Other teas are blended ...                      d ... with existing radiators.
5 The boiler can be connected ...                 e ... with certain scents.
6 Her work in dance has been compared ...         f ... with the Daily Mail.

# Verbs used with *with*: 4

Here are some more groups of verbs which are followed by a noun group and a prepositional phrase beginning with *with*:

■ **verbs concerned with doing something with another person**

| | | | |
|---|---|---|---|
| agree | do | negotiate | take up |
| check | exchange | pick | talk over |
| conclude | fight | play | talk through |
| debate | have | share | trade |
| discuss | hold | strike | |
| dispute | make | swap | |

*The university might acquire some more property if it **can agree** a deal with the city council.*

*Many prefer to **talk** these issues **through** with a careers adviser or close friend.*

*But who would choose to **pick** a fight with this man?*

*Further talks **are being held** with the protest leaders.* (passive)

Many of these verbs are **reciprocal verbs**: see Unit 88.

■ **verbs concerned with speaking to someone about an unwelcome subject**

| | | | |
|---|---|---|---|
| bore | bother | burden | confront |

*I **won't bore** you with private matters.*

*I pulled on a coat and boots and went round right away to **confront** Muriel with her stupidity and cowardice.*

■ **verbs indicating that someone has problems**

| | | | |
|---|---|---|---|
| be beset | be confronted | be faced | be weighed down |

*The oil and gas industries **are beset** with labour production problems.* (passive)

*As the fire burned, Stackpole and his wife **were faced with** making decisions on what they would save.* (passive)

■ **verbs concerned with thinking about or reacting towards something or someone in a particular way**

| | | | | |
|---|---|---|---|---|
| acknowledge | greet | meet | regard | treat | view |

*I asked them to **treat** me with respect.*

*Any newcomers **are** always **viewed** with suspicion.* (passive)

■ **verbs concerned with spending your time doing or dealing with something**

| | | |
|---|---|---|
| busy | concern | occupy | trouble |

The noun group following the verb is always a reflexive pronoun.

*The other women **occupied** themselves with their perpetual sewing.*

*She snapped on the lights and **busied** herself with preparing a quick dinner.*

■ **verbs concerned with beginning or ending a period of time or an event in a particular way**

| | | | | | |
|---|---|---|---|---|---|
| begin | close | end | finish | open | start |

*He **began** the day with a seven o'clock breakfast.*

*You may want to **end** the session with a hug.*

■ **verbs concerned with helping someone**

| | | | |
|---|---|---|---|
| assist | help | help off | help on |

*You **might be able to help** us with a problem.*

*I was then asked to **assist** them with raising the profile of the club.*

*He **helped** her **on** with her coat.*

■ **other common verbs**

| | | | | |
|---|---|---|---|---|
| charge | do | replace | threaten | trust |

*They now seem to be setting out to **replace** the people with robots.*

*1,000 of the world's 9,700 bird species **are threatened** with extinction.* (passive)

In the case of *do*, the noun group following the verb is always an **amount**.

*You **can do** quite a lot with quite a little money if you channel it in the right direction.*

**Productive use:** A prepositional phrase beginning with *with* is often used to indicate what someone uses to do something. An example is *An ordinary wooden door **has been reinforced** with steel plates*, which means that the steel plates have been used to reinforce the door.

## Different forms of the pattern

*What **were** you **charged** with?*

*The other animal we **associate** with Spain is the hardworking, long-suffering mule.*

*Sceptics are right to **treat** with caution the results produced using this method.*

*Each person will be given a box and **some photographs** to **decorate** it with.*

**A** In the sentences below, put a dotted line under the verb used with *with*. Then underline each of the other parts of the pattern.

1  I just wanted to check one thing with you.
2  We are confronted with the fact that we are aging.
3  Talk all this over with your husband.
4  His victory has been met with enthusiasm from all sides of the party.
5  And what do you suggest we replace it with?
6  It is an episode which few in Hollywood regard with any pride.
7  All the student need concern himself with is reality.
8  There are a lot of players I like to play golf with for a variety of reasons
9  He views with horror the relentless deterioration in Britain's trade balance over the past four decades.
10  Police have so far given no details of the offences with which those arrested will be charged.

**B** Fill in the gaps in the sentences below using the verbs in this list. Use each verb once.

begin    bore    conclude    confront    discuss    meet    replace    trust

1  I need to ................................. some matters with you.
2  When most companies are ................................. with problems, they try simply to fix them.
3  The floor boards had completely rotted and we had to ................................. them with special fast-drying concrete.
4  I won't ................................. you with all my personal and professional problems.
5  The President ................................. his day with a jog in suburban Louisville.
6  It may well be that if we ................................. a deal with Reed, other shareholders may decide to follow suit.
7  There is no way we're going to ................................. him with another large job.
8  The announcement was ................................. with dismay from trade unions.

**C** Put the different parts of these sentences in the right order.

1  her / with / he / a quick smile / exchanged ....................................................................................
2  with / they / each other / hatred / view ....................................................................................
3  he / talks / with / the other leaders / will be holding ....................................................................
4  scepticism / has greeted / the Government / with / such reports
   ............................................................................................................................................
5  the day / start / with / some / meditation or exercise ....................................................................
6  I'm / sorry / my troubles / to bother / with / you ..........................................................................
7  nothing / has / to replace / he / with / them ..............................................................................

# Reciprocal verbs: 1

Reciprocal verbs are used to refer to actions or relationships in which two or more people, groups, or things may be equally involved. Each of them has a particular combination of patterns.

## Pattern combination 1

● The verb is used with a plural Subject. This pattern is **pl-n V**.

| plural noun group | Verb group |
|---|---|
| They | were talking. |
| Those values | don't conflict. |

● The verb is also used with a Subject referring to one participant and followed by a prepositional phrase indicating the other. In most cases, the preposition is *with*. This pattern is **V with n**.

| | Verb group | *with* | noun group |
|---|---|---|---|
| We | 've been talking | with | our suppliers. |
| Their views | conflicted | with | those of the President. |

Verbs with this combination of patterns belong to the following meaning groups:

■ **verbs concerned with speaking and communicating**

| | | | |
|---|---|---|---|
| agree | communicate | meet | speak |
| argue | differ | negotiate | talk |
| chat | disagree | quarrel | |

*Her parents* never **argued**.
*He* **was arguing** *with his girlfriend and she hit him with a frying pan.*

*Chat, speak,* and *talk* are sometimes followed by *to*.

*I've been talking to Jim Hoffman.*

■ **verbs concerned with fighting, either physically or metaphorically, or competing**

| | | | |
|---|---|---|---|
| battle | compete | fight | tie |
| clash | draw | struggle | |

*Did he say why* **they were fighting**?
*About a thousand students* **fought** *with riot police in the capital.*

*Battle, compete, draw,* and *fight* are sometimes followed by *against*.

*Increasingly, local government* **is competing** *against the private sector.*

■ **verbs concerned with relationships**

| | | | | |
|---|---|---|---|---|
| break up | get along | get on | meet up | separate |
| co-operate | get divorced | go out | pair up | split up |
| fall out | get married | link up | part | team up |

*We'd only* **been going out** *for about six months at the time.*
*He* **used to go out** *with Kylie Minogue.*

*His demands increased until* **we finally broke up**.
*Just before Penny's marriage I* **broke up** *with a man I'd been seeing for over a year.*

*Part* and *separate* are followed by *from*, not *with*.

*I* **have parted** *from my wife by mutual agreement.*

The passive verb *get married* has a plural Subject or is followed by *to*.

*She gave a little party for me and Alexander after* **we got married**.
*He* **got married** *to Sue when he was very young.*

The passive verb *get divorced* has a plural Subject or is followed by *from*.

*We* **got divorced** *a few months ago.*
*He* **is getting divorced** *from his wife of 11 years.*

■ **verbs indicating that two or more things are similar or compatible, or are not similar or compatible**

| | | | | |
|---|---|---|---|---|
| agree | coincide | contrast | differ | match up |
| clash | conflict | correspond | match | |

*Do your needs* **clash**?
*Don't make any policy decisions which* **clash** *with official company thinking.*

*Correspond* is sometimes followed by *to*.

*The French grading system* **does not correspond** *to the English.*

*Differ* is followed by *from*, not *with*.

*How* **does** *your work* **differ** *from theirs?*

■ **verbs indicating that two or more things occur together, are in contact, or come into contact**

| | | | |
|---|---|---|---|
| coexist | collide | intersect | overlap |
| coincide | combine | merge | |

*The two Skyhawk jets apparently* **collided** *in mid-air as they were practising takeoffs.*
*A car* **collided** *with a motorcycle at a junction.*

# Practice

**A** Rewrite these sentences using the pattern **pl-n V**.

1 He was arguing with my mum every night, hour after hour.
*He and my mum were arguing every night, hour after hour.*

2 I disagree with Stephen about lots of stuff.
................................................................................................................

3 Warwickshire drew with Northamptonshire at Edgbaston.
................................................................................................................

4 I've just split up with my girlfriend.
................................................................................................................

5 We get on very well with them.
................................................................................................................

Now rewrite the following sentences using the pattern **V *with* n.**

6 When my husband and I broke up five years ago it was amicable.
................................................................................................................

7 Why don't Johnson and Kravis team up?
................................................................................................................

8 High-spending countries and low-spending countries can coexist.
................................................................................................................

9 The interests of the governors and the governed should coincide.
................................................................................................................

10 The Haywards Heath Building Society and the Yorkshire Building Society are to merge.
................................................................................................................

**B** Fill in the gaps in these sentences using *against*, *to*, or *from*.

1 He chatted ...................... me at the bar for a while.

2 The French fought ...................... the Communists for eight years.

3 Charlotte Pilcher is getting married ...................... James Studholme in July.

4 She also thinks that women's taste in music differs ...................... men's.

5 Kristina will be competing ...................... her sister Nicola for a place in the team.

6 In the previous year I had separated ...................... my husband after nineteen years of marriage.

**C** Divide the list of verbs concerned with relationships into three smaller groups:

1 five verbs indicating that people begin a relationship
................................................................................................................

2 six verbs indicating that a relationship ends
................................................................................................................

3 four verbs indicating that people have a relationship, or have a good relationship
................................................................................................................

# Reciprocal verbs: 2

## Pattern combination 2

- The verb is used with a plural Subject and is followed by a noun group. This pattern is **pl-n V n**.

| plural noun group | Verb group | noun group |
|---|---|---|
| MPs<br>They | have been debating<br>swapped | the issue.<br>gossip. |

- The verb is also used with a Subject referring to one participant and is followed by a noun group and a prepositional phrase indicating the other participant. The preposition is *with*. This pattern is **V n with n**:

| | Verb group | noun group | with | noun group |
|---|---|---|---|---|
| I | am not going to debate | the issue | with | you. |
| I | could swap | data | with | them. |

Verbs with this combination of patterns belong to the following meaning groups:

- **verbs indicating that people discuss something**

| debate | discuss | dispute | talk over | talk through |
|---|---|---|---|---|

*We **discussed** her options.*
*She'd never **discussed** it with her children.*
*The results of the test **are discussed** with a doctor.* (passive)

- **verbs indicating that two people or groups agree on future arrangements, or are trying to agree on them**

| agree | do | negotiate | sign |
|---|---|---|---|
| conclude | make | reach | strike |

*The US and Canada then **negotiated** an agreement that was completed in 1987.*
*The city's Peace Officers Association **is** currently **negotiating** a new contract with the city.*

'I came in here thinking *we **were going to do** a deal*,' Roberts said.
*European airlines are not ready to **do a deal with him**.*

- **verbs used with noun groups such as *talks* and a *conversation* to indicate that two or more people talk to each other**

| have | hold |
|---|---|

*Northern Ireland's Catholics and Protestants **are holding** talks today in Belfast.*
*He's also scheduled to **hold** talks with Jordanian officials before returning to Washington.*

*Talks **are being held** between the unions and the government at the moment but no agreement looks likely.* (passive)

- **verbs concerned with relationships**

| break off | form | make | patch up | resolve |
|---|---|---|---|---|
| establish | have | make up | renew | settle |

*The two West African states **had broken off** relations two years ago after bloody clashes erupted in the frontier area.*
*The Soviet Union **broke off** relations with Israel in 1967 at the time of the Six Day War.*

*Unless **France and Britain can resolve** their differences there will be no treaty on political union.*
*The former captain **has** now **resolved** his differences with team officials.*

In the case of *break off* and *make up*, when the noun group comes directly after the verb, it is always *it*.

*Then did she come here to **make** it **up** with him?*

- **verbs indicating that people give, say, or do things of the same kind to each other**

| exchange | swap | trade |
|---|---|---|

*They took photographs of each other and **exchanged** addresses.*
*The separatists **exchanged** fire with security forces at two places in the old city area.*

- **verbs concerned with fighting or competing**

| fight | fight out | have | play |
|---|---|---|---|

*We **had** a fight yesterday, and he walked out.*
*I **had** a fight with my husband.*

In the case of *fight out*, the noun group following the verb is usually *it*.

*Let the two of them **fight** it **out**.*

- *Share* also has this combination of patterns.

*My sister and I **shared** a bedroom until I was seven.*
*Livy wished she **wasn't sharing** a room with Caroline.*

**A** In the sentences below, put a dotted line under the verb used with the pattern **pl-n V n** or **V n with n**, or its passive. Then underline each of the other parts of the pattern.

1 For over two hours the police fought a pitched battle with the marchers.
2 They had clearly been having this conversation for some time.
3 When did you renew contact with your sister?
4 I've been having a chat with that son of yours.
5 And if you have any questions, you can talk them over with Mr. Bacon himself.
6 Why don't we talk it through tomorrow night?
7 Japan and South Korea have reached an agreement on the legal status of Koreans living in Japan.
8 It was reported that contact had been made with nationalist ex-soldiers fighting on the borders.
9 Britain and China have settled their differences over the plan for a new airport in Hong Kong.
10 The two have been trading insults and accusations since well before the start of the campaign.

**B** Rewrite these sentences using the pattern **pl-n V n**.

1 So I struck a deal with them.
*So we struck a deal.*
2 Above her head, he exchanged glances with Lloyd.

3 Mr. Bush discussed the proposed arms reductions with Mr. Gorbachev.

4 The only time I really had a conversation with him was at luncheon in the Elysee.

5 My husband was playing golf with the children on the green outside our house.

Now rewrite the following sentences using the pattern **V n with n**.

6 Nigeria and Cameroon share a common border.

7 My boyfriend and I discussed it. We just don't think it's necessary.

8 He and Grandpa were supposed to play chess today.

9 Patrick and I were having a discussion about games.

10 Israel and Bulgaria have re-established diplomatic relations after a break of twenty-three years.

# Reciprocal verbs: 3

## Pattern combination 3

● The verb is used with a plural Subject. This pattern is **pl-n V**.

| plural noun group | Verb group |
|---|---|
| They | embraced. |
| Their eyes | met. |

● The verb is also used with a Subject referring to one participant and followed by a noun group referring to the other. This pattern is **V n**.

| | Verb group | noun group |
|---|---|---|
| She | embraced | Jack. |
| Her eyes | met | Harry's. |

Verbs with this combination of patterns belong to the following meaning groups:

■ **verbs concerned with affectionate contact**

| embrace | hug | kiss |
|---|---|---|

*They **kissed**. She drove away.*
*She **kissed** me and turned out the light.*

■ **verbs concerned with relationships**

| date | divorce | marry |
|---|---|---|

*They **divorced** in 1976.*
*She **divorced** her Army husband at 23.*
*Norman **was divorced** by his wife Jo eight years ago.*
(passive)

■ **verbs concerned with fighting or competing**

| fight | meet |
|---|---|

*In the park, **three boys were fighting** and I said 'You can stop that immediately!'*
*I **had to fight** him even though I hate violence.*

*Sudan and Uganda **will meet** in the final of the East and Central African Challenge Cup on Thursday.*
*Manchester City **meet** Leeds at home tomorrow.*

■ **verbs indicating that two or more things are in contact, physically or metaphorically**

| cross | intersect | join | meet | overlap | touch |
|---|---|---|---|---|---|

*Her apartment was three miles out of Georgetown, at the junction where **two highways meet**.*
*Dentists may detect bone loss at the part of the jaw where the teeth **meet the bone**.*

■ *Meet* also has this combination of patterns when it is used to talk about one person meeting another person.

*John and I **met** in high school.*
*I **met** her about a month ago.*

■ *Match* also has this combination of patterns.

*The signatures **matched**.*
*They told him he couldn't board the plane unless the name on his ticket **matched** the one on his passport.*

## Emphasizing reciprocity

With most reciprocal verbs, a **reciprocal pronoun** (*each other* or *one another*) can be used after the appropriate preposition or after the verb, to emphasize that an action involves both or all the people mentioned as Subject.

*All across the world today **people are fighting** with each other and killing each other because of their racial and religious differences.*

*The fans **would exchange** information with one another.*

*They **hugged** each other.*

Each other and one another are also used to give ordinary verbs a reciprocal meaning.

*They **hate** each other.*

*We **gave** each other support.*

*Sara and I **looked** at each other.*

**A** Rewrite these sentences using the pattern **pl-n V**.

1 She married him in 1981. *They married in 1981.*

2 His militant views matched hers.

.......................................................................................................................

3 The experiences of women are beginning to overlap those of men.

.......................................................................................................................

4 Despite a declaration of cease-fire in Yugoslavia, Serbians were fighting Croats this morning in Osijek.

.......................................................................................................................

5 His fingers touched mine as I gave him the glass.

.......................................................................................................................

**Now rewrite the following sentences using the pattern V n.**

6 He and his first wife divorced in 1939.

.......................................................................................................................

7 Richard watched as Henry and Joanna embraced.

.......................................................................................................................

8 Catherine and John have been dating for five months.

.......................................................................................................................

9 His ashes will be immersed at the place where the Rivers Ganges and Jamuna meet.

.......................................................................................................................

10 She and her husband met ten years ago when he came to Moscow on a business trip.

.......................................................................................................................

**B** Rewrite these sentences using *each other* or *with each other*.

1 Police and demonstrators fought for four hours.
*Police and demonstrators fought each other for four hours.*

2 We embraced, laughing.

.......................................................................................................................

3 His guests seemed to agree about everything.

.......................................................................................................................

4 Counseling can help two people to learn to get along.

.......................................................................................................................

5 Is it true that women are more able to discuss personal things?

.......................................................................................................................

6 Lines of longitude all cross at the poles.

.......................................................................................................................

7 The Association says schools should not compete.

.......................................................................................................................

8 Increasingly, people needed better ways to communicate.

.......................................................................................................................

9 These orbiting particles collided, and ended up forming a flat disc.

.......................................................................................................................

# Ergative verbs: 1

Ergative verbs are verbs with a particular combination of patterns. The commonest type of ergative verb has the following patterns:

● The verb is used on its own. This pattern is **V**.

|  | Verb group |
|---|---|
| Her life | had changed. |
| My spirits | lifted. |

● The verb is followed by a noun group. This pattern is **V n**.

|  | Verb group | noun group |
|---|---|---|
| The war | had changed | her life. |
| Sunlight | can lift | the spirits. |

As you can see, the sort of person or thing indicated by the Subject of the pattern **V** may also be indicated by the noun group in the pattern **V n**.

Verbs with this combination of patterns belong to the following meaning groups:

■ **verbs concerned generally with change**

| alter | change | vary |
|---|---|---|

*Society **has changed**.*
*He thought his book **would change** society.*

■ **verbs concerned with physical or chemical change.** Many of these verbs relate to cooking.

| bake | cool | dry | fill up | melt |
|---|---|---|---|---|
| boil | cool down | dry out | flood | soften |
| burn | dissolve | fade | freeze | spoil |
| cook | drain | fill | heal | warm up |

*While the water **boiled**, I picked up the shopping and put it away.*
*Milwaukee residents have been advised to **boil their tap water** or drink bottled water.*

*Stir the mixture with a metal spoon until the sugar **has dissolved**.*
***Dissolve the sugar** in the warm water and add the dried yeast.*

*It is a good idea to brush the fish with oil while it **is cooking**.*
***Cook the fish** for 3-4 minutes on each side.*

■ **verbs concerned with something breaking or with something or someone being damaged or destroyed**

| blow up | burst | hang | snap |
|---|---|---|---|
| break | crack | mark | split |
| burn | crash | rip | tear |
| burn down | drown | shatter | wear away |

With most of these verbs, the Subject of the pattern **V n** refers to the person or thing causing the damage. With a few verbs, the Subject may refer to the person or thing that suffers damage or loss, as in *I **broke** my arm*.

*When he is captured, he **will hang**.*
*The convicted men were due to **be hanged** this week, having lost their appeal recently. (passive)*

*He slammed the door with such force that a window **broke**.*
*They threw stones and **broke the windows of buses**.*

■ **verbs concerned with the size, degree, or shape of something changing**

| bend | diminish | expand | shrink | tighten |
|---|---|---|---|---|
| contract | drop | grow | straighten out | widen |
| decrease | double | increase | stretch | |

*The cables are designed not to **stretch**.*
*Ease the pastry gently into the corners of the tin, making sure you **don't stretch** it.*

*With the use of random drug testing, the chance of being caught **has increased**.*
*Just one severe sunburn in childhood **can increase the chances of developing skin cancer**.*

■ **verbs concerned with change of an abstract kind**

| clear up | ease off | lift | strengthen | weaken |
|---|---|---|---|---|
| develop | improve | revive | turn around | wind down |

*In the course of the 1950s the situation **improved**.*
*We are convinced that he **could improve the political situation**.*

*Unemployment has soared as state industries **wind down**.*
*The recession went on and on, and I slowly **wound down the business**.*

# Practice

**A** These sentences are about damage and show the pattern **V n**. Rewrite them using the pattern **V**.

1 He snapped the stem of his wine glass.
*The stem of his wine glass snapped.*
......................................................................................................................

2 They burned down one of the city's main hotels.
......................................................................................................................

3 Eddie cracked the ice on the pond.
......................................................................................................................

4 She had torn her new dress.
......................................................................................................................

Now rewrite these passive sentences using the pattern **V**.

5 A warship was blown up in the harbour.
......................................................................................................................

6 The gold on the rim of the glass has been worn away.
......................................................................................................................

7 The rear window of her patrol car was shattered.
......................................................................................................................

8 Apparently, the Titanic's hull had been broken twice on or near the surface.
......................................................................................................................

**B** Fill in the gaps in the pairs of sentences below using the verbs in this list.

bake     change     clear up     cool     fade     improve     melt

1 a) I could smell loaves of bread .........*baking*........... in the oven.
 b) Most British housewives rarely ..........*bake*.............. their own bread.

2 a) The material had ................................. with wear.
 b) Light will ................................. the colours in organic materials.

3 a) In many cases this condition will ................................. of its own accord.
 b) Moisturizing cream will often ................................. the irritating rash.

4 a) Stir over low heat until the jelly has .................................
 b) ................................. the butter over a gentle heat.

5 a) The sooner the law ................................., the better for us all
 b) We've waited a long time for them to ................................. the law.

6 a) The flavour will ................................. if the vinegar is kept for a long time.
 b) Processing can ................................. the appearance and flavour of some foods.

7 a) Let the oil ................................. completely and then strain it.
 b) ................................. the rhubarb mixture until it is half-set.

# Ergative verbs: 2

Here are some more groups of ergative verbs with the patterns **V** and **V n**:

■ **verbs concerned with a change in the pace of something**

| accelerate | quicken | slow | slow down | speed up |
|---|---|---|---|---|

The pace of the negotiations **has quickened** in recent months.
The crisis has at least indirectly forced the President to **quicken** *the pace of change.*

The car never **slowed down**.
Narrowing the road **would slow down** *traffic.*

■ **verbs concerned with a thing, organization, or group of people dividing into two or more parts**

| break down | break up | divide | split | split up |
|---|---|---|---|---|

When the Soviet Union **split up**, Sahlins lost touch with the theater completely.
One of the largest commuter airlines in the country **may be split up**. (passive)

■ **verbs concerned with someone starting to have a feeling or emotion, or to be in a particular state**

| calm down | panic | revive | wake | worry |
|---|---|---|---|---|
| cheer up | relax | tire | wake up | |

Just **calm down** and tell me what's happened.
Frannie spent two hours on the phone with Dede, trying to **calm** *her* **down**.

He **woke** some hours later, completely refreshed.
She **woke** *Betsy* and they called the police.

■ **verbs concerned with something moving or being moved**

| bounce | move | settle | spin | turn over |
|---|---|---|---|---|
| break off | open | shake | tip up | |
| close | pile up | shift | turn | |
| get away | rock | shut | turn around | |

Her arms **were moving** like a ballerina's.
He was paralysed from the waist down and **could** only **move** *his left arm.*

The ground **shook** beneath his feet.
The shock waves **shook** *the ground* throughout most of Wales.

The door **opened** and Mrs MacMahon, carrying a tray, entered.
He **opened** *the door* and hurried out.

He found a part of the arrow that **had broken off**.
Edgar **broke off** *another chunk of chocolate.*

■ **verbs concerned with the driving or operation of a vehicle**

| back | land | sail | start | stop |
|---|---|---|---|---|
| halt | reverse | stall | start up | |

The van came to a halt, **reversed**, halted again.
A gunman opened fire as PC White **reversed** *the car* in a desperate attempt to escape.

Then my engine **stalled**, and had to be restarted.
She **stalled** *the engine*, and restarted it.

Most of these verbs have another **V** pattern in which the Subject indicates the person driving, operating, or travelling in the vehicle.

When she got out, the driver **reversed**, crushing her against the patrol car.

Verbs in this group which refer to movement also have the patterns **V prep/adv** and **V n prep/adv**: see Unit 93.

■ **verbs concerned with a place opening or closing**

| close | close up | open up | shut down |
|---|---|---|---|
| close down | open | shut | |

*Rumbelows said 200 of its 500 shops* **may close** *within two years.*
The company **is closing** *its copper cable factory at Bishopstoke, Hampshire.*

His new shop **opens** today at 659 Fulham Road.
I want to **open** *a dress shop.*

**A** Say whether the sentences below show the pattern **V**, or the pattern **V n** or its passive.

1 Nine nuclear power stations had been closed down. ...*V n (passive)*...

2 Stop the car! ................................

3 We can speed up the process. ................................

4 Southern Illinois was shaken by an earthquake this morning. ................................

5 She shut the door slowly. ................................

6 Suddenly their seat tipped up. ................................

7 The truck was accelerating. ................................

8 I turned the key in the lock. ................................

9 Has the engine stopped? ................................

10 Whole families have been split up by the fighting. ................................

11 Turn the fish pieces over carefully. ................................

12 The left rear tyre spun helplessly. ................................

**B** In each of the pairs of sentences below, one of the verbs from this list is missing. Mark where it goes and say what it is.

cheer up   panic   relax   revive   tire   wake up   worry

1 a) When she / she felt completely refreshed. ...*woke up*...
   b) I had to / her / every four hours to give her her medicine. ...*wake up*...

2 a) People were beginning to in the midday heat. ................................
   b) Anyone with this condition should avoid exercise which them. ................................

3 a) When one side of the boat began taking in water, people and rushed to the other side, causing the boat to sink. ................................
   b) Her screams the men and they fled. ................................

4 a) I was feeling a bit down, and she told me to. ................................
   b) Ethel suggested Paul should her daughter by visiting her while she recovered from a skiing accident. ................................

5 a) Seeing how free and easy he was, everyone and started talking freely too. ................................
   b) A high-carbohydrate dinner will you for sleep during the flight. ................................

6 a) In a few minutes the girls had enough to be able to tell their story. ................................
   b) Horrified staff tried to him but he was dead by the time he reached hospital.
      ................................

7 a) Don't, John, I'm not going to let you down. ................................
   b) What me is that we might get an increase in inflation. ................................

# 92 Ergative verbs: 3

**1** Here are some more groups of ergative verbs with the patterns **V** and **V n**:

■ **verbs concerned with an activity or situation starting, stopping, or continuing**

| | | | |
|---|---|---|---|
| begin | continue | halt | start |
| break up | end | resume | stop |

The blaze **started** in the kitchens of the thirty-six floor hotel.
The following year she **started a blaze** at her husband's parents' home.

For now, the fighting **has stopped**, but the guns haven't.
Today's agreement has done nothing to **stop the fighting**.

■ **verbs concerned with something coming into existence or becoming noticeable**

| | | | |
|---|---|---|---|
| develop | form | show up | turn up |
| evolve | show | spread | |

Some rare early photographs of the city of Jerusalem **have turned up** in Minnesota.
A search of the woods around the murder scene also **turned up a knife**.

A queue **forms** outside Peter's study.
**Form a queue** at the nearest doorway.

■ **verbs concerned with a machine or device working**

| | | | | |
|---|---|---|---|---|
| blow | light | play | run | work |
| explode | operate | ring | sound | |

A taped message from his mother **plays** in the background.
I think I**'ll play a record**.

When the final whistle **blew**, a lot of fans came onto the pitch.
We were waiting for the referee to **blow his whistle**.

**2** Another type of ergative verb has the following patterns:

● The verb is followed by an adjective group. This pattern is **V adj**.

| | Verb group | adjective group |
|---|---|---|
| The doors | slid | open. |
| The lock | snapped | shut. |

● The verb is followed by a noun group and an adjective group. This pattern is **V n adj**.

| | Verb group | noun group | adjective group |
|---|---|---|---|
| She | slid | the door | open. |
| The Major | snapped | his box | shut. |

Verbs with this combination of patterns belong to the following meaning groups:

■ **verbs concerned with something opening or closing, usually noisily or violently**

| | | | | |
|---|---|---|---|---|
| blow | slam | slide | snap | swing |

In a second someone was inside, and the door **slammed shut**.
He managed to drag her back inside the vehicle and **slam the door shut**.

A second later the door **swung open**.
Walking to the gate, I **swung it open**, crossed to the front door and rang the bell.

■ **verbs concerned with someone or something becoming detached from something**

| | | |
|---|---|---|
| pull | shake | work |

The adjective is usually *free* or *loose*.

He shook his head back and forth, and tried to **pull free**.
With a sob, she **pulled herself free**.

One of the pins **had worked loose from the outer plate**.
While we were still trying to **work it loose** we saw two more wild cats creeping towards us.

# Practice

**A** These sentences are about things starting, stopping, or continuing, and show the pattern **V**. Rewrite them using the pattern **V n** and the Subject given in brackets.

1 The countdown for the launch has begun. (they)
*They have begun the countdown for the launch.*

2 Our meetings rarely started on time. (we) ......................................................................

3 This idiocy must stop. (you) ......................................................................

4 His marriage broke up. (his affair) ......................................................................

5 The talks are continuing during the afternoon. (the two sides)
......................................................................

6 Production of chemical weapons has already halted in both countries. (both countries)
......................................................................

7 Play will resume on Wednesday. (the remaining teams)
......................................................................

8 He said that decisive action would be taken unless the protest ended. (the students)
......................................................................

**B** Fill in the gaps in these pairs of sentences using the nouns in this list.

bell   bomb   heating system   horn   matches

1 The ................................. wouldn't light.
He'd burnt himself trying to light .................................

2 A ................................. exploded in the capital last night, injuring two children.
The separatists also exploded a ................................. in a stationary bus.

3 He walked around to the front and rang the .................................
The ................................. rang, signalling the start of classes.

4 An oncoming truck sounded its .................................
The ................................. sounded as Lauren was pushed against the wheel.

5 The ................................. doesn't work.
We need to know if she understood how to work the .................................

**C** Rewrite the sentences below, using the verb and adjective given in brackets. The pattern may be **V adj** or **V n adj**.

1 The top drawer of his desk opened easily. (slide / open)
*The top drawer of his desk slid open easily.*

2 She shut the door. (slam / shut)
......................................................................

3 They could be injured if the window shuts. (blow / shut)
......................................................................

4 He opened his briefcase. (snap / open)
......................................................................

5 He paused before letting the gate shut behind him. (swing / shut)
......................................................................

# Ergative verbs: 4

Another type of ergative verb has the following patterns:

● The verb is followed by a prepositional phrase or, in some cases, an adverb. This pattern is **V prep/adv**.

|  | Verb group | prep. phrase/adverb |
|---|---|---|
| The smile | turned | into a grin. |
| The troops | had marched | away. |

● The verb is followed by a noun group and a prepositional phrase or, in some cases, an adverb. This pattern is **V n prep/adv**.

|  | Verb group | noun group | prep. phrase/adverb |
|---|---|---|---|
| Parents | can't turn | their house | into a fortress. |
| They | marched | the men | out. |

Note that the noun group may come after an adverb, as in *He slid back the door*.

Verbs with this combination of patterns belong to the following meaning groups:

■ **verbs concerned with change**

| change | convert | form | turn |
|---|---|---|---|

He **changed** into a fish.
I always try to **change** a dissatisfied customer into a happy one.

■ **verbs concerned with something breaking or dividing**

| break | divide | shatter | snap | tear |
|---|---|---|---|---|
| break up | separate | smash | split | |

It **shattered** into tiny pieces.
The steam **shatters** the rock into tiny fragments.

Let's **separate** into smaller groups.
The police wanted to **separate** them into smaller groups, but they insisted on staying together.

■ **verbs concerned with something moving somewhere**

| blow | move | slide | spread | transfer |
|---|---|---|---|---|
| bounce | pass | smash | squeeze | |
| dig | roll | spill | stick | |
| drop | rub | spin | swing | |
| float | shift | splash | tip | |

The red soil **blew** away in the wind.
A storm **blew** away the sand dunes.

It developed into a huge game, with water **splashing** everywhere.
Leaning over the fountain, Joanna **splashed** water upon her face.

Make sure that the person **can transfer** from wheelchair to seat with relative ease.
They learn a few technical skills, such as how to lift a frail old person and **transfer** that person from a chair or bed.

■ **verbs concerned with vehicles going somewhere**

| back | fly | land | reverse | sail | swing |
|---|---|---|---|---|---|

The traffic jam was caused by a caravan **backing** out of a driveway.
He **backed** his car out of the drive.

Most of these verbs have another **V prep/adv** pattern in which the Subject indicates the person driving, operating, or travelling in the vehicle.

They **reversed** out of the field the way they had come.

■ **verbs concerned with a person, group of people, or animal going somewhere**

| crowd | gather | pull | walk |
|---|---|---|---|
| gallop | march | transfer | withdraw |

The horse started **walking** away.
They **walked** their horses up the road.

We **gathered** in my office at 7:30 a.m. every day.
Now, in the greatest secrecy, he **had gathered** them all together.

■ **verbs indicating that something begins or ends in a particular way**

| begin | end | finish | open | start |
|---|---|---|---|---|

The meeting **opened** with a speech by the prime minister.
The local chairman **opened** the meeting with the usual pleasantries.

# Practice

**A** In the sentences below, put a dotted line under the ergative verb used with the pattern **V prep/adv**, or the pattern **V n prep/adv** or its passive. Then underline each of the other parts of the pattern and say which pattern it is.

1 The war has turned into a nightmare for them. .....*V prep*.....................

2 The house had been converted into a wooden fortress. ................................

3 Alan began to tear the portrait in half. ................................

4 The car reversed out. ................................

5 He backed the car down the driveway. ................................

6 He restarted the engine, swung the car around and drove back to Hillsden's apartment.
................................

7 When the plane landed at Stockholm's Arlanda airport, the hijacker gave himself up to police.
................................

8 Teddy galloped around the course at terrific speed. ................................

9 A large number of weapons, explosives and vehicles went missing when British troops were pulled out of Germany. ................................

10 Sharpe toyed with the idea of marching his own men into that open space, but he knew he was too late. ................................

**B** The following sentences are about something moving, and show the pattern **V n prep/adv**. Rewrite them using the pattern **V prep/adv**.

1 She dug her fingers into his arm.
*Her fingers dug into his arm.*
................................

2 He spilled coffee onto the carpet.
................................

3 They rolled the drum down the hill.
................................

4 He swung his legs backwards and forwards.
................................

5 He smashed his fist into her cheek.
................................

Now rewrite these passive sentences using the pattern **V**.

6 My hat was blown off.
*My hat blew off.*

7 The central hatch cover was slid back.
................................

8 The bottle was passed from hand to hand around the circle.
................................

9 The drum is spun around, creating an unsettling illusion of movement.
................................

10 The film is moved through the projector on a series of toothed wheels turned by a motor.
................................

# Verbs used with introductory *it*: 1

Sometimes the pronoun *it* does not refer back to something that has been mentioned, but points forward to a clause later in the sentence. We call this **introductory *it***.

In the following patterns (Units 94–96), introductory *it* is the subject.

## Verbs followed by a clause

| *it* | Verb group | clause |
|----|----|----|
| It | seemed | that he would keep his word. |
| It | may help | to talk about it. |
| It | looks | as if there will be a rebellion. |

**1** The verb is followed by a that-clause. This pattern is *it* V that.

Verbs with this pattern belong to the following meaning groups:

■ **verbs indicating that something happens or becomes known, or that something is logically the case.** With *turn out*, the word *that* is sometimes omitted, as in *It turned out she was married.*

| come about | emerge | follow | happen | turn out |
|----|----|----|----|----|
| come out | figure | get round | leak out | |

*It **happened** that Christopher Keene was available and interested.*

*It **emerged** that they shared a passion for sailing.*

*All eyes turned towards him, but it **turned out** he had nothing to say.*

■ **verbs used when indicating what a situation is, or seems to be.** With *appear* and *seem*, the word *that* is often omitted, as in *It seems I'm wrong.*

| appear | be | seem |
|----|----|----|

*It **appears** that the protest has thrown the government into a major political crisis.*

*Be* usually occurs in a negative clause, or is used with a modal or an adverb such as *just* or *simply*.

*It's **not** that I don't want a relationship, it's **just** that it would be really inconvenient.*

*It **may be** that another great change is on the way.*

*Seem* is sometimes followed by a prepositional phrase beginning with *to* which indicates whose opinion you are giving.

*It **seemed** to her that there was something odd about it.*

■ **verbs indicating how someone feels about a situation or event**

| help | hurt | matter |
|----|----|----|

*It **helps** that we work in the same business.*

*It **hurts** that people have such short memories.*

*Does it **matter** that you don't understand it?*

*Matter* is also often followed by a wh-clause, or a prepositional phrase beginning with *to* and a wh-clause.

*It **doesn't matter** how old you are.*

*It **doesn't matter** to them whether or not they sell your product.*

**2** The verb is followed by a to-infinitive clause. This pattern is *it* V to-inf.

Three of the verbs with this pattern indicate that something is helpful to someone, or is a good thing.

| (not) do | help | pay |
|----|----|----|

*I explained that sometimes it **pays** to know the regulations.*

*It **doesn't do** to exaggerate.*

The verb *hurt* also has this pattern.

*It **hurt** to breathe.*

**3** The verb is followed by a clause beginning with *as if*, *as though*, or, in informal English, *like*. This pattern is *it* V as if.

Verbs with this pattern are used when indicating what a situation seems or feels like.

| appear | be | feel | look | seem | sound |
|----|----|----|----|----|----|

*It **is** as if nothing at all has happened.*

*It **felt** as though a house had fallen on his leg.*

These verbs are sometimes followed by a prepositional phrase beginning with *to*.

*It **sounds** to me as though you've tried your best.*

## UNIT 94 Practice

**A** In the sentences below, put a dotted line under the verb used with a pattern described in this Unit. Then underline each of the other parts of the pattern.

1 It helps to talk.
2 If more families will now settle in the area, it follows that there will be more children in school.
3 It looked to me as if this gun had been used recently.
4 The break-down of the talks came as it emerged that two protesters died in a demonstration outside the capital.
5 It is simply that owning one's own home is regarded as important to people.
6 In terms of both attainment and behaviour it matters which school a child attends.
7 It doesn't do to grab more than one's fair share.
8 It feels as if spring is in the air.


**B** Fill in the gaps in the sentences below using the verbs in this list. Use each verb once.

be   come about   hurt   matter   pay   turn out

1 I do not know how it ................................. that he saw them.
2 I had bet everything on the race, but it ................................. that I lost.
3 He wasn't a bad man. It ................................. just that he believed in discipline.
4 I'm disappointed. It ................................. to lose.
5 Please help. It doesn't ................................. whether your contribution is large or small.
6 Whether you plan to stay in Britain or go abroad, it ................................. to read the holiday brochure very carefully before you book.


**C** Rewrite these sentences using the verb given in brackets with introductory *it*.

1 Everybody found out that the accusation had been made. (leak out)
   *It leaked out that the accusation had been made.*
2 I thought that I was an important part of their lives. (seem)
   ................................................................
3 Who won the game is not important. (matter)
   ................................................................
4 I think you'll have to move house. (look)
   ................................................................
5 I'm better off because I've got a tremendous family. (help)
   ................................................................
6 I don't think they're going to pay any attention. (sound)
   ................................................................
7 They don't mind whether or not they sell your product. (matter)
   ................................................................

# Verbs used with introductory *it*: 2

## Passive verbs followed by a clause

| it | Verb group | clause |
|----|------------|--------|
| It | is estimated | that a hundred people have now died. |
| It | was not disclosed | how much the sale will raise. |

**1** The verb is followed by a that-clause. This pattern is *it be V-ed that*. With some verbs, the word *that* is often omitted.

Verbs with this pattern belong to the following meaning groups:

■ **verbs indicating that something is said or shown**

| | | |
|---|---|---|
| be acknowledged | be confirmed | be reported |
| be agreed | be demonstrated | be revealed |
| be alleged | be disclosed | be rumoured |
| be announced | be emphasized | be said |
| be argued | be pointed out | be shown |
| be claimed | be proposed | be suggested |

*Eventually it was agreed that the present laws would continue to apply in the same areas for two years.*

*Last week it was reported that the new coach had asked Martyn to stand down as captain.*

*It was pointed out that several different solutions fitted the known data.*

■ **verbs indicating that something is thought or discovered**

| | | |
|---|---|---|
| be accepted | be envisaged | be known |
| be anticipated | be established | be learned |
| be assumed | be estimated | be noticed |
| be believed | be expected | be presumed |
| be calculated | be feared | be reckoned |
| be considered | be felt | be seen |
| be decided | be found | be suspected |
| be determined | be hoped | be thought |
| be discovered | be intended | be understood |

*They became concerned when it was discovered that more than nine thousand ballot papers had been forged.*

*It is expected that agreement will be reached by that date.*

**2** The verb is followed by a wh-clause. This pattern is *it be V-ed wh*.

Verbs with this pattern indicate that something is known or becomes known.

| | | |
|---|---|---|
| be decided | be established | be revealed |
| be determined | be explained | be seen |
| be disclosed | be known | be shown |
| be discovered | be learned | be understood |

*It has never been established whether either of the men survived.*

*It is not known who was behind the attack.*

## Verbs followed by an adjective group and a clause

| it | Verb group | adjective group | clause |
|----|------------|-----------------|--------|
| It | is | important | that you are honest. |
| It | would look | pretty silly | to turn the proposal down. |

**1** The verb is followed by an adjective group and a that-clause. This pattern is *it V adj that*.

Verbs with this pattern are used when indicating what a situation is, seems, or becomes. The word *that* is often omitted, as in *It is certain he will be there.*

| | | | |
|---|---|---|---|
| appear | become | look | remain |
| be | feel | prove | seem |

*I think it's important that you get to know them beforehand.*

*It quickly becomes apparent that he is not mad at all.*

*It looks likely that David has played his last game for the club.*

With *appear, be, become, remain,* and *seem,* the adjective group is sometimes followed by a wh-clause instead of a that-clause, depending on the adjective used.

*It is not clear why he is being held.*

**2** The verb is followed by an adjective group and a to-infinitive clause. This pattern is *it V adj to-inf*.

Verbs with this pattern are used when indicating what an action is, seems, or becomes.

| | | | |
|---|---|---|---|
| appear | become | look | remain |
| be | feel | prove | seem |

*It is important to use lawyers who are experienced in these matters.*

*It seemed reasonable to hope that the war would soon be over.*

The adjective group is often followed by a prepositional phrase beginning with *for.*

*It is becoming difficult for our club to cope.*

With *be, feel, look,* and *seem,* the adjective group is sometimes followed by an '-ing' clause.

*It was nice talking to you.*

**A** In the sentences below, put a dotted line under the verb used with a pattern described in this Unit. Then underline each of the other parts of the pattern.

1 It was clear that he had lost a great deal of weight.
2 It seems doubtful whether any foreign government would support the plan.
3 It was reported a few minutes ago that oil has come ashore on a headland in South Devon.
4 By the year 2050 it is expected that one out of four persons will be over 65.
5 If it was ever discovered how Beryl had died, they would both be in serious trouble.
6 I mean, it does feel important to have children because it's always been something I've wanted.
7 The 11-plus exam is being brought back, it was announced yesterday.
8 It is understood the airline will begin two weekly services to Cairns in September.
9 It is not known who was responsible for the bomb, which was hidden in a crate in a busy market place in the old city.
10 In ancient Greece, students wore sprays of rosemary in their hair because it was believed that it improved the memory!

**B** Make these statements less direct or definite by rewriting them using the verb given in brackets with the pattern *it be* V-ed *that*.

1 The drug can be used to prevent a heart attack. (think)
*It is thought that the drug can be used to prevent a heart attack.*

2 He only had a few weeks until he planned to retire after 41 years. (reveal)

3 A new town square with surrounding shopping should be developed on the site. (propose)

4 About three million dollars' worth of property has been destroyed. (say)

5 The vaccine will be successful. (hope)

**C** Match up the two halves of each sentence.

1 It appears increasingly likely ...          a ... to get doctors to work in country hospitals.
2 It became clear   ...                        b ... that a United Nations force will be sent there.
3 It is difficult ...                          c ... meeting you.
4 It was lovely ...                            d ... seeing him suffer like this.
5 It was kind of you ...                       e ... to take the trouble to write.
6 It is terrible ...                           f ... that the plane had crashed.

191

# 96 Verbs used with introductory *it*: 3

## Verbs followed by a noun group and a clause

| *it* | Verb group | noun group | clause |
|------|-----------|-----------|--------|
| It | bothered | her | that he hadn't asked for her. |
| It | seemed | a pity | to break up the peaceful scene. |

**1** The verb is followed by a noun group and a that-clause. This pattern is *it* **V n that**.

Verbs with this pattern belong to the following meaning groups:

■ **verbs used when indicating what a situation is, seems, or becomes.** The word *that* is often omitted, as in *It's a pity you weren't there*.

| be | become | remain | seem |
|----|--------|--------|------|

*It's a shame that you live so far away*.

*Of course it remains a possibility that Mr Meier was the intended victim*.

■ **verbs indicating how a situation makes someone feel**

| amaze | disappoint | frighten | sadden | worry |
|-------|-----------|----------|--------|-------|
| bother | disturb | hurt | shock | |
| concern | embarrass | please | surprise | |

*It frightens me that kids are now walking around with guns*.

*Does it worry you that you don't eat properly?*

Many of these verbs are sometimes followed by a wh-clause or a when/if-clause instead of a that-clause.

*It amazes me how many plastic shopping bags are given out by cashiers in large supermarkets*.

*It always pleases me when guests compliment me on the look of my food*.

■ **verbs indicating that an idea occurs to someone**

| dawn on | hit | occur to | strike |
|---------|-----|----------|--------|

*Suddenly it hit me that this was not how I wanted to live my life*.

*It didn't occur to me that he didn't know me*.

The noun group is sometimes followed by a wh-clause instead of a that-clause.

*Even in that first moment it struck me how utterly dependent he was*.

**2** The verb is followed by a noun group and a to-infinitive clause. This pattern is *it* **V n to-inf**.

Verbs with this pattern belong to the following meaning groups:

■ **verbs indicating what an action or situation is, seems, or becomes**

| be | become | remain | seem |
|----|--------|--------|------|

*It used to be a crime to help a slave escape*.

The noun group is sometimes followed by a prepositional phrase beginning with *for*.

*Death by poisoning would be simple to conceal here, because it was the custom for bodies to be burned*.

■ **verbs indicating how a situation makes someone feel**

| alarm | disturb | interest | scare | touch |
|-------|---------|----------|-------|-------|
| bother | frighten | pain | shock | upset |
| delight | hurt | please | surprise | worry |

*You are always in my thoughts and it pains me to think of you struggling all alone*.

*It pleased him to see that he'd delighted her with his choice*.

■ *Cost* and *take* also have this pattern. *Cost* is followed by an **amount**.

*It takes courage to face the unknown*.

*It costs a fortune to fly these people in from all over the country*.

*Cost* and one sense of *take* are sometimes followed by a noun group, an amount, and a to-infinitive clause.

*It cost him a lot to admit he needed help*.

*It took them a long time to reach the other shore*.

*Take* is sometimes followed by an amount, a prepositional phrase beginning with *for*, and a to-infinitive clause.

*It took seven years for a settlement to be reached*.

**A** In the sentences below, put a dotted line under the verb used with a pattern described in this Unit. Then underline each of the other parts of the pattern.

1 It seems a shame that it's taken him 32 years to change his image.
2 I couldn't face going to the hospital to visit my brother. It hurt me to see him so sick.
3 It shocked him to think he was capable of murder.
4 It took us at least two weeks to complete the assignment.
5 Didn't it strike you that he was awfully uptight and tense?
6 I could live for a week on what it cost to buy this shirt.
7 It struck her how self-centred she'd been, considering only her sorrow, not his.
8 It surprised him that so many had come to listen to him during lunchtime, but it saddened him that he did not see his brother in that audience.
9 It embarrassed her when friends insisted she was beautiful.
10 It was a pleasure to see my brother and his family.

**B** Rewrite each of the following pairs of sentences as one sentence.

1 Many of these people are regarded as frauds. This concerns me.
*It concerns me that many of these people are regarded as frauds.*

2 I wasn't as pleased to see John as I used to be. This bothered me.
.......................................................................................................................

3 The country is now in a position to mobilize its forces. This worries me.
.......................................................................................................................

4 She had not received either a note or a phone call from him. This disturbed her.
.......................................................................................................................

5 The Government never has enough cash for the public's needs but never fails to provide for MPs' salary increases. This amazes me.
.......................................................................................................................

6 He might have been on the wrong train. This hadn't occurred to me.
.......................................................................................................................

**C** Match up the two halves of each sentence.

1 It is my duty ...          a ... to let her down.
2 It takes experience ...    b ... to find a building here in the wilderness.
3 It seemed a shame ...      c ... to print thick, full-colour catalogues.
4 It costs a lot of money ... d ... to contemplate the operation and its risks.
5 It surprised her ...       e ... to know how to get through the process.
6 It frightened her ...      f ... to support my husband.

# Verbs used with introductory *it*: 4

In the following patterns (Units 97 and 98), introductory *it* is the Object.

## Verbs followed by *it* and a clause

**1** The verb is followed by *it* and a that-clause. This pattern is **V *it* that**.

Most of the verbs with this pattern indicate how a situation makes someone feel. These verbs have no equivalent passive pattern.

| appreciate | hate | love |
|---|---|---|
| (cannot) bear | like | (cannot) stand |

*I really **appreciate** it that you raised me in such a warm and happy family.*

*I **hate** it that you can paint contentedly while I'm feeling restless and bored.*

The verbs *arrange, have,* and *take* also have this pattern or its passive.

*Rumour **has** it that he is still alive.*

*I **take** it you haven't read the papers today.*

*So it **was arranged** that we should spend a week with Sally in London.* (passive)

**2** The verb is followed by *it* and a clause beginning with *when* or *if*. This pattern is **V *it* when/if**.

Most of the verbs with this pattern indicate how a situation or possible situation makes someone feel or react.

| accept | (cannot) handle | regret |
|---|---|---|
| appreciate | hate | (cannot) stand |
| (cannot) bear | like | (cannot) take |
| (cannot) believe | love | (cannot) understand |
| (cannot) endure | (not) mind | welcome |
| enjoy | prefer | |

*'I really **hate** it when you cry like that,'* Oliver said.

*I **can't stand** it when you expect me to give up my friends for you.*

*I **love** it when music does something to my emotions.*

*Frankly, we'**d prefer** it if you could find an adequate excuse to leave the country for the time being.*

The verb *help* also has this pattern, when used with *cannot*.

*I **can't help** it if you think I'm odd.*

## Verbs followed by *it*, a prepositional phrase beginning with *to*, and a clause

In the case of *put*, the clause is a that-clause. This pattern is **V *it* to n that**.

*I **put** it to him again that the money has got to come from somewhere.*

In the case of *leave* and *owe*, the clause is a to-infinitive clause. This pattern is **V *it* to n to-inf**.

*You just shut your eyes, and **left** it to the other people to clear up the mess!*

*I **owe** it to my country to fight for what's right.*

## Verbs followed by *it*, a prepositional phrase beginning with *as*, and a clause

Verbs with this pattern are used when indicating how someone sees or interprets a situation or action. The clause may be a that-clause, a to-infinitive clause, or a when/if-clause.

| accept | regard | see | take | view |
|---|---|---|---|---|

*They **will see** it as a major coup that they managed to blow up one of their top priority targets.*

*The Romans **regarded** it as undignified to compete naked in front of spectators.*

*I **take** it as a compliment when people call me aggressive.*

**A** Match up the two halves of each sentence.

1 I know you'd prefer it ...
2 I loved it ...
3 We couldn't believe it ...
4 I can't stand it ...
5 I'd love it ...
6 She couldn't handle it ...
7 He hated it ...
8 I would appreciate it ...

a ... when I told her the truth.
b ... when one of my horses takes a knock.
c ... if you would locate the file for me.
d ... that he cared enough to ask.
e ... when we were told we were only half-way.
f ... when she spoke so crudely.
g ... if I weren't around here any more.
h ... if you could come.

**B** Think of two kinds of event or situation you like, and two you hate.

I like it when ....................................................................................................................
I like it when ....................................................................................................................
I hate it when ....................................................................................................................
I hate it when ....................................................................................................................

**Now think of two things you would love to happen, and two you would hate to happen.**

I'd love it if ....................................................................................................................
I'd love it if ....................................................................................................................
I'd hate it if ....................................................................................................................
I'd hate it if ....................................................................................................................

**C** Rewrite these sentences using *it*, *as*, and the verb given in brackets.

1 I believe it is my responsibility to identify the problems. (see)
*I see it as my responsibility to identify the problems.*

2 Most analysts think it almost inevitable that the alliance will be scrapped. (see)
....................................................................................................................

3 Baron von Malchin wrote that he thought it was an honour to have known my father personally. (regard)
....................................................................................................................

4 They thought it was a positive sign that the university agreed to the contract extension. (see)
....................................................................................................................

5 The Dutch Presidency thought it was unhelpful to talk of independence for Slovenia and Croatia at that stage. (regard)
....................................................................................................................

6 The public now expect us to have three finalists in every championship by right and think it is abnormal when we don't. (view)
....................................................................................................................

# Verbs used with introductory *it*: 5

## Verbs followed by *it*, an adjective group, and a clause

**1** The verb is followed by *it*, an adjective group, and a that-clause. This pattern is **V *it* adj that**.

Most verbs with this pattern are concerned with how someone evaluates or judges a situation.

| believe | consider | feel | find | think |
|---------|----------|------|------|-------|

*I consider it essential that the photographer should do his own printing.*

*I find it remarkable that my lad seems unaffected by the insecurity he's lived with for most of his life.*

*It is thought unlikely that there will be compulsory redundancies.* (passive)

With *consider*, *find*, and *think*, the adjective group is sometimes followed by a when/if-clause.

*I found it disheartening when the horses were sold.*

*I think it best if you leave at once.*

The verb *make* also frequently has this pattern. The adjective that usually occurs with this verb is *clear*.

*From the very beginning he had made it clear that he did not have marriage in mind.*

The adjective is sometimes followed by a wh-clause instead of a that-clause.

*On the very first day, the United Nations made it absolutely clear what he should do.*

**2** The verb is followed by *it*, an adjective group, and a to-infinitive clause. This pattern is **V *it* adj to-inf**.

Most verbs with this pattern are concerned with how someone evaluates or judges an action or state.

| believe | consider | feel | find | judge | think |
|---------|----------|------|------|-------|-------|

*Most people find it hard to understand how living with one's own children could be lonely.*

*He suspected that Samantha had attended such parties previously and had not felt it necessary to tell him.*

*She dodged into the nearest toilet and remained there until she judged it safe to emerge.*

The verb *make* also frequently has this pattern.

*The reflection of the sun on the surface of the water made it impossible to see the bottom.*

## Verbs followed by *it*, a noun group, and a clause

Verbs with this pattern are used when indicating how someone evaluates or judges a situation or action. The clause may be a that-clause, a to-infinitive clause, or a when/if-clause.

| believe | consider | feel | reckon |
|---------|----------|------|--------|
| call | count | find | think |

*I sometimes find it a strain to be responsible for the mortgage and household bills each month.*

*I would consider it a favour if you would ask me home again next weekend.*

*The pilot called it a miracle that no one was killed.*

**A** Rewrite these sentences to form sentences showing whose opinion or viewpoint is being expressed, starting with the words provided. Then say what kind of clause follows the adjective group or noun group.

1  It is extraordinary that they should use a hospital as a fortress.
   We consider *it extraordinary that they should use a hospital as a fortress. (that clause)*

2  It is admirable that she wants to be independent.
   I think ...........................................................................................................................

3  It is unwise to spend large amounts of money on a few players.
   He believed ....................................................................................................................

4  At first it was difficult to relax.
   At first I found ..............................................................................................................

5  It is my duty to make sure they are given the proper atmosphere to succeed.
   I consider ........................................................................................................................

6  It seemed very strange when she said, 'I don't have to answer your question.'
   We thought ......................................................................................................................

7  It is a scandal that, in most states, fewer than 60 percent of children are immunized.
   Mrs Edelman called .......................................................................................................

8  It is likely that the tax officers' visits caught everyone by surprise.
   The spokesman thought ................................................................................................

9  It is not necessary to hold direct talks with the NLD.
   The government does not believe ................................................................................

10 It was important that every room had an individual feel and flavour.
   They felt ..........................................................................................................................

**B** Use *find* with *it* and a variety of adjectives from this list to express your feelings on each of the matters mentioned below.

   amazing   amusing   appalling   extraordinary   interesting   sad

1  People's breakfast habits are changing.
   *I find it interesting that people's breakfast habits are changing.* ...........................

2  There is little that can be done about this disease.
   ............................................................................................................................................

3  The press are prepared to publish unsubstantiated stories.
   ............................................................................................................................................

4  Alcohol is served in large quantities to young people.
   ............................................................................................................................................

5  People on the dole receive quite a good deal more money than students get, for doing nothing.
   ............................................................................................................................................

6  A 113-year-old Welsh church is being shipped to Japan to be made into a golf clubhouse.
   ............................................................................................................................................

# Verbs used with general *it*

Sometimes the pronoun *it* does not refer to anything at all, or refers very vaguely to the general situation. We call this **general it**.

## Patterns with general *it* as the Subject

**1** The verb can be used on its own, without anything following it. This pattern is *it* **V**.

Verbs with this pattern are all concerned with the weather.

| | | | | |
|---|---|---|---|---|
| brighten up | freeze | pour | snow | thunder |
| drizzle | hail | rain | be spitting | |

*She glanced out the window and saw that* **it was raining** *again.*

**It will brighten up** *in the next few days.*

**2** The verb is followed by an adjective group. This pattern is *it* **V adj**.

The verbs *be* and *get* are used when describing the weather, the temperature, or the light.

*It* **was chilly***, and he was glad of his coat and scarf.*

*We arrived just as* **it was getting** *dark.*

One sense of *get* is used with the adjective *late*.

*Well,* **it's getting** *late. I guess your wife will be wondering where you are.*

**3** The verb is followed by an adjective group and a prepositional phrase or adverb group. This pattern is *it* **V adj prep/adv**.

There is only one verb with this pattern, *be*. It is used to indicate your opinion of being in a place.

*It's* **nice here***.*

*It* **was awful in hospital***.*

**4** The verb is followed by a noun group. This pattern is *it* **V n**.

There is only one verb with this pattern, *be*. It is used when indicating the time or the date.

*It* **was four o'clock in the morning***.*

## Patterns with general *it* as the Object

Many of these combinations of a verb and *it* are sometimes considered to be phrases. Most of them are informal English. With phrasal verbs, the particle comes after the word *it*.

**1** The verb is followed by *it*. This pattern is **V** *it*.

Verbs with this pattern belong to the following meaning groups:

■ **verbs concerned with stopping doing something**

| | | | | |
|---|---|---|---|---|
| cool | cut out | hold | knock off | stop |

These verbs are always or usually used in the imperative.

*'***Hold** *it, Mom. Better not call the cops,' Frank said quickly.*

■ **verbs concerned with failure, success, and risk-taking**

| | | | |
|---|---|---|---|
| blow | (cannot) hack | lose | overdo |
| chance | have had | make | push |

*'I* **blew it***,' admitted Cook.*

*You'll* **make it***, don't worry.*

*Too much work can lead to exhaustion, so* **don't overdo it***!*

■ **verbs indicating how comfortable or well-off someone is**

| | | | | |
|---|---|---|---|---|
| be coining | be coining in | live up | rough | slum |

*He's had too comfortable a life, our friend. He* **can rough** *it for once.*

*He left Washington and he's now in Hawaii,* **living it up** *on his share of the money.*

■ **other verbs**

| | | | |
|---|---|---|---|
| clinch | settle | sweat out | watch |
| keep up | stick out | try on | |

*They're just* **trying it on** *– I don't believe they'll go that far.*

**Watch** *it, Sam. You're going to spill that if you're not careful.*

**2** The verb is followed by *it* and a prepositional phrase or adverb group. This pattern is **V** *it* **prep/adv**.

Verbs with this pattern are used to indicate someone's opinion of being in a place.

| | | | | | |
|---|---|---|---|---|---|
| enjoy | hate | like | love | prefer | (cannot) stand |

*My family* **hated it in Southampton***.*

*I* **love it here***. Everybody is so polite.*

**A** Fill in the gaps in the sentences below using the words in this list, and say whether the pattern is *it* **V** or *it* **V adj.**

cold   hot   raining   snowing   sunny   windy

1 Wear a sweater – it's *cold.* ................................ *it V adj* ........................

2 Sure you don't want a lift home? It's ................................ pretty hard. ................................

3 It's ................................ now. The roads between Larwick and here are starting to get blocked.
................................

4 It's ................................, but not very warm. ................................

5 If it's ................................ we could take the kite and see if we could fly it. ................................

6 If it's ................................ and people have been walking, they are given a large glass of fruit juice clinking with ice. ................................

**B** Use *it* to make statements which are true when you are reading this. Say something about:

1 the date: ................................................................................................................................

2 the time: ................................................................................................................................

3 the weather: ..........................................................................................................................

4 the weather yesterday: ..........................................................................................................

5 the place you are in: ..............................................................................................................

**C** In the lists of verbs with the pattern **V** *it*, find:

1 four verbs which indicate that someone is not successful
................................................................................................................................................

2 one verb which indicates that someone is successful ................................................................

3 three verbs which indicate that someone is well-off or living comfortably
................................................................................................................................................

4 two verbs which indicate that someone is not living comfortably ............................................

**D** The sentences below show the pattern *it* **V adj prep/adv**. Rewrite them using a verb with the pattern **V** *it* **prep/adv**, with *I* as the Subject. Use a different verb each time.

1 It's nice at work. *I like it at work* .... or ..........................................................................

2 It's really nice there. ..............................................................................................................

3 It's better here. ......................................................................................................................

4 It was horrible at school.
................................................................................ or ............................................................

# Verbs used with *there*

There are two patterns beginning with the word *there*, as described below. The verb *be* has these patterns much more frequently than any other verb.

There are two ways of forming a negative in patterns with *there*. The verb may be made negative, for example with *not* or *–n't*, or the noun group may be made negative, for example with *no*. You can say *There wasn't any evidence* or *There was no evidence*.

**1** Some verbs follow the word *there* and are followed by a noun group. This pattern is **there V n**.

| there | Verb group | noun group |
|-------|------------|------------|
| There | was | a loud bang. |
| There | seems | little hope of success. |

The noun group is the Subject. It agrees in number with the verb group: if the noun group is singular, the verb group is singular, and if the noun group is plural, the verb group is plural.

The noun group is usually indefinite: it begins with a word such as *a, some, any,* or *a few*. If the noun group is plural, there is often no determiner at all.

Verbs with this pattern belong to the following meaning groups:

■ **verbs indicating that something exists or happens**

| | | | |
|--|--|--|--|
| appear | exist | occur | seem |
| be | follow | remain | |

*Was there any genuine prejudice?*

*There was bound to be an increase in job losses.*

*There remain very serious problems.*

*There followed months of research.*

*Seem* and *appear* are usually followed by a noun group beginning with *little* or *no*, or with the pronoun *nothing*.

*There seems little chance of this happening.*

■ **verbs indicating that something comes into existence or starts to be seen**

| | | | |
|--|--|--|--|
| appear | come | emerge | grow up |
| arise | develop | grow | |

*There arises no question of loyalty to one's employers.*

*There emerges a picture of a woman who cares deeply for her man.*

*Then there appear a number of teachers with circles of devotees and students.*

**2** Some verbs follow *there* and are followed by a noun group and a prepositional phrase or adverb group. This pattern is **there V n prep/adv**. Most of these verbs also have the pattern **there V n**.

| there | Verb group | noun group | prep. phrase/adverb group |
|-------|------------|------------|---------------------------|
| There | was | no one | in the room. |
| There | remained | a risk | in such a situation. |

As with the previous pattern, the noun group is the Subject and is usually indefinite.

Sometimes the prepositional phrase or adverb group comes before *there*, as in *For every action there is an equal and opposite reaction*, or after the verb, as in *There was in the flat an ancient wood-burning stove*.

Verbs with this pattern belong to the following meaning groups:

■ **verbs indicating that something exists or happens**

| | | | |
|--|--|--|--|
| be | lie | remain | stand |
| exist | occur | seem | |

*There were no other wounds on the body.*

*There seems little wisdom in his proposals.*

In the case of *lie* and *stand*, the prepositional phrase or adverb group usually comes immediately after the verb or before *there*, rather than after the noun group.

*There lay between them something unspoken.*

*At one end of the room there stood a grand piano.*

**Productive use:** Any verb which indicates where someone or something is, or how they move, can be used with this pattern, for example *Near our camp there flowed a beautiful stream*.

■ **verbs indicating that something comes into existence or starts to be seen**

| | | | |
|--|--|--|--|
| appear | come | emerge | grow up |
| arise | develop | grow | |

*There appeared another little girl in her fantasy.*

*Out of all this there emerged many things that were positive, if also uncomfortable.*

**A** Rewrite these sentences using *there*.

1 A memorial service will be held at 2 p.m. on April 13.
*There will be a memorial service at 2 p.m. on April 13.*

2 At first the authorities denied that a hijack had taken place.
...................................................................................................................

3 Remarkably, no weather-related deaths or serious accidents have occurred.
...................................................................................................................

4 We haven't had any decent rain for four years.
...................................................................................................................

5 Do not stop if a passing motorist tells you that something is wrong with your vehicle.
...................................................................................................................

6 Some friction is inevitable during this ambitious phase.
...................................................................................................................

7 A series of explosions followed.
...................................................................................................................

8 One question remains: who should be tested?
...................................................................................................................

**B** Rewrite these sentences using the pattern *there* **V prep**.

1 Each gram of fat contains nine calories.
*There are nine calories in each gram of fat.*

2 The Museum contains many interesting objects and artifacts.
...................................................................................................................

3 That camp currently has about thirteen thousand people in it.
...................................................................................................................

4 This book contains over 100 mindbending puzzles to suit all ages and levels of ability.
...................................................................................................................

5 The waiting list has at least 100 names on it.
...................................................................................................................

6 The new Breeders LP actually has no songs on it.
...................................................................................................................

7 More than two hundred thousand people attended the rally.
...................................................................................................................

**C** Rewrite these sentences, forming the negative in a different way.

1 There were no marks on the body. *There weren't any marks on the body.*
2 There weren't any tables available. ...................................................................
3 There was no other traffic. .............................................................................
4 There isn't any alternative. ............................................................................
5 There were no fresh car tracks in the snow. ..........................................................

201

# Extra Practice

**A** For each verb in italics in the text below, underline each of the other parts of the pattern it is being used with, and say which pattern it is.

In the middle of the morning Mrs Pearson *walked* (1) into the Incident Room and *asked* (2) to speak to the officer in charge. Her white hair was uncombed and her cheeks were puffy with crying. 'You've got to stop it!' she *said* (3) when she was ushered in to Millson. 'They*'re saying* (4) terrible things in the village about my Lennie. It ain't right. It ain't right at all. And him only dead three days.' Millson put on a sympathetic face. 'What *are* they *saying* (5), Mrs Pearson?' 'They're saying Lennie was meeting the Book Lady on the sly and he *killed* (6) himself 'cos the police *were going to arrest* (7) him for murdering her. He *didn't* even *know* (8) her.'

1 ................................ 2 ................................ 3 ................................ 4 ................................

5 ................................ 6 ................................ 7 ................................ 8 ................................

**B** Now do the same with this text.

*Stepping* (1) from the car, Wade *called* (2), 'Hello, Alma! It's me. I'm just turning around.' She *nodded* (3) somberly, a tall woman in green trousers and plaid flannel shirt, mannish and abrupt, a woman who *kept* (4) herself aloof from the town but *seemed* (5) to love it nevertheless. She *drew* (6) the glass storm door closed and *started* (7) to shut the inner door, when Wade, instead of *getting* (8) back in the car, abruptly strode across the driveway and up the narrow freshly shoveled pathway to the door. Alma *swung* (9) the door open again, and Wade *entered* (10) the house. She *offered* (11) him a cup of tea, and he *accepted* (12) and *followed* (13) her into the kitchen.

1 ................................ 2 ................................ 3 ................................ 4 ................................

5 ................................ 6 ................................ 7 ................................ 8 ................................

9 ................................ 10 ................................ 11 ................................ 12 ................................

13 ................................

**C** Fill in the gaps in these sentences with *allow* or *let*. In one case, either is possible.

1 They would never ................................ her to stay now.

2 As a senior council officer, there is no way I can ................................ overspending.

3 Don't ................................ them wear you down.

4 My wife was ................................ to sit and sketch in one area.

5 I found the hidden key and ................................ myself into the house.

6 Is there any way that we can force them to ................................ us access to their garden?

7 The BBC should have instructed their staff not to ................................ him near a microphone, whatever his current claim to fame.

**D** The sentences below all contain the verb *talk*. Mark where a preposition should go, if appropriate, and say what it is.

1  I think you're talking rubbish there. ......................

2  What are you talking? ....................

3  It was nice to have someone like that to talk. ....................

4  A passer-by talked a gunman laying down his weapon moments after he shot a policeman in the leg yesterday. ....................

5  We talk all the time when we're on the pitch. ....................

6  He still talks Wolverhampton as his home. ....................

7  Some people tried to talk me joining the force, saying it'd be very tough. ....................

8  Armed with a sheaf of sketches and photographs, he talked his way the post of chief costume designer. ....................

**E** Here are some lines of text, as they appear in the Bank of English corpus. The same verb is missing from all of them. What is it?

```
         They were going to put him down but it ...... a shame.' I froze. Two lame lovers is
    his own, Madonna too risque. But Jackson ...... determined continually to raise the
              Perkins shook his head, amused. He ...... essentially a good-humoured man. 'Well,
         not have been with Lady Godetia. There ...... little point in sitting down with her
      carry Taro over in a cardboard box. This ...... peculiar to Bob and Pete, but Mr. and
       is thought to be the slowest ever. It ...... silly to rush back,' said Clive, 43, of
             both inside and outside Pakistan ...... surprised by the result. Was she?
          support (1092). Ten days ago it ...... that the rich world wanted to know
 the gross domestic product numbers, there ...... to have been a loss of momentum within
        General Philip Freeman actually ...... to have a handle on the opinionated,
```

**F** Here are some more lines of text. Which verb is missing this time?

```
    has discussed your symptoms with you and ..... a number of other questions about your
         on borders on the Gholan Heights. He was ..... about the boycott and the settlements and
           When they started up again Richard ....., 'And what about you, my dear ardent
       hardly knew what to reply. But she finally ..... him what he meant. As if you did not
 danced with the president's son -- King was ..... if his appearance amounted to an
         to do this. I had to help him. If he had ..... me to jump off the Brooklyn Bridge, I
      Justice has been done.' Ardiles had ..... the FA to reconsider the sending-off of
     be secured with Hooker assets. Hooker ..... the banks for an immediate injection of
            November 1992. Imagine you were ..... to design the perfect island. You might
 in the lucid way some alcoholics have, he ..... whether I was prepared to drink to anyone
```

**G** Which verb is missing from these lines?

```
 tentions. 'It's just not going to happen,' ..... a source close to Quayle about his dumping. If
           with assets of 161 billion.' Both ..... customer services had improved and pledged there
  by soldiers and police the Prime Minister ..... her visit was to see old friends in the
    ng to use the detainees or 'guests', as it ..... on calling them, as either bargaining-chips or
 ircumstances. Despite this, the Commission ..... on going ahead. Bryan told its members that it
          King of Corinth in Euripedes, he ..... on Jason marrying his daughter.
        Tannisho. Although Shinran always ..... on his fidelity to his teacher Honen, there wer
    influence -- in Lebanon. Yet it was he who ..... on this election. It has blown up in his face.
       today. At first, the Camelot spokeswoman ..... that the system was running yesterday. Then she
       's main rival for the party leadership, ..... that a Labour government must set itself an
```

## Extra Practice

**H** Fill in the gaps in these sentences with *look* or *see*, and say what the pattern is.

1 She's been *seeing* a lot of him. *V n of n*
2 She ................................. like a witch. .................................
3 He ................................. her stop and turn back to face the ocean. .................................
4 There he paused, turned and ................................. very steadily at John, meeting his eyes.
5 He opened the door of a small room which ................................. over the harbour.
6 You must let him ................................. through Dad's papers if that's what he wants.
7 I can't think what she ever ................................. in him.
8 It ................................. as if it might rain again.
9 She heard him before she ................................. him.
10 She has ................................. a winner from the start.
11 I ................................. George riding his bicycle at the other end of the street.
12 'I ................................. why you called it a delicate matter,' Simon said.
13 They ................................. it as an infringement on their own freedom of action.
14 She said he'd been out ................................. for work earlier in the day.
15 Liz ................................. her to the door, and returned frowning, shaking her head.
16 In the meantime, I'd told Mr Loveday to ................................. to the guests and gone upstairs.
17 I didn't think he ................................. very well when I met him downstairs last night.
18 I just want to ask you a few questions. I'm ................................. into the murder of Alan Mackenzie.

**I** The sentences below all contain a phrasal verb beginning with *go*. Each phrasal verb should be followed by a preposition. Fill in the gaps with the correct prepositions.

1 Many things are going up ................... price.
2 'You can't go back ................... your promise,' she said.
3 She went back ................... telling me how bad she felt.
4 With great reluctance I went along ................... this idea.
5 Smith keeps trying to get me to go out ................... his sister-in-law.
6 He was very popular and didn't go on ................... having a famous father.
7 It may well go down ................... the biggest rescue operation in recent maritime history.
8 Generally, if a farmer goes over ................... a completely organic system, there is a tendency for yields to fall.
9 I told my husband I was going to divorce him, and he threatened to kill me if I went through ................... it.
10 Since 1986, when British Gas was privatised, the price they pay for bulk supplies of gas has gone down ................... 8 per cent.

**J** For each sentence, say what comes after *me*: a noun group, an adjective group, or a bare infinitive clause. Then say whether the sentences are about *me* becoming, getting, or doing something.

1  She had made me a birthday cake. ......*noun group, getting something*..........................

2  It made me cry. ......................................................................................................................

3  They made me a professor. ....................................................................................................

4  He's always made me laugh. ..................................................................................................

5  It made me very angry. ..........................................................................................................

6  He made me a much better player. ........................................................................................

7  You made me feel special. ......................................................................................................

8  My mother had made me a new white dress. ........................................................................

9  She has made me a very happy man. ....................................................................................

10  It made me a little nervous. . ................................................................................................

11  Rovers have made me a very good offer. ..............................................................................

12  He made me look a fool. ........................................................................................................

**K** Fill in the gaps in these sentences with *say*, *speak*, or *tell*, and say what the pattern is.

1  She didn't ............*say*............ anything. ............*V n*............

2  She shook her head, still unable to ................................... ...........................

3  He ................................... them to be nice to me. ...........................

4  Many people that we met ................................... English. ...........................

5  They ................................... me I had to help them. ...........................

6  I'll ................................... you everything about it. ...........................

7  She ................................... as if Julie is still here. ...........................

8  Could you just ................................... us why you made that decision? ...........................

9  Did they ................................... when they'd be back? ...........................

10  A neighbour ...................................: 'We never let them go into the park on their own anyway.' ...........................

11  There are things going on right now that I cannot ................................... about. ...........................

12  I have to ................................... someone. I can't keep it to myself. ...........................

13  My father hasn't ................................... to Uncle Claude since then. ...........................

14  She ................................... something to the man, and looked at me again, laughing still. ...........................

15  The government has ................................... it wants to build a nuclear research centre. ...........................

16  The first thing we were ................................... was, 'If you want to watch the games, you're in the wrong place.' ...........................

# Verb Index

The numbers refer to Units, not pages.